Yellowcake
TOWNS

Mining the American West

Series Editors

Duane A. Smith
Robert A. Trennert
Liping Zhu

Yellowcake TOWNS

Uranium

Mining

Communities

in the

American West

MICHAEL A. AMUNDSON

University Press of Colorado

Published by the University Press of Colorado
5589 Arapahoe Avenue, Suite 206C
Boulder, Colorado 80303

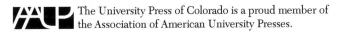 The University Press of Colorado is a proud member of
the Association of American University Presses.

The University Press of Colorado is a cooperative publishing enterprise supported, in part,
by Adams State College, Colorado State University, Fort Lewis College, Mesa State College,
Metropolitan State College of Denver, University of Colorado, University of Northern Colorado,
and Western State College of Colorado.

♾ The paper used in this publication meets the minimum requirements of the American National Standard for Information Sciences—Permanence of Paper for Printed Library Materials.
ANSI Z39.48-1992

Library of Congress Cataloging-in-Publication Data

Amundson, Michael A., 1965–
    Yellowcake towns : uranium mining communities in the American West / by Michael A.
Amundson.
        p. cm. — (Mining the American West)
Includes bibliographical references and index.
    ISBN 0-87081-662-4 (hardcover : alk. paper) — ISBN 0-87081-765-5 (pbk: alk. paper)
    1. Uranium mines and mining—West (U.S.)—History—20th century. I. Title. II. Series.
TN490.U7 A548 2001
338.4'762234932'0978—dc21

                                                                            2001008027

Cover design by Laura Furney
Text design by Daniel Pratt

Contents

Illustrations

Acknowledgments

MY INTEREST IN URANIUM MINING TOWNS began in the sum-
mer of 1990 while finishing my master's thesis and working as an intern at
South Pass City, Wyoming. I had to make several trips between the University of Wyoming in Laramie and South Pass City. Along the way I passed
through the small town of Jeffrey City, which had been little more than a
gas station called Home on the Range until the early 1950s when uranium
was discovered nearby. A processing mill was soon constructed, and a new
company town was born. During the energy crisis of the 1970s, Jeffrey City
boomed to over 4,000 residents but quickly busted when the uranium
bubble burst in the early 1980s. By the time I saw it, Jeffrey City was a
nuclear-age ghost town little bigger than the community-turned-museum
in which I was living and working. That summer I had the good fortune to
meet Sam Peterson, a retired mining engineer whose family had built Home
on the Range and who had seen the birth and death of Jeffrey City. His
support and interest in my research soon led me to others in Jeffrey City,

and I began to think I could study uranium mining towns when I entered the doctoral program at the University of Nebraska that fall.

In Lincoln I am indebted to my dissertation adviser, Frederick C. Luebke, for his guidance, patience, and good nature in seeing me through this project. I also owe thanks to John Wunder for his support and to the rest of my committee, including Kenneth Winkle, Frances Kaye, Dane Kennedy, and Parks Coble. I also owe a special thanks to former Atomic Energy Commission geologist William L. Chenoweth for his tireless work proofreading both the dissertation and this manuscript. Bill not only knew the history of uranium mining, but his knowledge of western geography was amazing. He is *the* source on the history of uranium mining in the American West.

This project could not have been completed without the incredible assistance provided by librarians and archivists who listened to my queries and provided terrific leads. I especially thank the librarians and interlibrary loan people at the Don L. Love Memorial Library at the University of Nebraska–Lincoln. Additionally, I thank librarians and archivists at the following institutions: the Special Collections Department at the J. Willard Marriott Library, University of Utah; Utah Historical Society; the Dan O'Laurie Museum in Moab, Utah; the American Heritage Center at the University of Wyoming; the Wyoming State Archives; the Western History Department, Denver Public Library; Colorado State University Libraries, the Museum of Western Colorado in Grand Junction; Umetco Minerals; Special Collections, University of New Mexico; New Mexico Historical Society; and the New Mexico State Archives.

Between the completion of my dissertation in 1996 and the publication of this book, I had the good fortune to teach at three institutions in the West. At Idaho State University in Pocatello, thanks to the history department, especially Bob Swanson, Peter Boag, and Ron Hatzenbuehler. At Mesa State College in Grand Junction, Colorado, thanks to Steve Schulte, Doug O'Roark, and Adele Cummins. At my current home, Northern Arizona University in Flagstaff, thanks go to the entire history department but especially to George Lubick, Val Avery, Larry MacFarlane, and Cindy Kosso. All of these people listened to me talk about uranium and prodded me to get things done when it seemed like the project had its own extended half-life. Additionally, thanks to the many undergraduate and graduate students at these schools.

My work on uranium mining in the history of the American West has twice been published by the *Western Historical Quarterly*. In 1995 the *Quarterly* published my article on Jeffrey City, and in 2001 it printed my work on the Orphan Mine at the Grand Canyon. My thanks to the editors and their assistants who helped me focus my work and also made it available to a wider audience. Special thanks to Clyde Milner, Anne Butler, Ona Siporin, and David Rich Lewis for their enthusiastic support.

I am indebted to Nancy Jackson, John Findlay, Andrew Gulliford, and Duane Smith for reading and commenting on earlier drafts of this work. Thanks to Francie Faure for the maps. Thanks also to Darrin Pratt, Laura Furney, Daniel Pratt, Cheryl Carnahan, and everyone at the University Press of Colorado for their wonderful support in getting this project completed.

Thank you to the many people who shared their lives and stories with me in Jeffrey City, Moab, Uravan, and Grants. A special thanks goes to Laura Gray-Rosendale and Steve Rosendale—plus Max and Nellie—for listening to me talk about yellowcake while hiking and biking the deserts and forests of northern Arizona. Finally, I owe special thanks to my parents, Arlen and Joan, and my sister, Kathy, who have supported me in everything I have ever tried to do. Although I owe these many institutions and people a great deal for their assistance, any errors are my responsibility.

Major Uranium Mills in the American West, 1942–Present

Manhattan Engineer District, 1942–1945

A. Durango, Colorado, United States Vanadium Green Sludge Plant
B. Uravan, Colorado, United States Vanadium Green Sludge Plant
C. Grand Junction, Colorado United States Vanadium Refinery
D. Monticello, Utah, Vanadium Corporation of America Mill Circuit
E. Naturita, Colorado, Vanadium Corporation of America Mill Circuit

Atomic Energy Conimission, 1947–1970

1. Tuba City, Arizona, Rare Metals Corporation of America
2. Canon City, Colorado, Cotter Corporation,°
3. Durango, Colorado, Vanadium Corporation of America
4. Grand Junction, Colorado, Climax Uranium Company
5. Gunnison, Colorado, Gunnison Mining Company
6. Maybell, Colorado, Trace Elements Corporation
7. Naturita, Colorado, Vanadium Corporation of America
8. Riffe, Colorado, United States Vanadium Corporation
9. Uravan, Colorado, United States Vanadium Corporation
10. Lowman, Idaho, Porter Brothers Corporation
11. Ambrosia Lake, New Mexico, Kermac Nuclear Fuels Corporation
12. Ambrosia Lake, New Mexico, Phillips Petroleum Company
13. Bluewater, New Mexico, The Anaconda Company
14. Grants, New Mexico, Homestake–New Mexico Partners
15. Grants, New Mexico, Homestake-Sapin Partners
16. Shiprock, New Mexico, Kerr-McGee Oil Industries, Inc.
17. Lakeview, Oregon, Lakeview Mining Company
18. Edgemont, South Dakota, Mines Development Inc.
19. Falls City, Texas, Susquehanna-Western, Inc.
20. White Canyon (Hite), Utah, Vanadium Corporation of America
21. Mexican Hat, Utah, Texas-Zinc Corporation
22. Moab, Utah, Uranium Reduction Company
23. Monticello, Utah, The Galigher Company
24. Salt Lake City, Utah, Vitro Corporation of America
25. Ford, Washington, Dawn Mining Company°
26. Gas Hills, Wyoming, Federal-Radorock-Gas Hills Partners
27. Gas Hills, Wyoming, Globe Mining Company
28. Gas Hills, Wyoming, Lucky Mc Mining Corporation
29. Riverton, Wyoming, Fremont Minerals, Inc.
30. Shirley Basin, Wyoming, Petrotomics Company
31. Split Rock Wyoming, Western Nuclear Corporation

Commercial Period, 1971–present

AA. Cebolleta, New Mexico, SOHIO Western Mining Company.
BB. Church Rock, New Mexico, United Nuclear Corporation
CC. Wellpinit, Washington, Western Nuclear Inc.
DD. Falls City, Texas, Pioneer Nuclear Corp.
EE. Panna Maria, Texas, Chevron.
FF. Ray Point, Texas, Susquehanna-Western Inc.
GG. Bear Creek, Wyoming, Bear Creek Uranium Comp.
HH. Highland, Wyoming, Exxon Minerals Comp.
II. Shirley Basin, Wyoming, Pathfinder Mines Corp.
JJ. Sweetwater, Wyoming, Kennecott Uranium Comp.
KK. Blanding, Utah, International Uranium Corp.°
LL. Lisbon Valley, Utah, Rio Algorn Mining Corp.
MM. Ticaboo, Utah, U.S. Energy Corp.°

°Denotes operational mills as of September 2001.

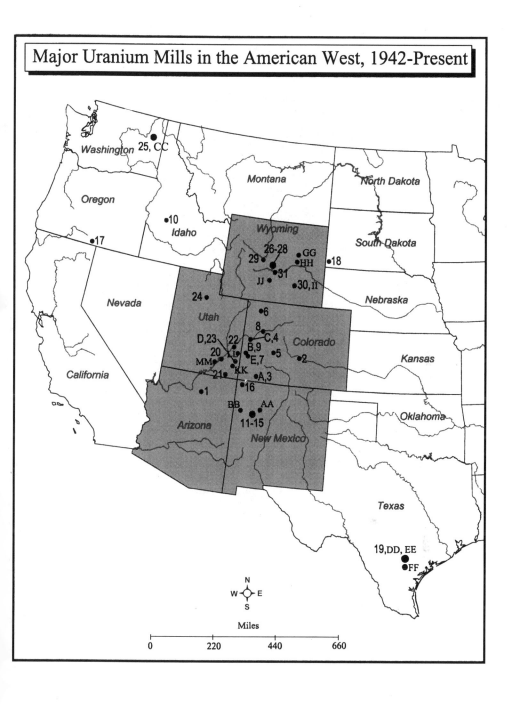

Major Uranium Mills in the American West, 1942-Present

Washington 25, CC

Oregon

Montana

North Dakota

Idaho ·10

South Dakota

·17

Wyoming

26-28

29· GG
·HH
·18

·31
JJ· ·30, II

Nevada

Utah

24·

·6

8

D,23 22· C,4
20 B,9 Colorado
L· ·5
MM· E,7
·21 KK ·2
·16 A,3

·1

Kansas

California

BB AA
11-15

Arizona

New Mexico

Oklahoma

Texas

19, DD, EE
·FF

N
W·E
S

Miles

0   220   440   660

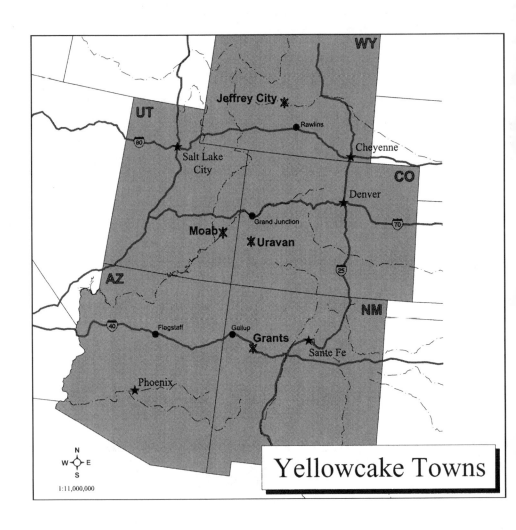

Yellowcake Towns

Introduction

SINCE THE END OF THE COLD WAR in 1989, Americans have begun to consider seriously the social costs exacted by the development of the atom. Recent disclosures have revealed radiation tests conducted on unknowing children. Similar studies have probed cancer rates in the intermontane West presumably caused by nuclear testing. Still others have examined the survival of cities such as Hanford, Washington, and Los Alamos, New Mexico, where the first bombs and reactors were manufactured.[1] But little scholarly attention has been directed to the supply side of the industry. Although some recent works have examined the environmental consequences of uranium mining and the cancer rates among its miners, there is little mention of the well-being of the communities impacted by the mining and milling of *yellowcake,* the industry's term for processed uranium ore.[2] This study analyzes the origins, development, and decline of four such yellowcake communities: Uravan, Colorado; Moab, Utah; Grants, New Mexico; and Jeffrey City, Wyoming.

Twice during the four decades of the Cold War, changing federal government policies caused "boom-and-bust" phases in the yellowcake communities. Although boom periods created severe problems with housing, schooling, and the like, the bust phases struck at the towns' very existence. Some, such as Moab and Grants, survived high unemployment, sharp drops in property values, and losses in local revenue by shifting to tourism. But other municipalities, like Uravan and Jeffrey City, had no foundation other than the production of yellowcake. Jeffrey City is nearly a ghost town, whereas Uravan is a federally classified remediation site. The history of these towns illustrates the interaction of outside forces and local boosters and their impact on communities that both mined and milled energy resources in the twentieth-century American West.

Although the role of uranium mining communities is new, it is deeply rooted in the region's history. Like all mining communities, the uranium towns were often located in remote places tied to larger trade networks. They were usually small, almost forgotten sites that became instant boomtowns when uranium was discovered. Like other such places, the communities were often deluged first by mostly male prospectors and later by families. This restless population overwhelmed the town's infrastructure and altered the community's character as it reshaped the landscape for mining and milling. The uranium industry also followed the traditional consolidation evolution from lone prospector to giant corporation.[3]

The study of company towns also sheds light on some uranium mining communities. Like their relatives in logging, coal, and copper mining, several uranium companies built new towns to support their workers in remote areas. In both Uravan and Jeffrey City, uranium mining companies provided inexpensive housing, recreation, schools, utilities, and shopping in addition to the usual jobs. Unlike the uranium boomtowns, these corporate communities were usually managed more effectively, with less economic and social upheaval. At the same time, Uravan and Jeffrey City, like all one-industry towns, were totally dependent on the uranium industry, and their residents were subject to colonial control—whether by the federal government, the market, or the company.[4]

Although the yellowcake towns were linked to other mining communities in these ways, the fact that they were supplying the raw material for the first atomic bombs and then for nuclear power plants places them in an entirely different context. As workers on the frontier of atomic science, uranium town residents often exhibited a unique "pronuclear" culture similar to citizens of the West's other atomic towns. In Hanford, residents named their high school football team the Bombers and placed mushroom clouds on their helmets. People in the yellowcake towns built "uranium cafés," held "uranium days," and even staged a "Miss Uranium" pageant where the lucky winner received a truckload of uranium ore.[5]

Understanding the forces at work in the international uranium market also provides a context for the history of the yellowcake towns. From the start of the Manhattan Project to the end of the federally subsidized market in 1970, the federal government completely controlled the market in the interest of national security. Uncle Sam subsidized prospecting, mining, and milling and was the only legal uranium buyer. This paternalism created the first big boom in the 1950s and a subsequent bust followed by a decade of stagnation. After 1970 the federal government's total control ended, and international market forces came into play. Another boom and bust followed. By the early 1980s the domestic uranium industry was dead.[6]

The history of the yellowcake communities is also a study in the intricacies of economic colonialism. Unlike westerners' traditional cry against control by eastern capital, the story of twentieth-century colonialism is a study of the integration of the western economy into the global economy. Like people in other hinterlands dependent on the extraction of natural resources, local boosters often pushed for uranium development in the yellowcake communities and later complained when they found themselves isolated and with very little influence in the global market.[7]

Such links are important to other fields of inquiry, but there must be limits. It is neither possible nor desirable in this study to pursue all related questions. For example, my examination of yellowcake communities is not intended to be an in-depth social history. These caveats aside, I reaffirm that the goal of this book is to analyze and compare the impact of changing federal policies on four uranium mining and milling communities. This approach reveals the typicality or uniqueness of the effects of outside forces and local boosters on a particular community. Further, the differing effects of corporate decisions on the various cities may also be detected. Because of this effort to compare similarities and differences among the four towns, the criteria for selection must be explained.

The communities in this study were chosen for several reasons. First, all four towns were home to uranium mining and milling operations. Second, all four communities existed and operated during the four decades of government dominance of the uranium industry. Third, uranium production played such a large role in these communities that its impact is easily detected. Fourth, two of the towns in this study were company towns and two were not, so the influence of corporate paternalism can be compared to that of independent governments. Fifth, each town was influenced more strongly by some policies than by others, allowing us to understand how national policies produced local variations. Finally, each community is located in a different state, so governmental differences—especially in the 1980s—can be detected. A brief look at each town provides an overview.

Uravan is located in west-central Colorado about 90 miles southwest of Grand Junction. A company town created by Union Carbide, the name *Uravan* is derived from the two main products processed there: *ura*nium and *van*adium. The town began, however, as a radium mining camp and only started to extract other minerals when market conditions proved favorable. During World War II, vanadium use in strengthening steel increased, and uranium became an unused part of the mill tailings. When the United States needed uranium to build the first nuclear bombs, the Manhattan Engineer District came to Uravan to process tailings for uranium. This mill remained in operation until 1945 when the town was closed.

Two years after the start of the new federal uranium program in 1946, Uravan reopened, and the population increased to over 800. But Union Carbide maintained its hold on the community, and Uravan never experienced true boomtown expansion. Indeed, the population never again matched its mid-1950s' peak. Operations at Uravan continued until the late 1970s when environmental regulations made them uneconomical. The mill closed in November 1984, and the town was shut down because of radiation problems in 1988.

Like Uravan, Moab played a role in the uranium industry before World War II. Situated on the Colorado Plateau in east-central Utah, the town's chief characteristic was its location in the canyon country near present-day Arches and Canyonlands National Parks. About 50 percent Mormon, Moab was rooted in agriculture and mining. After the war the town became a center for uranium prospecting and boomed after a major discovery in 1952. The population quadrupled in less than three years. In 1956 a mill was built, and city fathers proclaimed Moab the "Uranium Capital of the World."

During the 1960s, Moab's economic base diversified thanks to a new potash industry and increased tourism. Although impacted by the bust in the 1980s, Moab has prospered as a gateway town. In fact, few visitors to what is now billed the "Mountain Bike Capital of the World" even know about its past uranium identity.

Unlike Uravan or Moab, Jeffrey City, Wyoming, did not exist before the Cold War uranium procurement program in the 1950s. Created by Western Nuclear, Inc., to provide housing for its miners and mill workers at Wyoming's first uranium plant 90 miles northwest of Rawlins, during the first boom period Jeffrey City grew from a small post office for a ranching district into a trailer town of 750 inhabitants. During the industry slowdown in the late 1960s, Western Nuclear sold out to mining conglomerate Phelps-Dodge. This consolidation brought more money into the community just as a second boom began. By the mid-1970s Jeffrey City's population had grown to almost 4,000. Phelps-Dodge built more housing, streets, and parks. Unfortunately, the bust in the 1980s forced local employers to lay off hundreds of workers. With no alternative employment opportunities, people moved away. Within a few years, Jeffrey City's population had dwindled to several hundred people.

Like Moab, Grants, New Mexico, once proclaimed itself the "Uranium Capital of the World" because it was the center of New Mexico's uranium industry. Located on Route 66, 90 miles west of Albuquerque, Grants was a small agriculture community that claimed to be the "Carrot Capital of the World" before uranium was discovered in the early 1950s. Before the end of the decade, new discoveries at nearby Ambrosia Lake brought five mills into operation in the region, and most of the workers lived in Grants. The town's population increased 500 percent between 1950 and 1960. Like Moab, the character of Grants changed as it grew into another uranium capital. Also as with its Utah counterpart, the uranium boom industrialized Grants, expanded the community's size, and popularized its image. In the bust of the 1980s, though, the dependency on the uranium industry wreaked havoc. As unemployment grew to over 30 percent, businesses closed, homes were sold at a fraction of their cost, and the population—once projected to grow to 100,000—dropped from 20,000 to 10,000.

The details of why and how these changes took place constitute the substance of this book. Chapter 1 traces the early history of the U.S. uranium industry and the first uranium towns amid the carnotite deposits of the Colorado Plateau. From here the U.S. radium and then vanadium industries developed before the rise of atomic physics and the Manhattan Project gave discarded rock a new use. The chapter also recounts the federal government's growing involvement in the industry.

Chapter 2 describes the postwar transition to the U.S. Atomic Energy Commission (AEC) and its domestic uranium procurement program. Using a variety of new government incentives and guaranteed prices, the AEC created the first uranium rush to fuel the burgeoning U.S. atomic arsenal. By the late 1950s the U.S. uranium industry was a huge success.

Building on federal policy during the boom years 1946–1958, the next three chapters examine how the four communities responded to the boom. Chapter 3 shows how the new program affected employment, school enrollment, population, business growth, and physical expansion in the two company-controlled communities, Uravan and Jeffrey City.

Chapters 4 and 5 explore the rise of the two uranium capitals Moab and Grants during the 1950s uranium rush. Chapter 4 discusses Moab's growth and problems, and Chapter 5 examines the same issues in Grants. Rapid growth in population, school enrollment, business, and physical size are again investigated. Further, the place of uranium mining in each town's self-image is explored to show the transition to a uranium-dependent yellowcake community.

As uranium expansion increased beyond imagination in the 1950s, Congress decided it could no longer afford to purchase all the uranium ore being produced. As hopes for peaceful uses for atomic energy in power plants developed more slowly than expected, the uranium industry seemed headed for a state of overproduction. To ease this transition, the federal government instituted a new allocation program, a ban on imported uranium, and an extension, or "stretch-out," policy to keep domestic producers afloat until demand for nuclear power increased. Chapter 6 traces the development of these new policies during the period 1958–1970.

In the late 1950s and 1960s these four communities realized that their dependence on federal policy and industrial whim was likely stronger than imagined. As slowdowns and layoffs occurred, companies were forced to make decisions about their uranium futures. These decisions often led to consolidations, layoffs, and slowdowns that seemed to question the future of both the industry and the communities. The towns, meanwhile, sought to diversify their economies. Chapter 7 describes how these places survived the allocation and stretch-out periods.

By the early 1970s the government procurement program had ended, and a new commercial period began. Rising energy costs, created in part by the oil crisis, generated a second uranium boom. Although no longer the sole buyer of uranium, the government continued to influence the industry through international trade. Power companies planned dozens of new nuclear power plants, and demand increased. As uranium prices soared, Congress lifted the embargo, and imports began seeping into the seemingly endless U.S. market. By 1977 it seemed the boom would never end. Then the uranium market collapsed.

The reasons for the collapse were complex. Although many Americans blamed the March 1979 Three Mile Island incident for the falling price of uranium, that event was only a symptom of the problems created by growing environmental concerns, overproduction, delays in nuclear power plant construction, increased import dependency, and overzealous industrial speculation. As plans for new nuclear power plants were delayed and then scrapped, U.S. uranium producers petitioned the Reagan administration for help against low-cost imports. Arguing that the government had a legal duty to maintain a "viable domestic industry," the industry fought the government all the way to the Supreme Court. In 1988 the court ruled in favor of the government, which killed the U.S. industry. The factors that shaped the second great uranium boom and bust—the commercial period—are examined in Chapter 8.

Chapter 9 describes how the four yellowcake communities were affected by the commercial boom-and-bust period of the 1970s and 1980s. Like the earlier government program, the free market brought another expansion that transformed all four cities, especially Jeffrey City and Grants. New schools, businesses, and churches were opened as forecasters insisted that atomic power had a bright and prosperous future. For Moab and Uravan, the second boom had less of an effect than the first, but both towns bit into the expansion. For many, the future had never looked brighter. Then a bust hit again.

The drop in the price of yellowcake brought mill closings and job layoffs, followed by exodus. As people began to move, the local businesses that fed off the mining industry collapsed. Unemployment rates exceeded 30 percent in some towns, and property values plummeted. Newly built schools and water works were closed. In many communities the only remaining uranium jobs were in the reclamation projects that tried to control the millions of tons of waste. As the bust continued, town leaders considered nuclear waste storage as a possible solution to the job problem before looking to other ventures like tourism to keep their cities alive.

Chapter 10 examines the history of the uranium industry and the yellowcake communities since 1988. As during the stretch-out period, the continued commercial slump brought another round of consolidations in the domestic industry. But without government protection most U.S. producers saw little chance of success, especially after Russian uranium infiltrated the U.S. market in the early 1990s.

By the summer of 2001, the yellowcake towns had virtually disappeared. Uravan is in the process of remediation, and the remaining homes in Jeffrey City were recently sold and carted off. Moab's tourist industry has boomed to the point that few know of its past tie to the atomic age. Charlie Steen's home above the town is now a restaurant catering to tourists. Only Grants profits from its uranium history through heritage tourism. Visitors to the New Mexico mining museum can go "underground" and tour a reconstructed uranium mine before visiting the Uranium Cafe. Built in 1956, the café still serves "yellowcakes" for breakfast and "uranium burgers" for lunch. It seems a small reminder of the half-century history of uranium mining towns in the American West.

Notes

1. See especially, Eileen Welsome, *The Plutonium Files: America's Secret Medical Experiments in the Cold War* (New York: Dial, 1999); Valerie Kuletz, *The Tainted Desert: Environmental and Social Ruin in the American West* (New York: Routledge, 1998); Len Ackland, *Making a Real Killing: Rocky Flats and the Nuclear West* (Albuquerque: University of New Mexico Press, 1999); Tad Bartimus and Scott McCartney, *Trinity's Children: Living Along America's Nuclear Highway* (Albuquerque: University of New Mexico Press, 1991); Bruce Hevly and John M. Findlay, eds., *The Atomic West* (Seattle: University of Washington Press, 1998); Stephen I. Schwartz, *Atomic Audit: The Costs and Consequences of Nuclear Weapons Since 1940* (Washington, D.C.: Brookings Institution Press, 1998); Philip L. Fradkin, *Fallout: An American Nuclear Tragedy* (Tucson: University of Arizona Press, 1989); Michele Stenhjem Gerber, *On the Home Front: The Cold War Legacy of the Hanford Nuclear Site* (Lincoln: University of Nebraska Press, 1992); Stewart L. Udall, *The Myths of August: A Personal Exploration of Our Tragic Cold War Affair With the Atom* (New York: Pantheon, 1994); Peter Bacon Hales, *Atomic Spaces: Living on the Manhattan Project* (Urbana: University of Illinois Press, 1997).

2. Peter H. Eichstaedt, *If You Poison Us: Uranium and Native Americans* (Santa Fe: Red Crane, 1994); Raye C. Ringholz, *Uranium Frenzy: Boom and Bust on the Colorado Plateau* (New York: W. W. Norton, 1989); Gary Lee Shumway, "A History of the Uranium Industry on the Colorado Plateau," unpublished Ph.D. diss., University of Southern California, 1970. Government publications that cover the history of uranium development include Nielson B. O'Rear, U.S. Atomic Energy Commission technical memorandum 187, *Summary and Chronology of the Domestic Uranium Program (August 1966),* report prepared for the USAEC, Grand Junction Office (Grand Junction, Colo., 1966); Holger Albrethsen and Frank E. McGinley, *Summary History of Domestic Uranium Procurement Under U.S. Atomic Energy Commission Contracts: Final Report* (Grand Junction, Colo.: U.S. Department of Energy, 1982); U.S. Department of Energy, *United States Uranium Mining and Milling Industry: A Comprehensive Review* DOE-0028 (Washington, D.C.: Government Printing Office, 1984). The best source on geological reports and history is retired AEC geologist William L. Chenoweth. His published works include "The Uranium-Vanadium Deposits of the Uravan Mineral Belt and Adjacent Areas, Colorado and Utah," *New Mexico Geological Society Guidebook* (32nd Field Conference, Western Slope, Colorado, 1981); "Raw Materials Activities of the Manhattan

Project on the Colorado Plateau," *Four Corners Geological Society Guidebook* (10th Field Conference, Cataract Canyon, 1987); "Ambrosia Lake, New Mexico—A Giant Uranium District," *New Mexico Geological Society Guidebook* (40th Field Conference, Southeastern Colorado Plateau, 1989); "Uranium Resources in New Mexico," New Mexico Bureau of Mines and Mineral Resources, 1989; "A Summary of Uranium Production in Wyoming," *Wyoming Geological Association Guidebook* (42nd Field Conference, 1991); and "A History of Uranium Production in Utah," *Energy and Mineral Resources of Utah* (Utah Geological Association Publication 18, 1990.)

3. Classic overviews of mining history include Rodman W. Paul, *Mining Frontiers of the Far West, 1848–1880* (New York: Holt, Rinehart, and Winston, 1963) and William S. Greever, *The Bonanza West: The Story of the Western Mining Rushes* (Norman: University of Oklahoma Press, 1963). An excellent historiographical essay covering the rise and fall of western metal mining is Michael Malone, "The Collapse of Western Metal Mining: An Historical Epitaph," *Pacific Historical Review* 55, no. 3 (August 1986): 455–464. For the effects of mining on the environment, see Duane A. Smith, *Mining America: The Industry and the Environment* (Niwot: University Press of Colorado, 1993) and Richard V. Francaviglia, *Hard Places: Reading the Landscape of America's Historic Mining Districts* (Iowa City: University of Iowa Press, 1991). More recent approaches to mining community history include Malcolm J. Rohrbough, *Aspen: The History of a Silver Mining Town 1879–1893* (New York: Oxford University Press, 1986); Duane A. Smith, *Rocky Mountain Boom Town: A History of Durango, Colorado* (Niwot: University Press of Colorado, 1992); Andrew Gulliford, *Boomtown Blues: Colorado Oil Shale, 1885–1985* (Niwot: University of Colorado Press, 1989); Arthur R. Gomez, *Quest for the Golden Circle: The Four Corners and the Metropolitan West, 1945–1970* (Albuquerque: University of New Mexico Press, 1994); Susan Lee Johnson, *Roaring Camp: The Social World of the California Gold Rush* (New York: W. W. Norton, 2000); Mary Murphy, *Mining Cultures: Men, Women, and Leisure in Butte, 1914–41* (Urbana: University of Illinois Press, 1997).

4. James B. Allen, *The Company Town in the American West* (Norman: University of Oklahoma Press, 1966); Keith C. Peterson, *Company Town: Potlatch, Idaho, and the Potlatch Lumber Company* (Pullman: Washington State University Press, 1987); Robert W. Righter, *The Making of a Town: Wright, Wyoming* (Boulder: Roberts Rinehart, 1985).

5. For Hanford, see Gerber, *On the Home Front*, and Paul Loeb, *Nuclear Culture: Living and Working in the World's Largest Atomic Complex* (Philadelphia: New Society, 1986). Los Alamos is examined in Hal K. Rothman, *On Rims and Ridges: The Los Alamos Area Since 1880* (Lincoln: University of Nebraska Press, 1992). Las Vegas is covered in A. Constadina Titus, *Bombs in the Backyard: Atomic Testing and American Politics* (Reno: University of Nevada Press, 1986).

6. Histories of the famous Manhattan Project include Leslie R. Groves, *Now It Can Be Told: The Story of the Manhattan Project* (New York: Harper, 1962); Major General K. D. Nichols, *The Road to Trinity* (New York: William Morrow, 1987); Richard Rhodes, *The Making of the Atomic Bomb* (New York: Simon and Schuster, 1987); Richard G. Hewlett and Oscar E. Anderson Jr., *A History of the United States Atomic Energy Commission,* Vol. I, *The New World,* and Vol. II, *Atomic Shield, 1947/1952* (University Park: Pennsylvania State University Press, 1962, 1969). Economic histories of uranium include Marian Radetzki, *Uranium: A Strategic Source of Energy* (New York: St. Martin's, 1981); Anthony David Owen, *The Economics of Uranium* (New York: Praeger, 1985); Norman Moss, *The Politics of Uranium* (New York: Universe, 1982). The international uranium market is examined in Earle Gray, *The Great Uranium Cartel* (Toronto: McClelland and Stewart, 1982); June H. Taylor and Michael D. Yokell, *Yellowcake: The International Uranium Cartel* (New York: Pergamon, 1979); J. W. Griffith, *The Uranium Industry—Its History, Technology and Prospects* (Ottawa: Department of Energy, Mines, and Resources, 1967); Hugh C. McIntyre, *Uranium, Nuclear Power, and Canada-U.S. Energy Relations* (Montreal and Washington, D.C.: C. D. Howe Research Institute [Canada] and National Planning Association [USA], 1978). The changing definition of national security is discussed in Joseph J. Romm, *Defining National Security: The Nonmilitary Aspects* (New York: Council on Foreign Relations Press, 1993) and Michael A. Amundson, "Mining the Grand Canyon to Save It: The Orphan Uranium Mine and National Security," *Western Historical Quarterly* 32 (Autumn 2001): 320–345.

7. William G. Robbins explains the rise of global capitalism in his works, including *Colony and Empire: The Capitalist Transformation of the American West* (Lawrence: University of Kansas Press, 1994) and "The 'Plundered Province' Thesis and the Recent Historiography of the American West," *Pacific Historical Review* 55, no. 4 (November 1986): 577–597. Roger Lotchin shows how local boosters in California cities became dependent on federal largesse in the twentieth century in *Fortress California, 1910–1961: From Warfare to Welfare* (New York: Oxford University Press, 1992).

Yellowcake
TOWNS

Chapter
1

From Weed to Weapon:

U.S. Uranium, 1898–1945

IN THE EARLY DAYS OF WORLD WAR II, Cliff Hiett, a young vanadium mill worker from the small Western Slope town of Uravan, Colorado, was drafted into service. He left his family and joined thousands of other men, moving across five states in fifteen months during his training. Then an odd thing happened. Instead of being shipped overseas, Hiett received orders to return to Colorado. He would be, he was told, more valuable to the U.S. war effort at home than abroad. In fact, Hiett returned to his old job at the vanadium mill in Uravan, where he worked on the top-secret Manhattan Project. His efforts, and those of thousands of others, produced uranium for the atomic bombs that ended World War II.[1]

Cliff Hiett's story symbolizes uranium's dramatic transformation from worthless waste to a mineral on which national security depended. The atomic age commodified uranium into the most important metal in the world. At the same time, the Manhattan Project made uranium miners and millers strategic laborers and transformed the communities where they worked into national security towns. Ralph Waldo Emerson once said that a weed is a plant whose virtues are unknown. Uranium's rise to national security is a case study of such a change.

The early history of uranium revolves around work on radioactivity by French scientists Antoine Henri Becquerel and Pierre and Marie Curie. Using the mineral pitchblende as his source material, in 1896 Becquerel discovered that uranium was radioactive; as it decayed it spontaneously emitted particles and energy. Two years later the Curies isolated radium from uranium and learned that the new element could stop certain types of cancers. That discovery sparked a worldwide search for radioactive materials and brought the first uranium boom to the American West.[2]

One of the richest areas of radioactive materials in the United States was the mesa country of the Colorado Plateau, which contained impressive carnotite deposits. Carnotite is a canary-yellow to greenish-yellow compound containing deposits of uranium, vanadium, and minute amounts of radium. In fact, it took up to 300 tons of carnotite ore to produce 1 gram of radium. Nevertheless, radium's selling price of $70,000–$120,000 per gram made carnotite mining profitable, and a small rush soon developed. By 1910 a number of independent miners had developed operations at rock outcrops along the Dolores and San Miguel Rivers in western Colorado.[3] The collected ores were then sacked and hauled by mule to the railroad at Placerville, 50 miles away. From there, more than 90 percent of the pre-1910 ore was sent to European radium refineries.

To the progressive politicians of the day, this situation was intolerable. Although a 1912 Bureau of Mines investigation suggested that U.S. carnotite deposits contained nearly all the radium in the world, local producers were exporting it to Europe at little profit. Moreover, their inefficient habit of using only high-grade ore wasted almost five times as much ore as was actually shipped. As these small producers sold out to larger companies like the Radium Luminous Material Corporation, the Radium Company of Colorado, and the Standard Chemical Company of Pennsylvania, progressives in Washington seized on the idea of federally supervising the mining, milling, and distribution of radium. In 1913, Congress held a series of hearings on nationalizing the U.S. radium industry.[4]

Similar to the conservation program that had begun to save U.S. forests, progressives proposed that carnotite lands be withdrawn from the public domain to be properly exploited. As an example to both industry and Congress, the Bureau of Mines established a National Radium Institute to develop better methods to extract and refine radium from domestic sources.[5]

Joe Junior Camp #1 looking south, 1919. Standard Chemical Company's Joe Junior Camp produced radium from the area's carnotite ores from 1914 to 1923. In 1936 United States Vanadium built the company town of Uravan around the existing structures to extract vanadium from the mill's tailings. During World War II the Manhattan Project extracted uranium from these same piles. Uravan grew to around 1,000 residents during the 1950s boom. In the early 1980s it was determined that the entire town was radioactive, and it was soon dismantled and remediation began. The white boardinghouse, constructed in 1914, is one of only two remaining buildings. Courtesy, Ken Bonner and the Estalee Silver Collection.

As the campaign for government control of radium began, private companies, including Standard Chemical, decided to pursue their own course of action. In 1913 the company purchased land in western Colorado at the base of Club Mesa and began erecting a concentrating mill, lab, and boarding-inghouse. A small tent town, named Joe Junior for the son of company president Joseph Flannery, soon spread throughout the nearby Club Ranch's former hay fields.[6]

The Joe Junior Camp was located in the winding San Miguel valley, 4 miles above the river's confluence with the Dolores River and approximately 60 miles due south of Grand Junction, Colorado. In canyon country, however, roads seldom follow the cardinal directions but wind their way beside the river's serpentine path. Travelers coming into Joe Junior would have first seen Standard Chemical's millworks, a collection of dark, wood-frame buildings nestled at the foot of Club Mesa. Southeast of the mill stood a two-story, white-frame boardinghouse that housed single men and provided meals for a dollar per day. Surrounding these structures were a number of tents and lean-tos that housed the miners and their families. Across the main "street" stood a small frame clubhouse, a chemical labora-tory, and a tent school for the handful of children in the camp.[7]

Workers in the mines and at Joe Junior Camp lived an isolated life. With few automobiles or recreational opportunities, miners often worked seven days a week. In addition to their customary tasks of locating and developing ore bodies, producers also had to stuff the carnotite ore into 18 inch x 24 inch canvas sacks. These 70 pound sacks were then transported by mule from atop the mesas to the Joe Junior mill on the valley floor where the ores were separated. High-grade ores were sent directly to the railroad at Placerville, whereas lower-grade ores were first upgraded at the Joe Junior mill. It often took a week for the six-team wagons to make the 120 mile round-trip to Placerville.[8]

Although the progressives lost their campaign for government control of the industry in 1914, the beginning of World War I threatened demand until the use of a radium-based luminous paint in the war effort gradually led to an increase in Standard's production in 1918. In addition, the price of vanadium rose from between $1.80 and $2.50 a pound in 1916 to $5.50 a pound in 1917 and led carnotite companies to retrofit their plants to extract vanadium ore as well.[9] Standard increased its production by acquir-ing more claims and improving operating conditions in the area. Roads were built in the San Miguel valley that allowed gasoline trucks to replace the slower and more expensive horse-drawn wagons.[10]

By 1921, Standard Chemical was well on its way to becoming one of the major radium and vanadium producers in the world. Although the postwar depression slowed the vanadium and radium markets, an announce-ment the following year wiped out the Colorado carnotite industry. Early in 1922 Union Minere du Haut Katanga of Belgium announced that it had discovered a rich new source of pitchblende, another radioactive mineral, in its mines in the Belgian Congo (now the Democratic Republic of Congo). Although the deposit had been discovered before the war, the company had waited to make the announcement until its refineries were in place so it could corner the market on radium, which it did. With ore forty to a hundred times more pure than the Colorado carnotite, Union Minere eas-ily undercut its competition by selling radium at $70,000 per gram. In response, Standard Chemical closed the Joe Junior mill and Camp in 1923. Ten years later another pitchblende discovery in northern Canada ensured that the radium era was over in the United States.[11]

In sum, estimates suggest that from 1898 to 1923, miners on the Colorado Plateau processed about 67,000 tons of carnotite ore. From this amount, scientists produced only 202 grams—less than half a pound—of radium at a cost averaging $120,000 per gram.[12]

Although the radium era on the Colorado Plateau ended in the early 1920s, mining officials continued to study carnotite's vanadium content. Ferro-vanadium, used as an alloy to strengthen steel, could easily be extracted from Colorado carnotite. Sensing a new market, in 1927 Union Carbide and Carbon Corporation purchased the United States Vanadium Company's (USV) property in Rifle, Colorado, and made USV a wholly owned subsidiary. A year later USV expanded its holdings on the plateau by buying the Joe Junior mill and a number of adjacent claims from Standard Chemical.[13] In the early 1930s another company, the Vanadium Corporation of America (VCA), acquired the claims of the Colorado Radium Company and the Radium Luminous Material Corporation. VCA constructed a new town and rebuilt an unused mill owned by Rare Metals Company at Vancorum, just 13 miles southeast of the Joe Junior Camp. By 1935, two more companies had built vanadium mills in the area: North Continent Mines Company in Slick Rock, Colorado, and International Vanadium Company in Dry Valley, Utah.[14]

As vanadium production expanded on the Colorado Plateau, Howard Balsley, a former forest ranger from Moab, Utah, founded a small uranium-buying company. In fact, Balsley had been grubstaking radium, vanadium, and uranium miners since the turn of the twentieth century. Since vanadium had replaced radium as the metal of choice, Balsley realized that high-grade uranium ores were being discarded. If he could separate these ores, he might turn a profit. In 1934 Balsley signed a contract to supply uranium ore to the Vitro Manufacturing Company of Canonsburg, Pennsylvania, primarily for use as a pigment in pottery and glass factories. To supply his contract, Balsley bargained with more than 300 miners scattered across the Colorado Plateau. He then located central warehouses in Utah at Blanding, Monticello, Moab, Cisco, Thompson, and Green River. He also stored ore in the Colorado towns of Grand Junction, Meeker, Montrose, Naturita, Dove Creek, and Egnar. Thus by 1935, both vanadium and uranium mining had returned to the Colorado Plateau.[15]

In 1936, USV moved its Rifle plant to the Joe Junior Camp and began building a new model town around it. The town was christened Uravan for

Uravan looking south, 1936. This view shows the housing area of the new United States Vanadium company town of Uravan. Built on the site of the former Joe Junior Camp, the mill at Uravan processed the area's carnotite ore for the steel alloy vanadium. Courtesy, Estalee Silver Collection.

the principal ores of *ura*nium and *van*adium. USV built its mill on the southwest side of the San Miguel River on the site of the old Joe Junior refinery and built frame houses for its expected 250 employees on the opposite bank. To help alleviate the isolation, USV also erected a theater, medical clinic, store, community hall, guest houses, churches, and a school.[16] To power the mill and town, USV constructed three types of power plants — hydro, steam, and diesel.[17] Finally, the company established its own water system and connected each house to its own septic tank.[18]

Uravan's first years show a community planting roots. In the fall of 1936 a school was constructed by joining two cabins from a nearby Civilian Conservation Corps camp. In October the post office was opened, and the first mail arrived in the community.[19] In July 1937 the first child, a girl, was born in Uravan.[20] By the following year, in addition to the traffic of mill workers and miners, daily truck shipments brought foodstuffs, coal, and mail to the town. Since salt was needed for vanadium milling, USV acquired it from brine wells in nearby Paradox Valley. Most of the company's 250 workers labored six days per week. The monthly payroll ran about $60,000. Despite, or perhaps because of, the lack of a union, few labor problems occurred.[21]

Because of Uravan's size and industrial base, most workers knew one another. Further, most of the residents had either grown up in the nearby communities of Nucla, Norwood, and Naturita or had transferred with USV from Rifle.[22] In their leisure time, the workers and their families played cards and hosted parties. Because the town was "dry," alcohol had to be purchased 16 miles away in Naturita. Although management had nicer houses than the laborers, both groups intermingled. During the summer, residents played baseball and swam in the mill's cooling basin that doubled as the company pool. Schoolchildren studied in Uravan through the eighth grade and were bussed to Nucla for high school.[23]

By 1940, the vanadium industry had brought a certain prosperity back to the radium country of the Colorado Plateau. In addition to the seven vanadium mills in Colorado, two additional companies—International Vanadium Corporation and Blanding Mines—had built plants in Dry Valley and Blanding, Utah. VCA was building another mill at Monticello, Utah. Many independent mines were also operating throughout the plateau to supply the buyers.[24]

Uranium, however, was the vanadium producers' biggest waste product in the 1930s. Although some of the more highly concentrated materials were sold to Howard Balsley and then to Vitro for use as ceramic coloring, most unused uranium—along with silver, cobalt, and other heavy metals—settled into tailings piles at every vanadium and radium mill across the plateau.[25] As Europe went to war, demand for steel alloys became acute. Knowing that uranium, like vanadium, could be used as a hardening agent in steel, in 1937 USV added a uranium circuit to its Uravan mill. After two years this process had produced approximately 250,000 pounds of a uranium/vanadium concentrate known as *green sludge*.[26] Even at this late date, uranium was considered just another metal. That attitude soon changed.

Beginning in the early 1930s, physicists around the world started to reformulate understanding of the atomic world and began to see the tremendous potential of nuclear chain reactions.[27] Expanding on Pierre and Marie Curie's experiments with radioactivity, Ernest Rutherford, Frederick Soddy, and Leo Szilard established the present nuclear paradigm that atoms could be split, thereby producing large amounts of energy. In 1934 Madame Curie's daughter, Irene, along with her husband, Frederic Joliot, identified uranium as the best source of the new energy. In December 1938 German scientists discovered the basic fission process, but politics entered the picture. Many feared Hitler's Germany, having already seized Czechoslovakia's uranium deposits, would be the first to build a nuclear weapon.[28] On 2 August 1939, Albert Einstein wrote to President Franklin D. Roosevelt asserting that a nuclear bomb made from uranium was within reach.[29] Although uranium had changed from a worthless by-product to a possible miracle element, the most pressing need in 1941 was still for vanadium.

As the United States prepared to enter World War II, the federal government made sure ready supplies of vanadium would be available for alloy productions. In 1941 the government classified vanadium as a strategic metal and created a government-sponsored buying program to boost exploration and production of the mineral. The Metals Reserve Company (MRC), organized in 1942 as a part of the Reconstruction Finance Corporation, established a base price for vanadium ores. The U.S. Geological Survey and the Bureau of Mines operated a cooperative exploration and drilling program. As mining developed, buying stations were established in Moab, Thompson, and Monticello, Utah. To process the accumulated ore, MRC contracted with VCA and USV to construct and operate a mill in Monticello, Utah, and Durango, Colorado, respectively.[30]

As vanadium production spread throughout the plateau, a new uranium program began. In August 1942 the Army Corps of Engineers' Manhattan Engineer District (MED) established a secret program to develop an atomic bomb. Under the direction of Brigadier General Leslie R. Groves, the MED was responsible for engineering a bomb and procuring raw materials. Although the development of technical towns such as Los Alamos, New Mexico, and Oak Ridge, Tennessee, is well-known, scholars have neglected the raw materials activities of the project.[31]

In 1942 the greatest sources of uranium in the world were the veins and tailings piles of the two richest radium mines: the Shinkolobwe mine in the Belgian Congo and the Eldorado mine at Port Radium on Great Bear Lake, Northwest Territories, Canada. Although great effort ultimately secured 86 percent of MED's uranium from these two sources, in December 1942 MED also surveyed vanadium-processing plants on the Colorado Plateau. This analysis led to contracts to purchase tailings from the two largest plateau producers—the Vanadium Corporation of American and United States Vanadium—plus the recently organized Metals Reserve Company.[32]

The Manhattan Project transformed uranium from waste to the most important metal in national defense, which also increased the importance of the carnotite communities on the Colorado Plateau. From 1943 to 1945, MED purchased mill tailings in Blanding, Utah, as well as in the Colorado towns of Naturita, Durango, Slick Rock, Gateway, and Loma. In Moab, MED contracted with Vitro Manufacturing Company's local buyer, Howard Balsley, to purchase his stockpile of high-grade uranium ore. At Uravan and Durango, MED contracted with USV to reprocess the region's tailings into

8

a crude uranium sludge. Finally, in Grand Junction, MED constructed a refinery to concentrate the sludge sent from Durango and Uravan.[33]

In addition, the Manhattan Project also contracted with USV's parent company, Union Carbide and Carbon Corporation, to create the Union Mines Development Corporation (UMDC), a government-sponsored uranium resource investigation company. Organized into four separate divisions—bibliographic research, field exploration, exploration research, and metallurgical research—UMDC examined all available literature on uranium ore, conducted field investigations in thirty-six states and twenty countries, developed better exploration instruments such as an improved Geiger counter, and discovered better methods of refining plateau uranium ores. The UMDC also conducted geological surveys of the plateau states including three reports on Arizona, eighteen for Colorado, one for New Mexico, and twenty-two for Utah. Finally, MED purchased three promising uranium producing areas in Colorado and Arizona.[34]

On 12 May 1943, the U.S. government signed a top-secret contract, effective back to January, with United States Vanadium to operate its plant for uranium procurement.[35] In addition, MED contracted to build another unit at Uravan to assist the USV plant. Uranium ore would be secured from the area's many tailings, which would be brought to Uravan and run through one of the two plants to produce 3 tons per day of green sludge. This material was transported, along with similar matter from MED's Durango plant, to the Grand Junction refinery. The new Uravan sludge plant cost just over $300,000 and was operational by 15 July 1943. Together, the two plants employed about 180 workers at a monthly cost of $110,000.[36]

The growing MED presence could not have come at a better time. By early 1944 the Metals Reserve had become so successful at producing vanadium that all of its contracts were closed as of 28 February. Thus the MED boom, occurring just as the vanadium market was slumping, kept the carnotite communities of western Colorado alive.[37]

The change in production brought immediate changes to Uravan. The first order of business was security. Unlike the Metals Reserve, MED was a top-secret organization. To protect the secret mill, the army enclosed the area in wire fencing and constructed police gates at the town's entrance. At first, guards were posted 24 hours a day, and no vehicle could enter the town without proper identification. After a few months security diminished, and the gates remained open.[38] Although the U.S. Army still coded uranium S-37 and uranium oxide SOQ, most mill workers knew they were producing uranium sludge for the government, but they probably did not know to what end.[39]

Signs of the war were seen in Uravan. In addition to the reintroduction of a sizable industrial plant in the once quiet valley,[40] ration books, gasoline stickers, war movies, scrap drives, and savings bond drives soon appeared in the isolated town. To honor local servicemen, blue stars were placed in the windows of families' homes, and USV erected a military honor roll sign above the commissary.[41]

Like most U.S. production areas, Uravan also experienced a severe labor shortage. The town's isolation had often limited its available workforce, and the war exacerbated the situation. Further, three shifts were needed at both mills to keep the plants running around the clock.[42] To combat these problems, USV was permitted to hire boys at least sixteen years old and women no younger than eighteen.[43] At one point fifteen or sixteen women were working in the Uravan mill. Although several of the women were wives of company men, the majority had been recruited from outside the area.[44] In addition, the army returned a handful of drafted operators to work in the mills, including Cliff Hiett, whose story was related at the beginning of this chapter.[45]

Uravan's growing importance to the war effort is clear from MED's efforts to keep the town running at peak efficiency. Although the domestic labor shortage that plagued the entire country was acute in Uravan because of the heavy workload and the town's isolation, USV appealed to local draft boards to keep qualified workers on staff. The MED also assigned twenty-eight servicemen to work in Uravan's mills during the war. In addition to these special arrangements, Uravan workers might have stayed on the job for patriotic reasons, knowing they were contributing to the war effort. Despite these efforts, USV mill employees called for a strike in late May 1945, complaining about reduced pay, the company's seniority system, and the inability to settle past grievances. The company threatened to inform the striking workers' draft boards, thereby making them available for conscription, and negotiations brought the strike to a quick end a week later. Work in Uravan's mills had clearly become a national security priority.[46]

The influx of workers ballooned Uravan's population and stressed its infrastructure. Wartime population swelled to roughly 400. The number of school-age children peaked at 190, necessitating an addition to the Uravan school. To house the influx of government workers, in late 1942 the government let out contracts to build a series of one-, two-, and three-bedroom apartments northwest of the mill complex. Locals soon nicknamed these one-story, multiple-dwelling units "flattops."[47] Area newspapers, unaware of the secret uranium project, reported that the additional housing would be used by vanadium miners.[48]

From the completion of the Uravan mill in 1943 to the depletion of stockpiled tailings the next fall, MED processed about 150 tons of tailings in the USV plant and almost 400 tons in its own plant. USV's mill in Durango yielded almost 80 tons of the 20 percent sludge.[49]

Other vanadium companies around the Colorado Plateau contributed to the MED program. In Naturita, the VCA mill produced approximately 80 tons of uranium concentrate at 45–50 percent uranium oxide. In Moab, MED purchased the high-grade ore Howard Balsley had been accumulating. By late 1944, uranium sludge from the Colorado Plateau had been further refined into about 800 tons of uranium oxide.[50]

Adding up all the uranium sources in late 1944, MED concluded that there was enough material to operate all of its bomb facilities through the fall of 1945. Of the approximately 6,000 tons purchased by the Manhattan Project, two-thirds had come from high-grade Congo sources, one-sixth from Canadian pitchblende, and only one-seventh from Colorado carnotite. The domestic enterprise had been small and expensive, but given uranium's importance to national security, it was important to utilize domestic sources in case future uranium was needed.[51]

The successful outcome of the Manhattan Project became known to project members after the 16 July test at Trinity and was known to the world following the atomic bombing of Hiroshima on 6 August. Two days later another bomb was dropped on Nagasaki, and World War II was over. On the Colorado Plateau, MED told workers at Uravan's two plants that their work had been successful after the Trinity test, but the actual nature of that work was not discovered until the bombings in Japan.[52] Just a week after Nagasaki, the Moab *Times-Independent* ran a headline proclaiming "Atomic Bomb Element Produced Here."[53]

The Metals Reserve Company and the Manhattan Project had helped stabilize life on the Colorado Plateau. Local miners were given guaranteed prices for their ores, and nearby farmers and ranchers found ready markets for their products. Likewise, the major industrial companies—VCA and USV—prospered on government war contracts. Although the nationalization of the carnotite industry progressives dreamed of had given way to a joint government–private industry agreement, the role of the federal government in the uranium towns had certainly increased.

The Manhattan Project alchemists had transformed uranium from a nearly worthless waste product to one of the most important materials in the world. National security now demanded locating, developing, and maintaining uranium resources wherever possible. For the people of the Colorado Plateau's carnotite communities, the future appeared unlimited.

Certainly, the development of uranium resources would bring tremendous growth and money to towns like Uravan, Grand Junction, Moab, and Blanding, forever ending their cultural and economic isolation.

Notes

1. Hiett's story is told in John A. Hardcastle, "Halfway Between Nobody Knows Where and Somebody's Starting Point: A History of the West End of Montrose County, Colorado," unpublished M.A. thesis, Utah State University, 1998, 97–98. Because of the use of recently opened archives, Hardcastle's treatment of Uravan is the most thorough to date. A similar incident brought nearby Nucla resident Kenneth Bonner back to Uravan following a medical discharge from the army. See http://uravan.com/uravan/comments.htm#Kenneth_Bonner [14 August 2001].

2. Robert A. Meyers, ed., *Encyclopedia of Physical Science and Technology,* 2d ed. (San Diego: Academic, 1992), s.v. "Uranium," by William L. Chenoweth.

3. Early reports of Colorado's carnotite history can be found in two articles by Thomas F.V. Curran, then president of General Vanadium Company. See "Carnotite in Paradox Valley, Colo.," *Engineering and Mining Journal* 92 (30 December 1911): 1287–88, and "Carnotite-I," *Engineering and Mining Journal* 96 (20 December 1913): 1165–67.

4. Gary Lee Shumway, "A History of the Uranium Industry on the Colorado Plateau," unpublished Ph.D. diss., University of Southern California, 1970, 19–22.

5. Ibid.

6. Life and work in the Joe Junior Camp around World War I are described in Kenneth C. Nicholson, "Early Carnotite Mining in Colorado," *Engineering and Mining Journal* 159, no. 6 (June 1958): 100–101.

7. Estalee Silver, *Images of the Uravan, Colorado Area 1880–1990* (Grand Junction, Colo.: By the author, 1992).

8. Charles L. Parson, R. B. Moore, S. C. Lind, and O. C. Schaefer, *Extraction and Recovery of Radium, Uranium and Vanadium From Carnotite,* Department of Interior, Bureau of Mines, Bulletin 104, Mineral Technology 12 (Washington, D.C.: Government Printing Office [GPO], 1915), and Karl L. Kithill and John A. Davis, *Mining and Concentration of Carnotite Ores,* Department of Interior, Bureau of Mines, Bulletin 103, Mineral Technology 11 (Washington, D.C.: GPO, 1917).

9. Shumway, "History," 71–72.

10. Ibid., 74.

11. An excellent history of the radium era, including Canada's rise as a top radium producer in the 1930s, can be found in Robert Bothwell, *Eldorado: Canada's National Uranium Company* (Toronto: University of Toronto Press, 1984), 3–154.

12. William L. Chenoweth, "The Uranium-Vanadium Deposits of the Uravan Mineral Belt and Adjacent Areas, Colorado and Utah," *New Mexico Geological Society Guidebook,* 32nd Field Conference, Western Slope Colorado, 1981, 165–170.

13. J. B. Huffard, "Corporation Acquires Additional Vanadium Property in Colorado," *The Carbidea* (February 1929): 5.

14. Chenoweth, "Uranium-Vanadium," 168; Holger Albrethsen and Frank E. McGinley, *Summary History of Domestic Uranium Procurement Under U.S. Atomic Energy Commission Contracts: Final Report* (Grand Junction, Colo.: U.S. Department of Energy, 1982), A-24.

15. This information is from a letter by Howard Balsley describing his role in the early uranium activity on the Colorado Plateau. This document has been printed in a number of published sources, most recently in Robert Sullenberger, "100 Years of Uranium Activity in the Four Corners Region," *Journal of the Western Slope* 7, no. 4 (fall 1992): 1–18.

16. Several articles appeared in area papers regarding the building of the new "model town," including "Vanadium Corp. Building Town Called Uravan," Telluride *Journal,* 28 March 1936; "New Town Being Built in Paradox," Elk Mountain (Gunnison, Colorado) *Pilot,* 16 April 1936; and the Denver *Post,* 31 December 1937. These clippings were all found in the Uravan file, Western History Department, Denver Public Library.

17. "Uravan Is the Site of Mining, Milling Operations," *Colorado Prospector,* c. August 1939, Uravan file, Western History Department, Denver Public Library.

18. John and Lorraine Hill, interview by Clare Engle, 21 July 1970, interview 187, transcript, Utah Uranium Oral History Project, Marriott Library, University of Utah, Salt Lake City, Utah (hereafter UUOHP).

19. Marion E. Benedict, interview by Clare Engle, 6 August 1970, interview 101, transcript, UUOHP.

20. Tandie van Sell, "The Early History of Uravan and Uravan Area," tms., in possession of Estalee Silver, Grand Junction, Colorado.

21. "Mining Town: Vanadium Ore Mined and Milled on Immense Scale at Uravan, Thriving Montrose County Town," Montrose *Daily Press,* 24 August 1939; John R.J. Munro, interview by Clare Engle, 29 July 1970, interview 180, transcript, UUOHP.

22. Hill interview, UUOHP.

23. Hill and Munro interviews, UUOHP.

24. A. Q. Lundquist and J. L. Lake, "History and Trends of the Uranium Plant Flowsheet," *Mining Congress Journal* (November 1955): 42.

25. Rodney D. Millar, Lane T. Neilson, and Richard E. Turley, *A Study of the Utah Uranium Milling Industry, Volume II: Utah Energy Resources—Uranium* (Salt Lake City: Mechanical and Industrial Engineering Department and Utah Engineering Experiment Station, May 1980), 2.5.

26. Blair Burwell, "Construction, Operation, and Maintenance Report of Uranium Sludge Plants Operated by the United States Vanadium Corporation in the Colorado Area," copy on file with William Chenoweth, Grand Junction, Colorado; "Uranium Mill May Be Built at Uravan, Adding to What Is Already Great Property," Grand Junction *Sentinel,* 3 September 1939; Richard G. Hewlett and Oscar E. Anderson Jr., *The New World: Volume I, A History of the United States Atomic Energy Commission* (University Park: Pennsylvania State University Press, 1962), 292.

27. Richard Rhodes, *The Making of the Atomic Bomb* (New York: Touchstone, 1986), 13–28.

28. Ibid., 324–325, 385; Nicholas Dawidoff, *The Catcher Was a Spy: The Mysterious Life of Moe Berg* (New York: Vintage, 1994).

29. Quoted in A. Constadina Titus, *Bombs in the Backyard: Atomic Testing and American Politics* (Reno: University of Nevada Press, 1986), 5.

30. F. J. Hahne, "Early Uranium Mining in the United States," paper presented at the annual symposium of the Uranium Institute, 6–8 September 1989, London; Albrethsen and McGinley, *Summary History,* A-11.

31. William L. Chenoweth, "Raw Materials Activities of the Manhattan Project on the Colorado Plateau," *Four Corners Geological Society Guidebook,* 10th Field Conference, Cataract Canyon, 1987, 151–154; Leslie R. Groves, *Now It Can Be Told: The Story of the Manhattan Project* (New York: Harper, 1962); Major General K. D. Nichols, *The Road to Trinity* (New York: William Morrow, 1987), Rhodes, *Atomic Bomb.*

32. Chenoweth, "Raw Materials."

33. Ibid.

34. Ibid.

35. U.S. Army Corps of Engineers, Manhattan Engineer District, "Fixed Fee Design, Engineering, Construction, Equipment, and Operation Contract" with the United States Vanadium Corporation, 25 January 1943, Appropriation #212/30905, in files of Jack Frost, Umetco Minerals Corporation, Grand Junction, Colorado (hereafter MED-USV contract).

36. Ibid.

37. Chenoweth, "Raw Materials."

38. "When Uravan Went to War," in letter from Bob Ausmus to Estalee Silver, Grand Junction, January 1992. Original in possession of Estalee Silver, Estalee Silver Collection, Grand Junction, Colorado.

39. William Everett and Marge Haldane, interview by Clare Engle, 4 August 1970, interview 179, transcript, UUOHP.

40. David Lavender, *One Man's West,* 3d ed. (Lincoln: University of Nebraska Press, 1977), 276–277.

41. Ausmus, "Uravan Went to War."

42. Haldane interview, UUOHP.

43. U.S. Army Corps of Engineers, MED-USV Contract.

44. Haldane interview, UUOHP.

45. Van Sell, "Early History of Uravan Area," 42.

46. Hardcastle, "Halfway Between," 94–108.

47. Silver, *Images,* 14–15.

48. Stories of the construction contract appear in "Uravan Will Benefit From Housing Plan," Montrose *Daily Press,* 24 November 1942, and "Montrose Man Gets Contract Uravan Housing," Grand Junction *Daily Sentinel,* 10 January 1943. Details of the buildings can be found in "R. E. Wear Construction Company Is Awarded Contract to Build Housing Project at Naturita and Uravan," Montrose *Daily Press,* 11 January 1943.

49. Hewlett and Anderson, *The New World,* 292.

50. Ibid.

51. Ibid.

52. Hardcastle, "Halfway Between," 113.

53. "Atomic Bomb Element Produced Here," Moab *Times-Independent,* 16 August 1945.

Chapter
2

To Stimulate Production

and in

Interest of Security:

The First

Cold War Uranium Boom,

1946–1958

IN THE MID-1950s Gardner Games company marketed an electronic board game called *Uranium Rush*. The board was colored to look like a variety of western landscapes including "purple mountains," "green hill country," and "sandy desert." Each player was grubstaked with $15,000, and play proceeded by chance: each player spun an arrow that directed him or her toward the proper landscape for prospecting. As each mine was staked, the player had to decide whether to sell the claim or "develop" it. If the player chose the latter, he or she paid the government bank $1,000 and took an electronic "Geiger counter"—a small flashlight-like object—and held it against the game board. If the Geiger counter's light flashed, the player had discovered uranium and received $50,000 from the government bank.[1]

After testing the claim, the player picked one of thirty "government cards" from the deck and followed its instructions. These cards included bills for new Geiger counters, hospital fees following mountain lion attacks.

Uranium Rush board game. Like other forms of atomic popular culture, the 1950s board game *Uranium Rush* capitalized on the uranium boom. The iconography of the box top melds the traditional miner's mule, a western landscape, and new atomic symbols. Author's collection. Photo by Michael Amundson, 2001.

and rewards for finding oil, silver, gold, and copper prospects. Others reflected Cold War attitudes; one card ordered that the Geiger counter be skipped past the next player in case that player was an enemy agent; another gave the lucky player an extra $5,000 because the government bought the claim for an air force base; another awarded the player an extra $20,000 for discovering extra-high-grade uranium ore. One card forced the player to pay the bank $10,000 to clear title for the last claim because the ground was owned by an "Indian Tribe." The prospector with the most money when all claims had been staked won the game.

Although *Uranium Rush* was only one of many such toys at the time, it serves as an important symbol of uranium's transformation in the early days of the Cold War. Although the Manhattan Project had been top secret, the 1950s uranium boom was much advertised and very popular. In fact, the randomness of spinning a dial and selecting a card seemed to mirror the image that with a little luck, anyone could discover uranium, help preserve national security, and become a millionaire in the process. At the same time, the use of government cards suggested that Uncle Sam would regulate the whole affair and maintain security by being wary of "enemy agents."

On a deeper level, the creation and popularity of *Uranium Rush* and other Cold War toys represented the growing acceptance of atomic bombs in everyday American life. The possibilities of instant wealth and notoriety were sexier than the guardedness of national security considered necessary during the Manhattan Project. Although the veil of nuclear secrecy had been lifted and the effects of atomic bombs on the Japanese well documented, the American public separated the horrors of the atom bomb from the romance and awe of life in the nuclear world. The Manhattan Project's famed compartmentalization had seemingly been replaced by a sort of accommodation in which Americans joked about some aspects of atomic technology while repressing others. Patriotism and national security were rarely discussed by hopeful prospectors; Geiger counters, radioactivity, "glowing in the dark," and getting rich quick were more common topics. Little thought was given to how all the uranium would be used. A 1946 poll revealed that 47 percent of Americans were not worried at all or worried very little about the atomic bomb. People trusted science, the government, and God to protect them or suggested that such worry was useless.[2] Thus as the Atomic Energy Commission created and subsidized a massive search for uranium to use in atomic bombs, the U.S. public trusted its leaders and treated the uranium boom as another Old West adventure.[3]

The story began as World War II came to a close. V-J Day ended the war, but it did not conclude the Manhattan Engineer District's (MED) programs. As soon as the war ended, Congress met to decide whether to keep the atomic program under the control of the military or turn it over to some type of civilian command. The MED faced its own problems including postwar staff shortages as leading scientists left the project, debate over development of the hydrogen bomb, and procurement of new nuclear materials.[4] For the head of the MED, General Leslie Groves, the most pressing problem was administration. Although Groves had been in charge of the MED and its many resources during the war, he felt it was important to move control of the country's atomic program away from the War Department to a bipartisan, appointed civilian committee.[5]

For almost a year Congress debated how this new commission would work, who its possible members would be, and what responsibilities they would have.[6] Fifty-one weeks after the war ended, Congress passed the Atomic Energy Act. Citing the clearly evident power of atomic energy for military purposes, as well as the possible effects on social, economic, and political structures, this statute vested control of the country's atomic program in a five-member civilian board to be called the Atomic Energy Commission. Next, the act created a board of nine senators and nine representatives, called the Joint Committee on Atomic Energy (JCAE), to watch over the AEC and report back to their respective bodies.[7]

From its creation, the Atomic Energy Act sought to promote the use of nuclear energy for peaceful means as well as for defense. In fact, the act stated that atomic energy should be used for "improving the public welfare, increasing the standard of living, strengthening free competition in private enterprise, and promoting world peace."[8] To carry out this task, the AEC was empowered to establish four major programs designed to encourage private research, control scientific and technical information, establish federal research and development, and control all fissionable materials.[9]

The most important of these tasks for the domestic uranium industry involved government control. The law provided for federal ownership of all atomic reactors and production equipment. The act guaranteed that all fissionable materials—including uranium, thorium, and plutonium—would also be under government control. Further, it empowered the AEC to establish guaranteed prices for uranium ore if necessary. In short, these provisions made the federal government, through the AEC, the sole legal buyer, refiner, and producer of uranium ore for atomic energy use.[10]

The creation of the government market fulfilled the desire for the government to watch over the carnotite mining industry. Carnotite processing had been watched closely, including the progressives' unsuccessful attempts to monitor radium production and the controlled production of vanadium and uranium during World War II. But instead of continuing government uranium production, the Atomic Energy Act designated a system of guaranteed prices to encourage *private* businesses to explore and extract uranium, which could be sold only to the federal government.[11] This special trade condition, which economists call a monopsony, ensured a guaranteed market for private producers but also gave the government extraordinary power within the new uranium industry.[12]

Because of delays in selecting the first AEC members, the transfer of power from General Groves and the MED did not take place until 1 January 1947. For Groves and the MED, the almost yearlong lag proved difficult. The turnover phase was even worse for uranium producers as carnotite miners on the Colorado Plateau saw their government war contracts end and the price of uranium collapse.[13]

The boom that had enveloped the uranium mining camp of Uravan during the war ended shortly after V-J Day. Since the signing of its government contract in early 1943, the town's two treatment plants had worked around the clock, seven days a week, processing the area's vanadium tailings. By October 1945 there were no more tailings, and the MED contract ended. A secret MED report showed that the best and most easily accessible ore in the Uravan area had already been mined.[14] On the basis of this information, the government decided to close and then dismantle its plant in Uravan. United States Vanadium (USV) mothballed its Uravan mill and closed down the town.[15]

By the time the AEC assumed control on New Year's Day 1947, the U.S. uranium mining industry was at a standstill. Of the five former vanadium-processing plants that had operated on the Colorado Plateau during World War II, only one was still functioning, at half capacity. Uranium production was negligible, and only fifty-five men were at work in the area's mines.[16] To maintain the country's nuclear testing program, the commission turned to foreign countries as its primary source of uranium. By the end of 1947, the AEC had signed contracts with the MED's two major foreign suppliers, the Union Minere in the Belgian Congo and Eldorado in Canada.[17]

Although these contracts provided temporary relief, the AEC realized that more than 85 percent of MED uranium had been imported and that continuing that policy would make the United States overly dependent on foreign sources, possibly threatening national security. Therefore it was imperative to begin a widespread domestic uranium procurement program. The best place to begin would be the site of the last uranium production: the Colorado Plateau. The AEC created the Colorado Raw Materials Office in Grand Junction in December 1947 to spearhead the new ore and concentrate exploration and procurement program.[18] Finally, to enable the AEC to process future ore, in 1947 the commission contracted with the Vanadium Corporation of America and United States Vanadium to restart their mills in Naturita and Rifle, Colorado. The following summer the AEC acquired the Metals Reserve Company mill in Monticello, Utah, from the War Assets Administration.[19]

From its creation, the new Grand Junction office faced a serious dilemma. Because the new AEC concentrate contracts had been signed with the former vanadium giants VCA and USV, the plateau's many independent miners worried that a government-sponsored monopoly would be allowed to control carnotite production. This concern proved real when the VCA established uranium ore prices far below the typical miner's cost of production.[20] Throughout 1947 and early 1948, small mining companies worked to convince the AEC that expansion would not take place until independent producers, not just big companies, could turn a profit.[21]

Beginning in 1948 the commission embarked on a new program to expand the country's uranium industry. The AEC joined forces with U.S. Geological Survey (USGS) geologists and ordered government withdrawal of thousands of acres of public land from claim staking, conducted widespread airborne reconnaissance, and test drilled to chart uranium deposits throughout the West. If ore was discovered, the AEC leased the land for mining. If nothing was found, it returned the land to the public domain. Working from exploration camps in the field, geologists calibrated equipment and tested new Geiger counters. To ensure public disclosure, the AEC also published regular press releases and reports.[22]

As this work began, in April 1948 the AEC launched a series of programs, issued in the form of numbered circulars, to activate the domestic uranium industry by bringing independent miners into the fold. The first program included a government-guaranteed ten-year minimum price of $3.50 per pound of refined product for most plateau ores. The second offered a $10,000 bonus for the discovery and production of high-grade ores from noncarnotite deposits, and the third promised a government-guaranteed three-year minimum price of $1.50 per pound plus development allowances and premiums for higher-grade materials and for the delivery of low-grade plateau ores to the AEC purchasing agent.[23] Although the manager of the Grand Junction office believed the new program would stimulate domestic procurement, Colorado Plateau uranium miners argued that prices were still too low.[24]

Over the next two weeks, plateau producers and their congressmen pressured the AEC to raise its ore prices. To accommodate them the AEC issued Circular 4, which guaranteed two additional allowances for carnotite producers. First, the new program provided a "haulage allowance" of 6 cents per ton mile (maximum 100 miles) for ore delivered to the AEC. Second, the program added 50 cents per pound for higher-grade carnotite ores.[25] With these incentives in place, uranium mining on the Colorado Plateau increased almost immediately.[26]

To provide easy access to miners across the region, the AEC established a series of ore-buying stations throughout the plateau at which government contractors would weigh the ore, analyze it for its uranium content, and pay the producer based on the fixed schedule and bonuses. The first depot was located in Monticello, Utah, at the site of the government mill. As new deposits were found, ore-buying stations were built in the area once it became clear that the strike could support its own mill. When a mill contract was made, the AEC withdrew its station and sold the accumulated ore to the mill.[27]

The search for new domestic uranium deposits began in 1948 in the Uravan mineral belt on the Colorado Plateau and slowly radiated outward. Aided by guaranteed prices and haulage allowances, local weekend prospectors began to search the backcountry for uranium. To aid the amateur, popular magazines published articles on how to look for uranium.[28]

In 1949 the AEC issued the booklet *Prospecting for Uranium*. This handbook included chapters that listed the major uranium-bearing minerals; explained different types of ore deposits, testing and prospecting with radiation-detecting instruments, and assaying and selling procedures; described laws and regulations concerning mining claims; addressed frequently asked questions; and finally provided an appendix of price schedules, sources of Geiger counters, and geological information.[29]

To clarify the many rules and regulations in effect, in 1949 the AEC combined several aspects of its circulars under the umbrella of a new Circular 5. This latest program merged Circulars 3 and 4, increased the price for uranium oxide, and established premium prices for higher-grade ores. In effect, Circular 5, especially after it was amended in 1951, became the basic purchasing guideline for the domestic procurement program through 1962.[30]

Stabilized by Circular 5, the first government-sponsored peacetime uranium rush began in 1949 and continued until 1958.[31] Working outward from the Uravan mineral belt, AEC and USGS geologists drilled thousands of exploratory holes and made airborne reconnaissances while thousands of amateur prospectors scoured the countryside looking for familiar outcroppings. As new finds were made, the AEC established ore-buying stations and considered mill sites. After reopening the five former vanadium mills, the AEC awarded contracts for mills at Hite and Salt Lake City, Utah, and Grand Junction, Colorado.[32]

These newly discovered uranium deposits assured that the United States would have atomic ores as the Cold War began. President Harry Truman had pledged in 1947 to resist global communism, and the country began to use nuclear diplomacy during the Berlin crisis in 1948. At the same time, the Pacific testing program required uranium. China's fall to communism and the discovery of the Soviet bomb the following year, followed by the recommendations of the NSC-68 (National Security Council) report in 1950, led the United States to embark on a nuclear arms race that continued to fuel government demands for even more yellowcake.

The first steps toward meeting these demands began when the first major uranium discovery of the postwar era occurred in the spring of 1950 when a Navajo named Paddy Martinez discovered uranium on land owned by the Santa Fe Railway northwest of Grants, New Mexico. According to the story, Martinez talked with some prospectors who showed him their ore samples. Saying he had seen similar rocks elsewhere, Martinez took the prospectors northwest of Grants to an outcrop at Haystack Butte. Santa Fe Railway geologists noted that some of the area's vegetation had a purplish tint like plants near other known uranium prospects. Martinez, who was familiar with the surrounding countryside, used that clue to show the geologists several places with similar "locator" plants. These areas also yielded uranium deposits. Encouraged by the prospects, the giant Anaconda Copper Mining Company soon discovered a large new ore body on the Laguna Pueblo reservation east of Grants. In late 1951 Anaconda signed an AEC contract to build a uranium-processing mill at Bluewater, a small railroad town west of Grants.[33]

As the uranium boom pushed into New Mexico, Charles A. Steen, a young geologist from Texas, was about to change the entire domestic industry. Unlike most weekend prospectors who used Geiger counters to search for uranium, Steen had a degree in geology from the Texas School of Mining and Metallurgy. By the end of the 1950s, Steen's rags-to-riches story was the most celebrated of the era and inspired others to look for uranium.

Charlie Steen had worked in South America as a geologist during World War II. After the war he completed a year of graduate work at the University of Chicago. After a stint with Standard Oil, Steen became interested in uranium. Intrigued by an article about the postwar rush, he borrowed money from his mother and in 1948 packed his wife and three children off to Utah.[34]

After checking out a number of sites, Steen settled on the Big Indian Mining District south of the tiny village of Cisco, Utah. Although he staked a number of claims, Steen failed to find uranium before his money ran out in 1950. He sold out and moved his family to Arizona. When they returned to Cisco a year later, Steen rented a $15-a-month shack without electricity or running water. When his wife contracted pneumonia and the bills mounted, Steen was sure his dream would be postponed again.[35]

Steen asked for more money, and amazingly, several hundred dollars were forwarded. Then his mother showed up, saying she had sold her Houston home to grubstake her son. Steen bargained with a friend for a used diamond drill. By early July 1952 Steen had moved the rig onto his Mi Vida (Spanish for "my life") claim in the Big Indian Wash about 40 miles southeast of Moab.[36]

Steen kept a sharp lookout for the familiar canary-yellow carnotite ore that would mean uranium. He figured the drill should reach carnotite approximately 200 feet below the surface. As the drill worked its way down, Steen removed cores that were a dirty gray. At 197 feet the drill broke deep in the hole. There was no way to retrieve it and still no sign of uranium. Frustrated, Steen tossed a few of his core samples into his jeep and headed back to Cisco, arriving on July 18. The owner of the local gas station asked if he had had any luck. When Steen tried a few of his gray samples under the man's Geiger counter, the needle jumped. Instead of yellow carnotite, Steen had found a million-dollar body of pitchblende.[37]

Before announcing his claim, Steen invited several close friends to join him in staking almost forty more claims near the Mi Vida. Over the next six months, Steen fought off critics who claimed he had "salted" the pitchblende because the AEC had earlier reported that the Big Indian Wash had no uranium. In October he started a small shaft near the drill hole and then went to Moab to form a company. In exchange for a few shares of stock, Moab lawyer and former state senator Mitch Mellich drew up the papers for the Utex Exploration Company. On Steen's thirty-first birthday in December, the shaft hit a 14-foot-thick lode of pitchblende just 68 feet down. The average assay showed that the ore measured 0.34 to 5.0 percent uranium oxide. It was the biggest strike in the history of the Colorado Plateau and was worth at least a million dollars.[38] At about the same time Steen's strike was reported, another rags-to-riches prospector named Vernon Pick made a million-dollar discovery near the small town of Hanksville, Utah.[39] Like Paddy Martinez's discovery in New Mexico, Steen's and Pick's strikes brought a flood of new prospectors to uranium country, all dreaming of striking it rich.

One such dreamer was businessman Bob Adams of Rawlins, Wyoming. In 1952 Adams read an article about Charlie Steen's discovery in Utah.[40] Adams, a restaurant owner, had also heard uranium talk from the AEC and Geological Survey crews who came into his restaurant after trips into the nearby hills. When Neil McNiece, a Sunday prospector from Riverton, Wyoming, discovered the "Lucky Mc" mine that year north of Rawlins, Adams was ready to act. He fitted his plane with radiation detectors and began to scan the hills north of Rawlins. Adams discovered uranium in the Crook's Gap area in 1954, and in March of 1955 he founded a small mining interest called the Lost Creek Oil and Uranium Company.[41]

From Wyoming, the uranium rush shifted back to the Ambrosia Lake area of New Mexico. Like the Charlie Steen saga, the story of septuagenarian Stella Dysart's uranium discovery is steeped in romance. A successful Los Angeles businesswoman in the 1920s, Dysart had invested in New Mexico land in hopes of striking oil on her property. After securing a sheep range called Ambrosia Lake northwest of Grants in 1925, Dysart spent the next twenty-five years drilling for oil. Paddy Martinez's discovery to the south in 1950 led Dysart to shift to uranium. She showed her drilling logs to a young geologist named Louis B. Lothman. He drilled 360 feet down and found a 17-foot-thick uranium seam. Another rush to Grants ensued. By 1956, discoveries showed that almost 70 percent of the nation's uranium reserves were below Ambrosia Lake. Unlike earlier deposits, these discoveries were too deep for small mining companies to develop properly. Instead, big companies including Phillips Petroleum, Homestake Mining, and Kerr-McGee were brought in. By 1958, four mills were operating at Ambrosia Lake.[42]

As more and more strikes were made, journalists throughout the nation chronicled the romance and intrigue of the new uranium kings and queens. Beginning with trade magazine stories in the late 1940s, the rags-to-riches tales of "uraniumaires" soon became Sunday features. Charlie Steen especially became the focal point of these stories. A typical 1953 article in the *American Mercury* called Steen the "new Horatio Alger."[43] Other stories exposed Steen's new lifestyle, describing Charlie and his wife taking the company plane to Grand Junction to have the laundry done or flying to Salt Lake City for rhumba lessons, Charlie driving around town in a new red cadillac, or Charlie going up in his plane to get better television reception.[44] Indeed, the number of uranium stories listed in the *Reader's Guide to Periodical Literature* rose from thirty in 1953 to over seventy in the two years following Steen's discovery.[45]

Movies also picked up on the uranium frenzy. Although Union Carbide and Carbon Corporation joined forces with the U.S. Bureau of Mines and the AEC to produce a documentary film called *The Petrified River: The Story of Uranium,* Hollywood produced a string of more memorable B movies about uranium. In Laurel and Hardy's final film, *Utopia,* released in 1950, Stan and Ollie inherited a Pacific Island on which uranium was soon discovered and a mad rush to the island ensued. Another film that year focused on the risk to national security posed by illegally selling uranium to a foreign country. In the *Bells of Coronado,* Roy Rogers starred as an undercover insurance investigator pursuing a "mysterious murderer plotting to sell stolen uranium to an unfriendly power." Four years later Mickey Rooney starred in *The Atomic Kid,* a farce based on a story by Blake Edwards. In the film, Rooney and costar Robert Strauss go searching for uranium in a remote corner of Nevada. Following hot leads, Rooney wanders into "doom town," the uninhabited village constructed on the Nevada test site, just as the army is detonating another atomic weapon.

Mill dignitaries with drums of yellowcake, c. 1958. Charlie Steen, *center,* father of uranium in Moab, leans against a drum of yellowcake outside the Moab mill. Also shown are Mitch Melich, *left,* and Roy Hollis, *right.* Courtesy, Dan O'Laurie Canyon Country Museum, URECO collection, Moab, Utah.

Somehow Rooney's character survives and "quickly senses the huge commercial potential in being the first human being to survive an atomic blast." Two other films were Leo Gorcey, Huntz Hall, and the Bowery Boys in the 1955 *Dig That Uranium* and Dennis Morgan and Patricia Medina in the 1956 film *Uranium Boom.* Whereas the poster for *Dig That Uranium* shows two cowboys in Nashville garb with drawn six-shooters, protecting a sparsely dressed woman, the *Uranium Boom* poster shows a buxom brunette and two prospectors holding Geiger counters. The poster is highlighted with the word EXPLOSIVE and the phrase "The inside story of the atom-age boomtowns!"[46]

Other forms of popular culture paid homage to uranium's get-rich-quick ethos. The television version of the *Amos and Andy* show featured a uranium mine in 1957. In January 1958 the *Lucy and Desi Comedy Hour* featured Lucy, Desi, Fred, and Ethel plus guest star Fred MacMurray hunting for uranium outside Las Vegas. The Roy Rogers television show, also featured on View-Master cards, showed Roy rounding up uranium claim jumpers in 1956. Two board games, including *Uranium Rush* described earlier, appeared in the 1950s. Ny-Lint Toys even produced a steel toy truck called the *uranium hauler.* One can imagine a kid with his uranium hauler dreaming of becoming the next Charlie Steen.[47]

The notoriety of the uranium rush in popular culture and the media supported uranium companies in the penny-stock markets. Small prospecting and mining companies in need of capital began issuing inexpensive stocks through Salt Lake City brokers. Hoping to raise funds through volume sales, most companies offered certificates for pennies. For thousands of Americans who wanted to participate in the uranium rush without getting dirty, penny stocks were just the thing. By June 1954, 7 million shares—almost three times the daily volume on the New York Stock Exchange—were sold in a single day. For the lucky investors in companies such as Lisbon Uranium, investments rose from 20 cents to $3.12 a share in just six months. Others were less fortunate. After stories began to circulate about suspected con men and crooks, the Securities Exchange Commission cracked down on brokerage houses, and the uranium market collapsed just eighteen months after it had begun. Despite its fall, the extravagance of the penny-stock market helped popularize and bankroll the domestic uranium industry.[48]

Although uranium ore discoveries, popular culture, and penny-stock fortunes made big headlines, the main objective of the AEC raw materials program was to acquire uranium concentrate, or "yellowcake," from uranium mills. Between 1947 and 1950, six mills were opened in the uranium belt of western Colorado and eastern Utah. As exploration expanded and new discoveries were made elsewhere, new mills were opened in New Mexico, Arizona, and South Dakota. After 1955 the strikes in New Mexico and Wyoming, combined with expanded ore reserves in Utah and Colorado, led to an upswing in mill contracts. Five new compacts were executed in 1955, seven in 1956, and six in 1957.[49]

Mill contracts were negotiated under authority of the Atomic Energy Act of 1946 and pertinent AEC regulations. Before negotiating a contract, the AEC required that each prospective company submit a proposal showing it could meet the commission's requirements for an adequate ore supply, technical capability, and financial responsibility. If these conditions were met, the AEC and the company arranged a contract for the construction and operation of a mill based on processing so many tons of ore per day. Yellowcake prices were negotiated, taking into account ore cost, estimated milling costs (including plant amortization), metallurgical losses, and profit. Ore haulage costs were also added, based on the average distance between the mine and mill site. In some cases contracts also provided that mills would receive a specified amount of ore from independent producers.[50]

These terms were so favorable they almost guaranteed that a mill would turn a profit. The problem was meeting the AEC's requirements. Therefore most mill contracts were not signed with the ore discoverer but with big companies like VCA, USV, and Anaconda. In Ambrosia Lake, where deposits were found anywhere from 300 to 1,000 feet underground, high capitalization costs enabled the large mining companies of Kerr-McGee Oil, Homestake Mining, and Phillips Petroleum to buy out the prospectors. Still, the stories of Charlie Steen and Bob Adams attest to some people's will to compete in the growing uranium business.[51]

Since his first discovery, Steen had dreamed of building his own uranium mill to serve the independent miners of Utah and Colorado. After forming the Utex Exploration Company to dig his shaft and mine the ore, Steen joined forces with the Combined Metals Reduction Company—a substantial western miller—to create the Uranium Reduction Company (URECO) in March 1954. Before signing an AEC contract, the company needed to meet the commission's difficult criteria.[52]

After surveying the different uranium concentration methods, URECO decided on the new resin-in-pulp process. Financing for the project came from a $6.2 million mortgage to the New York Life Insurance Company, and the Chemical Corn Exchange Bank of New York City lent URECO $3.5 million for construction and capital purposes. An additional $2.3 million

was raised by selling debentures to various companies and private investors. No common stock was issued. Finally, to ensure future ore, URECO
joined forces with Floyd B. Odlum's Atlas Corporation, which had acquired
extensive ore reserves near Steen's Mi Vida mine. With these conditions
met, URECO signed a seven-year, 1,500-ton-per-day contract on 1 June
1955. When the mill began operation in 1957, it was the second-largest in
the world and provided over 25 percent of the nation's yellowcake for the
next few years.[53]

Like Steen, Bob Adams dreamed of becoming a big player in the uranium field. After locating uranium north of Rawlins, Wyoming, Adams decided that his Lost Creek Oil and Uranium Company would try to obtain
its own milling license from the AEC. At first, the process of acquiring the
$3–$4 million needed to construct a mill was discouraging. Adams suggested that the penny-stock market had turned off potential investors. He
said, "We got a cold turndown from the first Denver bank we talked to. . . .
The word *uranium* frightened the bank and it wasn't having any part of
it."[54] In Rawlins, Adams had similar luck. Many small contributors were
willing to invest $5,000–$10,000, but no one would take a big plunge.
Then Dr. C. W. Jeffrey, a seventy-three-year-old Rawlins physician and
philanthropist who had made a fortune in oil, offered Adams $250,000.
Adams could now convince the big bankers to support his plan. By August
1956 the Lost Creek Oil and Uranium Company had secured $4.25 million
and signed a contract to build its mill at Split Rock, a few miles northeast of
a small post office called Home on the Range.[55]

By the late 1950s, Home on the Range was just one of many new lo-
cales in the federal government's growing uranium procurement program.
From a virtually dead industry in 1946, the domestic market had expanded
in every way, including total ore production, total amount of known ore
reserves, annual drilling totals, and total number of processing mills. At the
start of the government procurement program in 1947, production consisted of only 67 tons of uranium concentrate, or U_3O_8, in ore from the two
former vanadium mills on the Colorado Plateau. By 1958, production had
increased to over 12,000 tons. At the same time uranium ore reserves increased from just 2,200 tons U_3O_8 in ore in 1947 to a high of 181,800 tons in
1958. To process this supply, the number of mills grew from two in 1947 to
twenty-eight by 1958. Finally, from a small mineral belt in western Colorado, by 1958 uranium production had expanded across eight states.[56]

Although the domestic uranium industry grew tremendously during
the first eight years of the AEC program, the commission felt a continued
high rate of discovery was essential for substantial production to continue

Dr. C. W. Jeffrey, *left,* and Bob Adams, *right,* at Jeffrey City, Wyoming, September 1957. Adams, former restraunteur from Rawlins, Wyoming, was the father of Wyoming uranium. He discovered the atomic ore and built the state's first processing plant. He is shown here the day the mill was dedicated with his largest investor, Dr. C. W. Jeffrey, for whom Adams named his company town. Courtesy, Riverton, Wyoming, *Ranger.*

after government programs terminated in 1962. Therefore, on May 24, 1956, the AEC announced that its procurement program would continue for the period 1962–1966.[57] The future of the industry seemed bright.

The government-sponsored uranium procurement program was successfully providing the uranium needed to build atomic bombs and preserve national security in the growing Cold War. The AEC had successfully taken over the program from the Army Corps of Engineers and had established a civilian-controlled atomic energy program. The government had then introduced programs that created a highly successful private uranium industry. New discoveries were made and put into production. This program assured Americans of uranium independence, contributed to the growing postwar economy, and successfully—if not intentionally—separated uranium's economic opportunities from its horrific end use.

On the other hand, the uranium boom wreaked havoc on the communities directly affected and set in place new forces that would change those communities. Small agricultural centers like Moab, Utah, and Grants, New

Mexico, and industrial towns like Uravan, Colorado, and Jeffrey City, Wyoming, were thrust into the atomic age whether they liked it or not. These communities became "atom-age boomtowns" seemingly overnight, and their economies, landscapes, and identities were eventually overhauled as they became dependent on the industry and federal government. Their stories are the subject of the next three chapters.

Notes

1. Gardner Games, *Uranium Rush,* c. 1957.
2. Leonard S. Cottrell Jr. and Sylvia Eberhart, *American Opinion on World Affairs in the Atomic Age* (Princeton: Princeton University Press, 1948), 108–111. This poll and its revelation are discussed in Spencer R. Weart, *Nuclear Fear: A History of Images* (Cambridge, Mass.: Harvard University Press, 1988), 134.
3. This attitude is expressed in Kevin Rafferty, Jayne Loader, and Pierce Rafferty's classic Cold War documentary *Atomic Café,* 1982.
4. Leslie R. Groves, *Now It Can Be Told: The Story of the Manhattan Project* (New York: Harper, 1962), 373–400; Major General K. D. Nichols, *The Road to Trinity* (New York: William Morrow, 1987), 215–255.
5. Groves, *Now It Can Be Told,* 391.
6. Richard G. Hewlett and Oscar E. Anderson Jr., *The New World: Volume I, A History of the United States Atomic Energy Commission* (University Park: Pennsylvania State University Press, 1962), 482–530.
7. *Atomic Energy Act of 1946, U.S. Statutes at Large* 60 (1946), 755–775.
8. Ibid.
9. Ibid.
10. Ibid.
11. Ibid.
12. A discussion of the debate on these matters can be found in Hewlett and Anderson, *The New World,* 493–495.
13. Richard G. Hewlett and Oscar E. Anderson Jr., *A History of the United States Atomic Energy Commission Volume II: Atomic Shield, 1947/1952* (University Park: Pennsylvania State University Press, 1969), 147–148.
14. R. D. Nininger and P. L. Guarin, "S-37 and T-37 Resources of the United States," *Manhattan Project History,* microfilm, reel 11, 6.1, 26.
15. Jack F. Frost, Umetco Minerals Corporation, telephone interview by author, 28 October 1993.
16. Holger Albrethsen and Frank E. McGinley, *Summary History of Domestic Uranium Procurement Under U.S. Atomic Energy Commission Contracts: Final Report* (Grand Junction, Colo.: U.S. Department of Energy, 1982), 4, and Jesse Johnson cited therein.

17. Ibid.; Nielson B. O'Rear, *Summary and Chronology of the Domestic Uranium Program (August 1966)*, report prepared for U.S. Atomic Energy Commission, Grand Junction Office (Grand Junction, Colo.: Government Printing Office [GPO], 1966), 1.

18. Robert Bothwell, *Eldorado: Canada's National Uranium Company* (Toronto: University of Toronto Press, 1984), 200–204; ibid., 2; Albrethsen and McGinley, *Summary History*, 3–4.

19. Rodney D. Millar, Lane T. Neilson, and Richard E. Turley, *A Study of the Utah Uranium Milling Industry, Volume II: Utah Energy Resources-Uranium* (Salt Lake City: Mechanical and Industrial Engineering Department and Utah Engineering Experiment Station, 1980), 2.6; Albrethsen and McGinley, *Summary History*, A-90.

20. "Uranium Prices Quoted by VCA at Naturita," Moab *Times-Independent*, 26 June 1947.

21. "Uranium Producers Organize to Seek Fair Price for Their Ore From Atomic Energy Commission," Moab *Times-Independent*, 1 May 1947; Loren L. Taylor, "Local Uranium Miners Getting Raw Deal," Moab *Times-Independent*, 27 November 1947; "Uranium Producers Organize to Market Ores Cooperatively," Moab *Times-Independent*, 11 March 1948; Loren L. Taylor, "Definite Price for Uranium Ore Is Needed," Moab *Times-Independent*, 8 April 1948.

22. Albrethsen and McGinley, *Summary History*, 7–8.

23. U.S. Atomic Energy Commission, "U.S. Atomic Energy Commission Announces Program to Stimulate Production of Domestic Uranium," press release no. 96, 10 April 1948. This and subsequent press releases were found in the personal files of William L. Chenoweth, Grand Junction, Colorado.

24. Ibid.; "Atomic Commission Announces Schedule of Prices on Uranium," Moab *Times-Independent*, 18 April 1948; "Uranium Producers Disappointed With New Price Schedule," Moab *Times-Independent*, 18 April 1948.

25. "Atomic Commission Announces Increase in Uranium Price," Moab *Times-Independent*, 13 May 1948; U.S. Atomic Energy Commission, "Temporary Additional Allowances, Colorado Plateau Area Carnotite-Type and Roscoelite-Type Ores," addition to Circular 4, 15 June 1948.

26. "Much Assessment Work Underway on Carnotite Properties Through District," Moab *Times-Independent*, 20 May 1948.

27. Albrethsen and McGinley, *Summary History*, A-90; O'Rear, *Summary and Chronology*, 7–8.

28. "How to Hunt for Uranium," *Popular Science* (February 1946): 121–123; "How to Find Uranium," *Time* (21 April 1947): 86; "Out Where the Click Is Louder," *Time* (18 July 1949): 53.

29. U.S. Atomic Energy Commission and U.S. Geological Survey, *Prospecting for Uranium* (Washington, D.C.: GPO, 1949, revised 1951).

30. U.S. Atomic Energy Commission, "Domestic Uranium Program Circular 5, Revised," *Federal Register,* Document 53-8282, 15 October 1953. A copy of this document was found in the personal files of William L. Chenoweth, Grand Junction, Colorado.

31. "Uranium Mining Underway Throughout Carnotite Belt: Low Price Schedules, Plus Fair Transportation Allowance, Give Assurance of Profitable Industry," Moab *Times-Independent,* 24 June 1948.

32. "Exploration Widens the Uranium Ore Belt," *Business Week* (3 March 1951): 102–104; "The Uranium Boom," *Time* (13 October 1952): 95–96.

33. A brief survey tracing the expansion of uranium ore–producing areas can be found in O'Rear, *Summary and Chronology,* 21–23. The folklore surrounding Paddy Martinez's uranium discovery is discussed in a number of books and articles. See especially Merle Armitage, *Stella Dysart of Ambrosia Lake* (New York: Duell, Sloan and Pearce, 1959), 48–50, 125–126 for two different stories, as well as New Mexico Energy Institute, *Uranium Industry in New Mexico* (Albuquerque: Energy Resources Board, 1976), 2–5; Wayne Winters, "Uranium Boom at Grants," *New Mexico Magazine* (March 1951): 13–15, 52; "Paddy Finds Yellow Rock, It's Rich Claim," Moab *Times-Independent Energy Supplement,* 17 February 1955; Victor L. Devers, "A History and Economic Analysis of the Uranium Industry in New Mexico," unpublished M.A. thesis, University of New Mexico, 1962, 9.

34. Raye C. Ringholz recounts Steen's story in *Uranium Frenzy: Boom and Bust on the Colorado Plateau* (New York: W. W. Norton, 1989), 22–24.

35. Steen's story can also be found in Maxine Newell, *Charlie Steen's Mi Vida* (Moab, Utah: By the author, 1976), and Al Look, *U-Boom: Uranium on the Colorado Plateau* (Grand Junction, Colo.: Bell, 1956), 19–35.

36. Popular magazines of the time also carried Steen's story. See "Broke and Hungry Prospector Hits Uranium Jackpot," *Business Week* (1 August 1953): 28–30; "The Cisco Kid," *Time* (3 August 1953): 60–61; J. P. McEvoy, "Uranium's New Horatio Alger," *American Mercury* (November 1953): 15–18; "Special Report: Striking It Rich in the A-Age," *Newsweek* (19 April 1954): 100–105.

37. "Geologists Report Pitchblende Find," Moab *Times-Independent,* 4 September 1952; "Assay Report Good on Pitchblende Find," Moab *Times-Independent,* 4 December 1952. Steen's discovery is also recounted in Ringholz, *Frenzy,* 52–58, and Newell, *Mi Vida,* 15–16.

38. Technical reports of Mi Vida can be found in Charles A. Steen, George P. Dix Jr., Scott W. Hazen Jr., and Russell R. McLellan, "Uranium-Mining Operations of the Utex Exploration Co. in the Big Indian District, San Juan County, Utah," *Information Circular 7669,* U.S. Bureau of Mines (Washington, D.C.: GPO, 1953); Burt Meyers, "Uranium Jackpot," *Engineering and Mining Journal* 154, no. 4 (September 1953): 72–75; Burt Meyers, "Big Boom at Big Indian," *Engineering and Mining Journal* 155, no. 4 (April 1954): 96–99.

39. Look, *U-Boom,* 37–58.
40. Bob Peck, "Bob Adams: Steen Story Caught His Eye," Riverton (Wyoming) *Ranger,* 19 June 1980.
41. "The History of a Successful Uranium Venture," *Wyoming* 1 (June-July 1957): 28–31.
42. Armitage, *Stella Dysart*; "Uranium Jackpot," *Time* (30 September 1957): 89–90; "Boom That Gives U.S. Top Spot in Uranium," *U.S. News and World Report* (16 August 1957): 120–121.
43. McEvoy, "Uranium's New Horatio Alger," 15–18.
44. "Broke and Hungry Prospector," 28–30; "The Cisco Kid," 60–61.
45. *Reader's Guide to Periodical Literature* (New York: H.W. Wilson, 1953–1955).
46. Union Carbide and Carbon Corporation, *The Petrified River: The Story of Uranium,* 1956; Leo Joannon, dir., *Utopia,* 1950; Republic Pictures Corporation, *Bells of Coronado,* 1950; Republic Pictures Corporation, *The Atomic Kid,* 1950; Ben Schwalb, prod., *Dig That Uranium,* 1955; Sam Katzman, prod., *Uranium Boom,* 1956.
47. *The Amos and Andy Show,* "The Uranium Mine," c. 1957; *The Lucy and Desi Comedy Hour,* "Lucy Hunts Uranium," 3 January 1958; *The Roy Rogers Show,* "Uranium Fever," 1956; Ny-Lint Toys, *Uranium Hauler,* c. 1958.
48. For a firsthand account, see "Uranium Makes a Wilder West," *Life* 37, no. 3 (19 July 1954): 12–15. A good summary of the penny stocks is in Ringholz, *Frenzy,* 179–193.
49. O'Rear, *Summary and Chronology,* 13–17.
50. Ibid., 14; Albrethsen and McGinley, *Summary History,* 8–9.
51. Albrethsen and McGinley, *Summary History,* B-7.
52. "Uranium Mill Assured for Moab Says Wimpfen at Chamber of Commerce Meeting," Moab *Times-Independent,* 10 December 1953; Mitch Mellich, "A Historic Look Back: How the Uranium Reduction Company Got Its Start," pamphlet, Uranium file, Museum of Western Colorado, Grand Junction.
53. Mellich, "Historic Look Back"; Robert Bernick, "$4 Million Uranium Mill Set for Moab," Salt Lake City *Tribune,* 13 April 1954; Albrethsen and McGinley, *Summary History,* A-86.
54. "History of a Successful Uranium Venture," 28–31.
55. Albrethsen and McGinley, *Summary History,* A118–A122.
56. U.S. Energy Research and Development Administration, *Statistical Data of the Uranium Industry* (Grand Junction, Colo.: GPO, 1976), 19. Ore reserves for this period are based on a price of eight dollars per pound U_3O_8.
57. O'Rear, *Summary and Chronology,* 17; Albrethsen and McGinley, *Summary History,* 9.

Chapter 3

Uranium Company Towns
in the American West

WHEN THE GOVERNMENT-SPONSORED uranium boom began in 1948, the company town of Uravan was ready. Constructed in the 1930s on the site of a former radium camp, the town owed its existence not only to the mineral market but also to its parent company, Union Carbide. As in company towns throughout the nation, Uravan's population had waxed and waned as the company reacted to changing market conditions. Further, Uravan's existence was based on the belief that large mining companies that struck deposits in isolated areas needed to provide low-cost housing and other amenities to entice workers. But there were complications. Because the same company controlled not only employment but often housing, shopping, and medical and recreational facilities, many workers who lived in company towns felt a loss of personal control. This trade-off—good wages and low rent in exchange for corporate paternalism—was the essence of the company town. Throughout U.S. mining history this way of life had been a practical alternative; it would continue into the uranium era.

The government procurement program brought a series of problems to the uranium towns including growing populations, school enrollments, housing shortages, and crime. Further, the tax hikes, bond issues, and federal grants most communities employed to ease the initial problems often led to even more difficulties. But these problems did not occur in company towns. In communities like Uravan and, later, Jeffrey City, Wyoming, the major problems residents faced were how to deal with the company that controlled their lives and the sense of dependence associated with living in a one-industry town. Like such communities everywhere, uranium company towns were totally dependent on the success or failure of their company in its chosen marketplace. Because the federal government controlled the uranium market, residents of Uravan and Jeffrey City undoubtedly felt increasingly dependent on the federal government as well.

During the uranium era, the company town remained a viable alternative when conditions were right. First, the company had to have the rights to a substantial amount of ore to warrant the creation of a new community. Second, the ore body had to be remote or distant enough from existing communities to eliminate the possibility of commuting. Third, the company had to provide low-cost housing, medical care, and recreational opportunities to keep its workers happy. If these conditions were met, the yellowcake company town usually bypassed the exploration boom period experienced by independent towns. In essence, uranium company towns began life dependent on uranium and were already yellowcake communities. Two towns—Uravan, Colorado, one of the first postwar yellowcake communities, and Jeffrey City, Wyoming, one of the last company towns constructed during the government period—typify this kind of uranium mining community.[1]

Uravan

On the day the Grand Junction *Sentinel* reported that an atomic bomb had been dropped on Hiroshima, United States Vanadium (USV)[2] vice president Blair Burwell issued a statement recognizing the role of Colorado's carnotite region in developing the materials for the new weapon. An article published two weeks later thanked local Chamber of Commerce and business leaders for assisting Uravan during the war. Unfortunately for Burwell and Uravan residents, the town's wartime success did not carry over into the postwar period. With the completion of the Manhattan Project, the government closed down and then dismantled its sludge plant. Union

Carbide soon disbanded its Uravan mill and then mothballed the town in late 1945.[3]

Uravan remained closed during the congressional debate over the proposed Atomic Energy Commission and the subsequent delay in selecting its commissioners. To safeguard the town and keep the mill and mines in functional order, Union Carbide kept a few men working in the area. Although the post office remained open, the town's library and reading room were closed, and the books were given to the nearby town of Nucla.[4] Population numbers are not available during this period, but school figures show that enrollment dropped from 190 school-age children in 1944 to 79 in 1945, 26 in 1946, and just 7 in 1947.[5] The town's decline was further revealed when the Federal Public Housing Authority, trying to ease the housing crunch for returning veterans in nearby Grand Junction, offered to move the government's sixty-eight flattop apartments from Uravan without charge. The buildings remained.[6]

When the domestic uranium procurement program began in 1947, Uravan made a complete turnabout. Having already signed contracts to open three plateau mills, the AEC signed a contract with Union Carbide (UCN) to reopen its Uravan uranium mill. Effective 1 July 1949, the new contract provided for the company to process up to 500 tons of ore per day.[7]

When the Uravan mill began operating in December 1949, the town was little changed from the Manhattan Project era four years before. Situated on the southwest side of the San Miguel River, the town flanked the large mill that sloped down the western wall of the canyon. South of the plant were most of the businesses, including the school, store, bar, boardinghouse, and recreation hall. Residential areas D and E were also south of the mill. Further south and across the stream sat residential block F. North of the mill stood several bunkhouses, the town medical clinic, and the company's offices. Across the stream were residential blocks A and B, and still further north were the flattop apartments, the main house of Club Ranch, and the ranch's hay fields.[8]

Because of its operation as a company town and its location amid long-standing uranium claims, Uravan did not experience an exploration rush like other communities did. Instead, during its first two years of operation under the AEC contract, Union Carbide gradually added workers to its mill operations. By 1952, UCN's operations had grown to the point that a controlled "company boom" existed. At this time the company began to publish a bimonthly company newsletter called *Photo News*. Covering operations in Rifle, Grand Junction, and Uravan, this pamphlet became the unofficial town paper and chronicler as Uravan again grew into a community.[9]

Life in Uravan in the early 1950s revolved around work. Nearly every resident was employed in UCN's mines, mill, or labs. In addition, the company employed a few people as secretaries, ore and concentrate haulers, construction and maintenance workers, and medical personnel. Union Carbide also subcontracted out for people to run the boardinghouse, company store, and tavern. The only noncompany personnel allowed to live in the community were the postmaster and school workers.[10]

To meet its AEC contract requirements, Union Carbide operated its mill twenty-four hours a day, seven days a week, 365 days a year. To maintain this schedule, the company hired three shifts. The change in shifts was regimented by a loud whistle from the mill.[11]

From the reopening of Uravan in late 1949 through the early 1960s, housing the many employees and their families remained a constant problem. Unlike open towns where the free market allowed local entrepreneurs to lease individually owned lots to trailer owners, company towns like Uravan were dependent on the main corporation to develop suitable housing. This circumstance produced both positive and negative results. On the plus side, land ownership by one major company did not allow unplanned, unsightly boomtown development to occur. Conversely, the lack of competitive building forced all potential Uravan residents to live in company housing or outside the town. Further, Union Carbide's construction monopoly meant that although the company was supposedly more in tune with the town's needs than private builders, the quality of homes did not benefit from free-market competition.[12]

As people came to work in the mill, an informal pecking order for suitable housing was established based on tenure, job importance, whether one was salaried or an hourly worker, and family need. The variety of housing ranged from fine houses for the superintendent and company doctor to miners' shacks. New single workers often found a room in one of the bunkhouses located throughout the town. For men with families, the choices were more difficult. If space was available, they could live in one of the many company houses that lined the valley floor in small residential blocks. The oldest of these units dated from Uravan's beginnings in 1936.[13]

The second option was the government-owned flattop apartments. Sixty-eight units had been rapidly constructed for the Manhattan Engineer District in 1943, and the government maintained half of the units for AEC and U.S. Geological Survey (USGS) officials and exploration crews but sublet the rest to Union Carbide as company housing. The thirty-four three-, four-, and five-room apartments were grouped around a circular drive.[14] If no housing was available, a man could either live with his family outside town or live by himself in a bunkhouse and move his family to town when space became available.[15]

Cletus and Estalee Silver experienced the housing situation in Uravan in the spring of 1951. As part of the first boom that came to Uravan after the mill reopened, the Silvers were unable to find suitable accommodations in the town. The couple paid seven dollars a day for a motel room in Norwood, 40 miles to the south. After several months the Silvers moved into the big house at Club Ranch (the company had purchased this historic ranch after World War II). The couple soon managed to get a flattop apartment and then a small Quonset hut that had been renovated into a house. After their son became ill in 1959, the company offered the family a house in the salaried section, even though Cletus remained an hourly worker.[16]

Once in a company house, employees at Uravan found the accommodations only adequate, but pluses included the low rent, lack of property taxes, and company assistance. Most houses available in the early 1950s dated from 1936. They consisted of an uninsulated wooden frame built on a concrete slab. The oldest homes had a living room, bedroom, bathroom, and combination kitchen/dining room. They were heated by a coal stoker. The newer houses had two or even three bedrooms and gas heat. The larger, nicer homes were reserved for the mill and mine superintendents, the company doctor, and key company personnel. None of the houses had telephones.[17]

Union Carbide worked hard to maintain Uravan's outward appearance. The company painted the outsides of all of the houses at least once every few years and provided fencing materials, grass seed, and trees for the yards. For the interiors, Union Carbide provided paint, plumbing, and electrical work. The company also allowed renters to add basements and rooms at their discretion. Despite all this, many renters wanted better homes.[18]

Next to Union Carbide, the Uravan school was the town's largest employer. Records show that at least a grammar school had existed off and on since the Joe Junior Camp was formed back in 1919. United States Vanadium built a new frame school when Uravan was created in 1936. Record enrollment was 161 in 1942. The influx of people during the Manhattan Project boosted the school census to 190 in 1944 and forced the company to enlarge the school building. When the Manhattan Project was completed and the government plant closed, school enrollment dropped to 79 in 1945, 26 in 1946, 7 in 1947, and 9 in 1948. When mining and milling resumed under the AEC in 1949, the school grew along with the town.[19]

The school continued to grow throughout the early 1950s. From the end of the school year in 1952 to Christmas the following year, enrollment increased by 60 students (33%) and overwhelmed the small school.

To meet the growing demand, 50 first graders and 24 sixth graders were moved to temporary classrooms in the company recreation hall until a new three-room addition to the school could be built.[20] By August 1954 elaborate plans had been made to continue to add to the school until eventually a completely new school emerged around the old structure in the shape of a "U." The old section was renovated, and the center of the "U" was enclosed for a gymnasium and library.[21]

As enrollment continued to expand, the school district decided to replace the old facility with a new school and gymnasium. In the fall of 1955 the original frame building was moved to open space for the new school. With support from a district-wide bond issue, a modern steel school was constructed on the site of the old building. Across the street the district constructed a new steel gym next to the old frame school.[22]

The location of the new gym posed a problem in the industrial town. Pedestrians were forced to cross the main road ore trucks took to the mill. To circumvent potential problems, the company installed an underpass to allow pedestrians to reach the new structure safely. Two years later the company built a fenced walkway from the footbridge over the San Miguel to the school. Several outlets were built along the route to allow walkers access to the town.[23]

Overall, though, Union Carbide did not have unusual power in the school. The Uravan school was part of a district encompassing the west end of Montrose County. People in the district elected their own board members, passed bond issues for expansion, and hired and fired administrators and teachers. Even though Union Carbide was probably the largest taxpayer and two of its employees constituted 40 percent of the board, the only direct links between the company and the school district were the fact that the company provided housing for teachers and that during the boom years, wives of company men were often hired as local teachers.[24]

As with most company towns in the American West, Uravan's main reason for existence—a profitable mineral lode in a sparsely populated region—was also its major detraction. The isolation combined with a lack of civic government forced Union Carbide to provide not only recreational and commercial outlets for its residents but medical care and civic services as well.

Union Carbide hired a doctor and a nurse to maintain a small clinic in town. The company provided the doctor with a house, a fully furnished clinic, the right to maintain a private practice beyond company duties, and a $500 a month stipend.[25] The job included conducting exams for prospective employees, giving workers their annual exams, and providing emergency care. Examinations and treatments were carried out in a five-bed hospital equipped with an X-ray machine, oxygen apparatus, and separate operating and delivery rooms. The company also hired one full-time and several part-time nurses, usually wives of company men. Because turnover among doctors was high, the nursing staff became the stabilizing element in the town's health care.[26]

Union Carbide also maintained a well-trained fire crew that operated company-owned equipment. Initially formed to keep the mill from burning, the fire crew also fought residential fires. The volunteers were called to duty by a loud whistle from the mill.[27]

Surprisingly, Uravan had no police force. Instead, the county sheriff responded to problems from his office 40 miles away. Apparently, the threat of losing one's job and home deterred would-be criminals.[28]

In the mid-1950s residents started building a church for the small community. They began with a Sunday school and vacation Bible school for youngsters, and in 1955 Uravan residents established their own interdenominational community church. Mormon residents continued to travel to nearby Naturita to worship, and area Catholics went to Nucla, so the new church had mostly Protestant parishioners. At its peak in the late 1950s, the church boasted about 100 members, about half of whom attended regularly. Housed in the community recreation hall, stocked with donated supplies, supported by a transient population, and served by volunteer ministers from the Village Mission, the Uravan community church did not appear to offer much. But for the isolated worshipers the services were needed, and the church became a "good cornerstone in the community."[29]

Throughout the 1950s Uravan had few elderly residents. As in most company towns, residency was tied directly to work. If a person quit, was fired, or retired from the company, he or she had to leave town. One resident noted that the community lacked the type of long-standing grudges and friction often associated with small towns because anyone who retired left the town. Similarly, Uravan had no cemetery, and any resident who died had to be interred in a nearby community.[30]

Recreational activities provided an important escape for Union Carbide employees and their families. By far the biggest attraction was the company swimming pool across from the mill in a large concrete cooling reservoir, originally used by the town's power plant. The pool was Olympic-sized, 122 feet long by 64 feet wide. The company built showers, lockers, sidewalks, fencing, a high dive, a water filtration system, and lighting for night swimming. Not surprisingly, the pool attracted visitors from nearby towns and ranches and became the center of summer life. Swimming lessons were provided, and local swimmers competed in regional amateur matches.[31]

Other group recreation included school basketball teams, bowling in nearby communities, and a crude golf course.[32] Unlike the situation in other towns, UCN built and maintained several recreational facilities including a company park for summer baseball and softball, a tennis court, and the multifunctional community recreational hall. The latter was used in a variety of ways including as a classroom for the overflowing school and as a community library, gym, and movie theater. The structure also hosted the community church and Sunday school services, dances, a carnival, and a variety of club meetings including Boy Scouts, Cub Scouts, Brownies, Rifle Club, Lions Club, Athletics Club, PTA, and union meetings.[33]

The image most often associated with a company town is the company store. Usually situated in a prominent location and often the largest non-production structure in town, the traditional company shop was usually a general store type of business with many departments and sometimes a saloon. The traditional company store usually held a monopoly in the community, and it often used special company scrip and charged high prices. Customers paid high prices, drove long distances for other choices, or did without.[34]

In Uravan the company store did not fit the traditional mold. Uravan's store was known as the San Miguel Trading Center. It was near the school on the south end of the main street, close to the highway intersection. The store was well maintained with a variety of grocery items plus dry goods, meats, a taproom, filling station, and a soda fountain. Its manager, P. H. Peters, also oversaw operation of the town's bunkhouse, boarding facilities, and movie theater.[35]

Several residents suggested that the store's prices were somewhat high, but they were comparable to those charged by other area merchants and were actually lower than the cost of traveling to shop elsewhere. One resident noted that trips to shop out of town had to be planned well ahead of time. To alleviate this situation, the San Miguel Trading Center gladly took special orders.[36]

During the first uranium boom, Uravan was characterized by orderly expansion. From its reopening in 1948 with just a handful of people, Uravan grew to almost 1,000 residents in just ten years. As its population expanded, Union Carbide tried to construct more housing and enlarge recreational facilities. West End voters also saw to it that the community had a good school and teachers. In many aspects Uravan was a model town that was trying to become like any small U.S. town. Still, the community could not escape its company town status. Uravan residents worked for Union Carbide, paid their rent to Union Carbide, and bought their groceries from a store leased by Union Carbide. Adults were regulated by a company whistle, and their children played with children of fellow employees.

Although Union Carbide's control kept Uravan from becoming a boomtown, the company's growing reliance on the federal government's purchase of uranium made the community a yellowcake community. As long as government demand continued, Uravan would continue to exist.

Jeffrey City

In the spring of 1956, nearly a decade after the reopening of Uravan, Robert W. Adams of Rawlins, Wyoming, set about securing an AEC uranium milling contract for his company, Lost Creek Oil and Uranium. His new mill would be near the recently constructed government ore-buying station at Split Rock, a lonely point strategically located between the uranium lands of Crook's Gap to the south and the Gas Hills to the north. Situated nearly in the center of Wyoming along the winding Sweetwater River, Split Rock was 60 miles from the closest towns of Casper, Lander, Riverton, and Rawlins. The local post office, a small gas station called Home on the Range, served the area's ranchers.[37]

With its AEC contract finalized, Lost Creek Oil and Uranium Company began fulfilling the details of its compact. Adams, wanting to ensure he would always have enough ore for his new mill, obtained more mining claims in the area.[38] Because his contract required the company to supply housing for its workers, Adams began to plan and build a trailer town, which he christened Jeffrey City, near Home on the Range.[39]

The name *Jeffrey City* was derived from Adams's largest benefactor, Rawlins physician C. W. Jeffrey. When Adams first began capitalizing on his dream to build a uranium mill, Dr. Jeffrey came to his aid when Denver banks would not. After securing several small investments, he obtained $250,000 from Jeffrey. Adams then convinced bigger bankers that his plan was sound. By August 1957, the Lost Creek Oil and Uranium Company had secured $4.25 million.[40]

Adams worried that the name Lost Creek Oil and Uranium suggested a paper corporation instead of the major corporate player he wanted it to be. After all, he had found uranium, had secured a government contract to process it, and was building a town to house his workers; his company warranted a more progressive-sounding name. So in May 1957 Adams changed the name of his company to Western Nuclear Corporation.[41] By

Dedication of the Split Rock mill near Jeffrey City, Wyoming, September 1957. The opening of a uranium mill was a momentous occasion for western towns. Western Nuclear's mill was the first for the state of Wyoming. Note the dignitaries on stage in front of the building and the marching band and baton twirlers at left center. Here, people bowed their heads as the benediction was read. Courtesy, Riverton, Wyoming, *Ranger.*

the time the Split Rock mill opened that spring, *Uranium* magazine reported: "As the area's first mill, Western Nuclear [WN] no doubt has an advantageous contract with the AEC. With its excellent battery of managers seasoned in mine and mill management. WN ranks as an outstanding small integrated uranium company."[42] Bob Adams seemed well on his way to becoming a leader in the nuclear industry.

The new trailer town of Jeffrey City initially took form on land Adams purchased from Sam and Beulah Peterson, proprietors of the small store and gas station at nearby Home on the Range. Although the couple had been willing to sell some of their land to Adams's company, Beulah was not ready to relinquish control of her beloved post office. Stories abound that

Western Nuclear, Inc., Wyoming's first uranium mill, Jeffrey City, Wyoming, c. 1957.
Courtesy, Riverton, Wyoming, *Ranger.*

when she received mail addressed to Jeffrey City and not Home on the
Range, she would mark "return to sender, address unknown" on the enve-
lope and send it back.[43]

In the 1950s Jeffrey City was a company camp, not a boomtown. Western Nuclear constructed, owned, and managed the entire townsite. In fact,
the town's welcome sign, built by Western Nuclear, read "Jeffrey City—
Home of Wyoming's First Uranium Mill." An early description noted there
were 26 permanent houses for selected company personnel, a 36-room
bachelor dormitory, 4 trailer courts filled with 145 trailers, a modern restaurant and bar, bathhouses, and a combination firehouse and dispensary.
It is interesting that instead of building workers' shacks as USV had done
in Uravan two decades prior, Western Nuclear opted to install trailer courts
and trailers in this postwar age. Western Nuclear also installed the town's
water and sewage system and built a huge Quonset building that served as
the community's first school, meeting place, laundromat, church, and movie

house. Within three years the company added a swimming pool, a community church, and a school building.[44]

A 1961 topographical map hints at the landscape developed by Western Nuclear in Jeffrey City. In the beginning, Jeffrey City consisted of six city blocks platted just to the south of highway 287 and west of Home on the Range. Western Nuclear constructed two parallel roads, 1st Street South and 2nd Street South, running parallel to the highway, and five perpendicular streets labeled A–E. On E, the westernmost of the north-south streets, Western Nuclear constructed the large Quonset hut that served as company and community headquarters. The rest of the community was divided by function, with the bunkhouses and stores on 1st South and the family homes located off 2nd South. The eastern boundary of the community was Home on the Range. Across the highway and several miles to the north stood the Split Rock mill.[45]

As a company town, Jeffrey City had no formal system of elected government. Western Nuclear provided a townsite manager and employed a four-man crew to maintain roads and take care of other civic needs. A fifteen-man volunteer fire department, crucial to a community of densely packed trailers, operated equipment supplied by Western Nuclear.[46] Fremont County provided a justice of the peace and deputy sheriff for the town, although the nearest jail was 25 miles away in Lander.[47] The only semblance of popular government was the Jeffrey City Community Council, a fifteen-member organization that served as a liaison between the company and the community.[48]

Jeffrey City, with its 500 residents, was hardly the metropolis it aspired to be. The Denver *Post,* in its *Empire* magazine, described it as an "atomic age frontier town." Despite the town's "scrawny" appearance, its inhabitants seemed content. The *Post* quoted one housewife as saying, "I've been in lots of towns like this, but Jeffrey City is more pleasant than any of them. Everybody seems to like it here and a lot will stay as long as they can."[49]

Life in the early days revolved around work. In Shirley Basin, another uranium mining community 60 miles to the east, a 1973 study concluded that people moved to such towns primarily to find a job or to move up to a better-paying one.[50]

Jeffrey City residents enjoyed movies or went to bars after work. In good weather the surrounding area invited hunting, fishing, and rock hounding. A single television station was boosted in from Casper.[51]

During the first few years, local schoolchildren were taught in the Western Nuclear Quonset building. As the number of children increased and the community's future seemed more stable, in 1958 Western Nuclear set aside land to build a grade school. Located near the company's head-quarters, the elementary school opened in the fall of 1959.[52]

By 1958, Jeffrey City had emerged from the sagebrush of the Wyoming plain, but the community was still a small mining and milling camp of 500 residents. Nevertheless, Bob Adams had created both a company and a community from scratch. The future of Jeffrey City depended on the government's continued need for uranium. Thus by 1958, Jeffrey City was a true yellowcake community. As long as the federal government needed yellowcake, Jeffrey City's future looked bright.

Uravan and Jeffrey City represent one result of the discovery of uranium during the government-sponsored boom of the 1950s. In each community, strong paternalistic companies established order, constructed comfortable, affordable housing, and provided recreation for their residents. Residents in each company town found themselves increasingly tied not only to Union Carbide or Western Nuclear—their "official" employer and provider—but also to their unofficial overseer, the federal government. Thus the uranium company town provides a new example of the growing power of the federal government in the post–World War II West.[53]

Notes

1. The classic description of company towns is James B. Allen, *The Company Town in the American West* (Norman: University of Oklahoma Press, 1966). See also Robert W. Righter, *The Making of a Town: Wright, Wyoming* (Boulder: Roberts Rinehart, 1985) for another example of a modern energy company town.

2. In 1955 Uravan's parent company, Union Carbide and Carbon Corporation, reorganized its atomic energy companies, and United States Vanadium became part of a new division known as the Union Carbide Nuclear Company. To avoid discrepancies, the name Union Carbide or UCN will be used throughout this chapter except when discussing the company prior to the government's uranium program of 1948. In that instance United States Vanadium or USV will be utilized.

3. R. D. Nininger and P. L. Guarin, "S-37 and T-37 Resources of the United States," *Manhattan Project History,* microfilm, reel 11, 6.1, 26.

4. Estalee Silver, interview by Clare Engle, 6 August 1970, interview 171, transcript, Utah Uranium Oral History Project, Marriott Library, University of Utah, Salt Lake City, Utah, 11 (hereafter UUOHP).

5. Estalee Silver, interview with author, October 1993 (hereafter Silver, interview by author).

6. "Say 68 Apartments at Uravan May Be Moved Here for Vets," Grand Junction *Daily Sentinel,* 1 November 1946.

7. Holger Albrethsen and Frank E. McGinley, *Summary History of Domestic Uranium Procurement Under U.S. Atomic Energy Commission Contracts: Final Report* (Grand Junction, Colo.: U.S. Department of Energy, 1982), A-39.

8. *Uravan Housing Area Map,* map (Uravan, Colo.: Union Carbide, n.d) in files of Umetco, Grand Junction, Colorado.

9. From its creation until July 1955, this paper was titled *USV Photo News.* After Union Carbide reorganized its atomic energy components into a new division called Union Carbide Nuclear in August 1955, the name of the paper changed to *UCN Photo News.*

10. Silver, interview with author.

11. Bernie Jones, interview with author, 28 October 1993. Jones was the Uravan townsite manager for a number of years and was often referred to by the spurious nickname "Mayor of Uravan."

12. Ibid.

13. Dr. and Mrs. Leroy Edward Ellinwood, interview by Clare Engle, 23 July 1970, interview 178, transcript, UUOHP; Lark Washburn, interview by Clare Engle, 22 July 1970, interview 198, transcript, UUOHP. Housing selection in other company towns is discussed in Richard V. Francaviglia, *Hard Places: Reading the Landscape of America's Historic Mining Districts* (Iowa City: University of Iowa Press, 1991), 99–115.

14. "R. E. Wear Construction Company Is Awarded Contract to Build Housing Projects in Naturita and Uravan," Montrose *Daily Press,* 11 January 1943; Silver, UUOHP interview.

15. Mr. and Mrs. Lloyd Larrison, interview by Clare Engle, 5 August 1970, interview 177, transcript, UUOHP, see especially p. 30; Ellinwood interview, especially pp. 27–28; Ralph Thull, interview by Clare Engle, 5 August 1970, interview 203, transcript, UUOHP, especially pp. 35–38; Silver, UUOHP interview, especially pp. 2–3.

16. Silver, interview with author. The discussion of housing is prevalent in most UUOHP interviews regarding Uravan. See especially the Ellinwood, Larrison, Silver, and Thull transcripts.

17. See the following UUOHP interviews for discussions of various structures: Ellinwood, Larrison, Silver, Thull, and Washburn.

18. Francaviglia, *Hard Places,* 101–103; Jones, Larrison, and Washburn interviews.

19. Silver, interview by author.

20. "Uravan School Expands," *USV Photo News* 13 (February 1954): 17.

21. "New 4 Room School Addition at Uravan Completed," *USV Photo News* 16 (August 1954): 14.

22. "Uravan School Expands," *USV Photo News* 13 (February 1954): 17; "Signs of Progress," *UCN Photo News* 28 (August 1956): 4; "Uravan School Completed," *UCN Photo News* 29 (November 1956): 15.

23. "Making It Safe for Youngsters at Uravan," *UCN Photo News* 40 (fourth quarter 1958): 7.

24. Silver, interview by author.

25. Ellinwood interview.

26. *Photo News* 10 (September 1953) through 39 (October 1958) show five different doctors practicing in Uravan, including three in 1953 alone.

27. Jones, interview with author.

28. Ellinwood and Washburn interviews.

29. Washburn interview; Silver, UUOHP interview; Larrison interview.

30. Silver, UUOHP interview.

31. Swimming activities are mentioned in a number of issues of *Photo News* and oral interviews in UUOHP. See especially "Record Numbers Attend Swimming Classes," and "Uravan Swimmer Establishes New Record," *UCN Photo News* 22 (August-September 1955): 7. Discussion of the pool is also found in John and Lorraine Hill, interview by Clare Engle, 21 July 1970, interview 187, transcript, UUOHP, 15.

32. References to sports and recreation are found throughout the 1950s in *Photo News*. For a sampling, see "Uravan Baseball News," *USV Photo News* 3 (June-July 1952): 3; "Uravan Women Softball League Champs," *USV Photo News* 5 (October-November 1953): 16; "Uravan Also Has Junior-High 'A' and 'B' Basketball Teams," *USV Photo News* 13 (February-March 1954): 15; "Tennis Courts Completed," *UCN Photo News* 33 (July-August 1957): 11; "Calling All Uravan Golfers," *UCN Photo News* 22 (August-September 1955): 12–13.

33. "The Uravan USV Community Center," *USV Photo News* 20 (April-May 1955): 12–13.

34. Francaviglia, *Hard Places,* 39–40.

35. "The West's Foremost Mining Camp Managers: San Miguel Trading Center, Inc., and the Fremont Trading Company," advertisement in special energy edition of the Moab *Times-Independent,* 17 February 1955. The following interviews also contain references to shopping: Ruth M. Quackenbush, interview by Clare Engle, 3 August 1972, interview 196, transcript, UUOHP, 9; Germaine Steele, interview by Clare Engle, 1 August 1970, interview 185, transcript, UUOHP, 30–32.

36. Quackenbush and Steele interviews, UUOHP.

37. Sam Peterson Jr., interview by author, 13 May 1992.

38. "Lost Creek Expanding," *Uranium* (April 1957): 30.

39. Although the February issue of *Uranium* magazine still called this location Home on the Range, the next month's copy referred to the area as "Jeffrey City, the name given the former wilderness location of the Lost Creek Uranium mill." See "Lost Creek Mill at Home on the Range," *Uranium* (February 1957): 30; "Top of the News," *Uranium* (March 1957): 7.

40. "The History of a Successful Uranium Venture," *Wyoming* 1 (June-July 1957): 28–31.

41. "Western Nuclear Corp. Is the New Name for Lost Creek Oil and Uranium," *Uranium* (May 1957): 26; ibid., 31.

42. "Western Nuclear Corp.," *Uranium* (August 1957): 12.

43. Peterson interview; "Survey of Wyoming Uranium," *Uranium* (August 1957): 16.

44. Dorsey Woodson, "Frontier Town–Atomic Age Style," Denver *Post, Empire* magazine, 2 February 1961, 6–7; James E. Quinn, *Western Nuclear, Inc. Uranium Mill* (Denver: Denver Equipment Company, [1960]), 2. This report was found in the private collection of Richard Fairservis, former Jeffrey City townsite manager, Riverton, Wyoming.

45. *Crook's Peak Quadrangle, Fremont County Wyoming,* map (Denver: U.S. Geological Survey, 7.5 Minute Series, 1961).

46. Woodson, *Empire.*

47. Richard Fairservis, former Jeffrey City townsite manager, interview by author, 22 September 1993.

48. John R. Adams, and Muril D. Vincelette, interview by author, 20 May 1992. John R. Adams is the youngest son of Bob Adams and at that time was chairman of the board of Energy Fuels Corporation. Muril D. Vincelette worked at Jeffrey City for Western Nuclear in the late 1950s. Much of this is also found in *Empire.*

49. Woodson, *Empire.*

50. John F. Eastman, "Blue Collar Community: A Descriptive Analysis of the Family Life Style of Uranium Workers in an Atypical Social Environment," unpublished M.A. thesis, University of Wyoming, 1972, 21. This attitude is also supported in Phil Eugene Kiner, "A Case Study of Rural Employment in Wyoming's Uranium Sector," unpublished M.A. thesis, University of Wyoming, 1973.

51. Woodson, *Empire.*

52. Dedication of the Jeffrey City School, Wednesday, September 30, 1959, 8:00 P.M., commemorative napkin on file at the Wyoming State Archives, Cheyenne.

53. Gerald D. Nash, *The American West in the Twentieth Century: A Short History of an Urban Oasis* (Albuquerque: University of New Mexico Press, 1973), 229–235.

Chapter
4

The Uranium Capital
of the World I:
Moab

IN ADDITION TO THE COMPANY TOWNS of Uravan and Jeffrey City, the 1950s' government-sponsored uranium boom brought sweeping changes to several independent small towns in the Rocky Mountain West. These communities, lacking corporate paternalism and control, were over-run by individuals responding to the government's buying program, pro-duction bonuses, and exploration services. Like mining camps throughout history, western towns such as Grand Junction, Colorado, and Moab, Utah, became jumping-off points for explorations into the hinterlands. As the industry took off in the late 1940s, the old Utah vanadium towns of Monticello and Blanding flourished again along with Uravan, Naturita, and Durango, Colorado. The boom spread when new strikes were made near Grants, New Mexico, in 1950. Two years later Charlie Steen's pitchblende discovery brought the rush to Moab. Strikes the following year in the Gas Hills region of central Wyoming began opening that sparsely populated area. Then in 1955, a dis-covery at Ambrosia Lake, New Mexico, brought another boom to Grants.

The newcomers found these boomtowns unable to cope with the growing numbers of people. Like most small towns at the time, they were closer to horse and buggy days than to the atomic age. After a decade of depression followed by five years of war, many had experienced little civic improvement since the New Deal in the 1930s. Towns that had made improvements were deeply in debt with newly installed water, lighting, or sewer systems that were supposed to last another generation.

At the center of the new boom were Grants and Moab. Although Moab had been home to a small uranium industry before World War II, neither community was ready for the changes that occurred because of government programs in the 1950s. As people inundated the towns, local government and infrastructure were quickly overstretched. Housing, utility, commercial, and educational facilities became inadequate. To survive, Grants and Moab were forced to construct trailer courts and new subdivisions, provide them with new sources of water and electricity, build new retail centers, reroute traffic, and build new schools.

Grants and Moab not only met this challenge head-on but did it with flare, embracing the uranium boom by giving up their pastoral images of farming and ranching for an industrial portrait. Moab, once known as a garden spot, and Grants, the so-called Carrot Capital, soon vied for the same nickname of "Uranium Capital of the World." Local entrepreneurs constructed Atomic Motels and Uranium Cafes. Beauty pageants dubbed their winners "Miss Uranium" or "Miss Atomic Age" before presenting them with prizes, including truckloads of atomic ore. In short, the uranium rush modernized these nineteenth-century towns, cloaking them in atomic attire while discarding the past for future promise.

Generally, the impact of the uranium rush on the community followed a basic sequence. As the uncontrolled explosion of expectant capitalists—prospectors, construction workers, merchants, and government workers—overwhelmed the existing infrastructure, a lack of ready housing forced the arrivals to live in temporary accommodations such as motels, trailers, and even tents. If a big strike was not found, the rush pushed on to the next community. If a promising new discovery was made, the men soon sent for their families, exacerbating the boom problems. As the newly constructed trailer lots filled, landowners allowed newcomers to rent vacant lots and backyards, adding problems of sanitation and zoning. Schools reported new enrollment records, and utilities—such as power lines and water, sewer, and telephone systems—were quickly overrun. Local government officials had to act quickly and with great foresight to approve new tax hikes, seek federal aid, and pass bond issues. They were aided by the uranium companies, which bought land and built their own subdivisions to house company workers. Like the Levittowns first coming into existence, these company suburbs often mark the first departure from the traditional grid town plat.

As communities began to meet the demands of the boom and embrace the growing atomic industry, their increasing dependence on uranium marked their transition to a new phase: the yellowcake community. Heralded by such events as the completion of a refining mill, the leveling off of population, or the adoption of a pro–uranium industry attitude, the birth of the yellowcake community came at different times to different towns. To understand this evolution, it is necessary to examine each community's history through this period so the similarities and differences become more readily apparent. Moab will be examined first, and Chapter 5 considers Grants.

When word of the atomic bombing of Japan reached Moab, the local press noted that key elements of the bomb had been developed locally and that the area's carnotite industry could become "very active" in years to come.[1] As congressional debate over the control of atomic activities commenced in the fall of 1945, local investigations began to probe the possible monopoly status of the two local carnotite companies, Vanadium Corporation of America (VCA) and United States Vanadium (USV), in the U.S. vanadium industry. Other inquiries sought to repay the small-time vanadium producers for the uranium the Manhattan Project had milled from their waste material.[2] These were the major uranium activities until 1948, when the AEC established an equitable price for uranium ore. Over the next year, prospectors began to trickle into Moab in what could be termed the exploration phase of the uranium boom.[3]

The town prospectors found was much the same as it had been for the last seventy years. The area's history dated from 1854, when Mormon missionaries from Salt Lake City established the Elk Mountain Mission. After several Indian attacks, the missionaries abandoned the post and returned north to defend Salt Lake City during the Mormon war of 1857. The valley remained for the natives until a group of non-Mormon ranchers from Colorado brought cattle into the area around 1875. A post office was established in 1879, and the biblical name Moab was chosen. In 1890 Grand County was created with Moab as its county seat. Over the next fifty years the town grew into a commercial center for agriculture, mining, and tourism.[4] The 1941 Works Projects Administration (WPA) *Guide to Utah* listed Moab as having a population of 883 and indicated that:

Though isolated it has a small business district, selling everything from hay and gasoline to malted milk and liquor—the only "legal" liquor in the county. Squat red adobe houses stand neighbor to more pretentious firebrick houses. In the evenings neon lights illuminate the business district, but after midnight, except on Saturdays, the town does a complete "blackout."[5]

By 1949, despite ongoing reports that Moab would be the heart of a new uranium boom, the town's appearance and character were basically unchanged from the WPA description.[6] As uranium prospectors began trickling into the community, the town still served as a supply point for the area's farmers and ranchers, as the center of county government, and as a primitive jumping-off point for tourists rafting on the Colorado River or going to Arches National Monument. The pace of life was slow; local people shopped downtown, went to church on Sundays, and supported high school activities. Annual events included the Red Rock Roundup rodeo, carnival, and beauty contest held each October when the town celebrated its frontier past. Occasionally, Moab also served as host to western movies filmed in the region.[7] A 1949 article in a Salt Lake newspaper described Moab as a "friendly place, where people of all ages greet the stranger walking down the street with a cheerful 'hello' and even stop their cars to offer to drive him to his destination."[8]

A 1954 map of Moab attests to the continuity of the town's landscape. Situated in a valley that runs northwest to southeast, Moab had been laid out on the cardinal directions in a five-block by five-block grid between the Slick Rock Hills and Mill Creek. Because of the juxtaposition of the vertical grid in a horizontal valley, the town lacked the traditional long main street and instead followed U.S. Highway 100 as it snaked its way through town. Visitors coming to town from the north passed over the Colorado on a long bridge at the head of the valley. They drove southeast through pastures and orchards and entered the town on North Main Street. After passing several blocks of commercial buildings, the highway turned east on Center Street for four blocks before turning south again on East Fourth Street and heading out of town.[9]

The debate over control of the nation's atomic industry and the ensuing struggle between small producers and the big companies curtailed the expected prospecting rush into the Colorado Plateau. As the AEC was about to establish its new incentive program (Circulars 1–3) in the spring of 1948, a few rumblings began to be heard about the future of uranium in Moab and on the plateau.[10] When the government increased the uranium price under Circular 4, uranium activity expanded again.[11] But the publication of Circular 5 in the spring of 1951 marks the shift toward an increasing uranium presence in Moab. A March newspaper article reported that the Moab area was the second-largest uranium-producing region in the country. Throughout that fall and the following spring, the paper recorded that the uranium rush rivaled nineteenth-century gold rushes. Then, on 4 September 1952, the newspaper noted that a young geologist had found pitchblende. When the assay proved good, the rush was on.[12]

Charlie Steen's 1952 pitchblende discovery signals the transition from exploration to boom period. Seemingly overnight, news of the major strike brought hundreds of hopeful prospectors and their families to Moab. Over the next four years, Moab underwent a complete transformation as uranium altered the community's size and character. Indeed, Moab soon called itself the Uranium Capital of the World. To understand this transformation, it is important to examine each of the dilemmas the uranium boom created, as well as the solutions the city formulated to alleviate them.

Moab's fundamental problem was that population expanded ahead of infrastructure. The 1950 census reported the town's population as around 1,200. After Steen's discovery, local accounts cited a 33 percent increase to about 1,800 by 1954. As uranium industry construction began, the population soared to more than 4,000 in 1956. As in boomtowns throughout history, this rapid acceleration quickly outpaced the town's ability to cope.[13]

From the beginning, Moab's civic leaders recognized the problems the boom created for the town, as well as the potential for even greater ones in the future. In a revealing article titled "The Official Outlook," Mayor J. W. Corbin and the five-man city council outlined Moab's present state and its future just two weeks after taking office in January 1954:

> Most of us are wondering about the future of Moab, how big will it grow, what changes to expect and how will it affect us as individuals. Whether we like it or not seems to matter very little as the forces being brought to bear are not to be stayed. WE ARE A BOOMTOWN. Our economy seems assured with our budding uranium industry, ranching, farming, and tourists. . . .
>
> Your Mayor and your City Council are fully cognizant of these conditions and are fully aware of the responsibilities therein. We realize the time for farsighted planning is now. We realize the time for action is now. In view of these facts we are consulting and asking for the best advice available to us, but we will need the help of the citizens of the community. We will make mistakes and we ask your forbearance for they will be honest ones.
>
> Some of the problems we are faced with are these: our water and sewage, the need for a building code, the necessity of a zoning ordinance, the

existing and the proposed new subdivisions. These are but a few but they are necessary for an orderly growth in any budding hamlet.

At the present time the City of Moab is destitute for funds. We must have money to carry out these proposals. You will see some new forms of revenue: we will possibly increase some of the old. In conclusion may we add—Your City Officials will go to bed each night with this prayer, "Dear Lord, please let our friends remain friends, and please don't let our fellow citizens, friends or not, cuss us, but help us, Amen."[14]

Although not specifically mentioned in Mayor Corbin's letter, Moab's most immediate concern was housing. The town had living quarters for about 2,000 people plus four motels, and the rush of people following the Steen discovery quickly exceeded the accommodations. For the first time in mining history, boomers brought self-contained travel trailers and parked them in the city's courts. By late 1953 the trailer parks were full, so newcomers began parking their trailers in the orchards north of town and along the Colorado River. Others set up tents along the river or slept in sleeping bags in the city parks. Locals, realizing the value of their land, began to rent their front yards and empty lots to accommodate more trailers. A young man visiting the area described it this way:

> The streets were full of people. You'd drive around the streets of Moab and you'd see literally people living in tents, small trailer homes. We stayed out at the old city park at that time because we just brought sleeping bags with us, just kids out of school . . . and we had a lot of company, a lot of guys sleeping in sleeping bags out there.[15]

The overflow of humanity brought sanitation problems, especially on the outskirts of town where most of the tent and trailer towns had been established. In July 1954 a state health commissioner reported that large numbers of people were living without garbage or sewage disposal and getting their water from open ditches.[16]

In an attempt to alleviate the sewage problems, city leaders contracted for a new plant to be opened in 1956. A number of difficulties—from a national steel strike to an incapacitating illness to problems with the designing architect—delayed the project several times. By late 1957 the project was still not completed, and the local paper described the fiasco as the "city's big headache."[17]

Although construction had expanded, it still lagged behind the increasing population. An early 1954 housing check reported that the town was 300 homes short of its immediate needs. Throughout the year new subdivisions were designed, new businesses were opened, and the city adopted a zoning ordinance. But it was not enough; the dilemma of boomtown life continued.[18]

Faced with the housing shortage, Charlie Steen became the leader in an effort to provide quality new homes in Moab.[19] After finding a recently purchased motel inadequate, Steen announced in January 1954 that his Utex Exploration Company had purchased a large tract of land north of Moab to build the first 10 of 150 planned new homes for key company personnel.[20] Nicknamed "Steenville," the tract was sort of a company subdivision, built and sold by Steen's company.[21] Other entrepreneurs followed close behind. By July, residential building permits topped $300,000 as plans were issued for a 107-unit tract dubbed "Uranium Village" and another 50-home subdivision.[22]

To ease immediate housing problems while these new subdivisions were built, new motels, apartment buildings, and trailer courts were also constructed.[23] As more and more people opted for trailers, the business became very competitive. A local dealer promoted a variety of new and used mobile homes and temporary housing units called "takealong huts." A competitor in Grand Junction, advertising "Mobile Homes for a Mobile Nation," offered prospective customers free air transportation to and from Moab.[24]

Although the housing problem continued to plague Moab throughout 1954 and into 1955, important long-term steps were initiated. They included the enactment of ordinances governing trailer courts and the new subdivisions, provisions for garbage removal, adoption of a building code and zoning ordinance, establishment of a board of health, enactment of a master street plan, revision of water and sewer ordinances, creation of a planning commission, and the hiring of a planning consultant.[25]

Moab's school system also demanded modernization even before the uranium boom. In 1952 the city's 547 students were packed into an eighteen-year-old building designed for 400–500 pupils. The school boasted 22 faculty members and a total budget of $179,062. The county tax for school uses was 7 mills for operation and maintenance and 1 mill for future buildings. To alleviate problems, a 1949 plan to build a new 8-room elementary school was already under way as the uranium expansion began. In the fall of 1952 the board of education realized that the structure would quickly be outdated. As enrollment increased in the spring and summer of 1953, the board began to negotiate with Charlie Steen about purchasing a 16-acre site within his new subdivision to build a new school. Eventually, the board purchased the land for the same price Steen had paid for it.[26]

As enrollment expanded to almost 700 by the spring of 1954, the board of education made plans for a new elementary school to be built on the new lot. Funding became a problem because property taxes were increasing much slower than enrollment. The crisis was complicated by the fact that although Moab was the home base of the new boom, most of the mines—including Steen's Mi Vida—were located in neighboring San Juan County.[27] Thus to pay for the $600,000 project, Moab residents overwhelmingly passed a bond election in April, and work started immediately on a 15-room school. Complete with a gym, auditorium, library, and kitchen, the new Helen M. Knight School opened in the fall of 1955.[28]

With the school nearing completion, the board of education faced two new difficulties as newcomers continued to pour into the community. By 2 September enrollment neared 900, and students were forced to sit on windowsills or meet outdoors.[29] The first problem was apparent: despite the addition of the new school, the town's growing population required even more classrooms. This need led to the second dilemma. The bond passed to build the school had maximized the district's legal indebtedness. To build another facility, Moab would have to seek federal aid. Thanks to a public law that provided federal funds for districts heavily impacted by government activity, Moab was able to land a $173,800 federal grant to build another 8-room elementary school.[30]

Although building plans were made to accommodate boom conditions, the delay between planning and opening forced Moab schoolchildren into cramped conditions. Until the Knight school was completed in the fall of 1955, up to 670 students were jammed into a building designed for 500 pupils. Even after the new facility opened, burgeoning elementary enrollment forced the board of education to hold double sessions in 8 classrooms the first year and for all grades 1–6 in 1956.[31]

Public utilities were also impacted by the uranium rush. The most notable example was the local telephone system, a critical communication service that linked outside capitalists to the isolated town. In 1952 Moab's local Midland Telephone boasted service to 275 local customers plus an additional 5 northbound and 4 southbound circuits for long-distance traffic. Only 2 operators were required to handle the business.[32]

Then came the prospecting boom of 1954. As local prospectors staked their claims, a communications rush developed. The switchboard was jammed with long-distance calls from Salt Lake City, Grand Junction, Denver, and beyond. Stories abound of prospectors staying up late just to use one of the available telephones. One anecdote tells of a man in Salt Lake City who became so frustrated when he could not place his call to Moab that he got in his car and drove the 150 miles home. When he arrived the phone was ringing; it was the operator placing his call.[33]

As service deteriorated with the rush, Midland Telephone and Mountain States Telephone (the long-distance company) poured hundreds of thousands of dollars into the system. By 1956 the town boasted over 800 phones in service, over 30 northbound and 12 southbound long-distance circuits, and 7 operators. The number of full-time employees nearly doubled from 40 to 75 over the same time period.[34]

As the population of Moab increased, the city also faced problems with its water system. Although the Colorado River flowed through the valley, the city obtained its civic water from underground wells. The increase in population placed new demands on this supply and raised health questions as newcomers, many of whom were living outdoors, increased the chance of contamination. When early restrictions on watering lawns could not keep up with the population, the city drilled new wells to increase supplies. Then in 1957 the city purchased a ranch east of town for its water rights, thereby doubling supplies.[35] Although this curtailed problems temporarily, an unusually dry year in 1958 caused more water shortages. Concerns were raised about inadequate water pressure in the event of a fire, and restrictions were again placed on private use in July 1958.[36]

The local post office faced similar boom problems. As was the case in many small towns, preboom Moabites did not have home delivery but went to the post office each day to collect their mail from assigned boxes. When the boom hit, the boxes were quickly occupied, forcing the postmaster to assign each box to two and even three occupants. Still others received their mail through general delivery, which led to long lines as the one full-time clerk and a part-time assistant served them. Postal receipts jumped from $12,000 per year in 1952 to over $41,000 just two years later. As stopgap measures, three new clerks and 384 new boxes were added in July 1954. A move to a new building during the summer of 1955 and the start of home delivery the following year greatly alleviated the problems.[37]

Retail trade in Moab also expanded because of the uranium boom. In 1952 the city had six grocery stores, three eating places, three dry goods stores, four motels, a drugstore, and a lumberyard. Bank deposits in the town totaled just under $3 million, and just over 110,000 pounds of freight were loaded annually.[38] By 1956 the town had eight groceries, eleven eating establishments, six dry goods stores, eleven motels, two drugstores, two lumberyards, a theater, jewelry store, radio station, brokerage house, several new service stations, and a taxi service. Bank deposits exceeded $5.7 million, and freight loadings surpassed 4.5 million pounds.[39]

As more and more outsiders moved into Moab, crime increased, and the city had to expand its police force. Before the rush, Moab was patrolled by both a county sheriff and a city marshal. The two agencies worked together and shared the same four-occupant jail in the Grand County courthouse.[40] As petty crime grew, the city hired an extra officer to work weekends, warned citizens to lock their doors at night, and bought a new police car.[41] In July 1954 the city opened a new police station, and the county hired a deputy sheriff. According to one account, these efforts met the city's needs.[42] But when problems with area youths continued over the next two years, the city council implemented a curfew prohibiting those under age seventeen from being on the streets after 11 P.M.[43] When vandalism, the writing of bad checks, and burglary continued, the two law enforcement agencies found their shared jail space inadequate, a problem that continued for several years.[44]

The influx of newcomers into Moab reinforced the existing racial imbalance. In 1950, 100 percent of Moab's 1,274 residents were listed as "white" in the census. Ten years later only 3 African Americans and 10 "others" were listed among the town's 5,995 inhabitants.[45] Although there was not the outward show of the Jim Crow discrimination or segregation occurring at the time in the South, *Ebony* magazine reported in 1955 that Moab's lone black prospector, Augustus "Maxie" Maxwell, worked as a custodian for Charlie Steen and lived in Steen's motel. Maxwell stated that "many citizens have told me that I have as much right here as anyone else."[46]

The 1950s uranium boom changed the character of Moab from a sleepy supply town to a modern, industrial yellowcake community. Although the transformation encompassed most of the problems and solutions discussed here, the other changes can be summarized in three main categories: the effect of the uranium boom on mundane activities, the increasing use of "uranium" or "atomic" in everyday names, and the emergence of a true economic dependence on uranium.

The uranium boom affected nearly every aspect of life in Moab, and the boom conditions transformed the village into a city. Still, news stories from the local paper suggest that the uranium boom kept people away from rodeos, elections, and even local movie shoots. A select group of headlines attests to this change: "No Cowboys—No Rodeo—They Went Uranium Mining," "Politics Shaded by Uranium in Light Primary Turnout," "Universal International May Make Movie Here if Housing Can Be Had," "Uranium Is Hot—Politics Are Not," and "Movies Can't Compete With Uranium in Moab."[47]

The increased use of atomic-age nomenclature attests to the way the community adopted uranium into its psyche and marks the beginning of an

Uranium Jewelry Sign, Moab, c. 1960s. The remnants of the town's parking meters, a failed attempt to control transportation during the boom, can be seen. Courtesy, Dan O'Laurie Canyon Country Museum, Toots McDougald Collection, Moab, Utah.

atomic subculture. One of the town's first subdivisions was called Uranium Village. A Uranium Building was constructed. The name of the rodeo was changed from Red Rock Roundup to Uranium Days Rodeo. In 1957 local women competed for the title Uranium Queen.[48] Not surprisingly, the newspaper boosted the area's new industry by first calling the town the Uranium Center before settling on the grander title, Uranium Capital of the World.[49]

The strongest component of Moab's transformation into a yellowcake community began in 1953 when local companies began to discuss building a uranium-processing mill in the town.[50] In August Charlie Steen's Utex Exploration Company contacted the AEC about a Moab mill. In January 1954 the AEC announced that an ore-buying facility would be constructed there. Then in April 1954 Steen announced plans to build a $4 million mill in Moab. To gather the needed capital, Steen combined Utex with the Combined Metals Reduction Company to form the Uranium Reduction Company (URECO). The new company was fully financed and did not offer public stock.[51]

During the first uranium boom, atomic nomenclature entered the landscape of many yellowcake towns. Here Arctic Circle sells prospecting equipment. Courtesy, Dan O'Laurie Canyon Country Museum, Toots McDougald Collection, Moab, Utah.

In May 1954 the AEC opened its ore-buying plant as URECO began outlining its plans for what would become the nation's largest uranium mill. The company decided on a new resin-in-pulp process that had been tested but never used in a commercial plant. In June 1955 URECO signed its AEC contract, and construction continued until October 1956, when the $9 million operation was finally completed. The new mill delivered its first yellowcake in November 1956, and by the following spring it was the nation's second-largest yellowcake producer, supplying one-quarter of total U.S. production.[52]

When the new mill opened, Moab's landscape was already beginning to reflect its increasing uranium dependence. The increased transportation as a result of exploration had combined with the growing population to cause greater traffic on the town's roads and in the business area. In 1953 the Utex Exploration Company notified the public that its drivers had been instructed to obey all traffic rules, and it encouraged citizens to report any contrary behavior.[53] The following year a new bridge was com-

Moab, Utah, Uranium Center of America. Photo by Michael Amundson, 2001.

pleted across the Colorado to provide better traffic flow. When the boom intensified in 1954 during mill construction, business increased so much in downtown Moab that parking meters were installed the following year. They caused so many complaints that they were removed in 1957. When the mill was completed north of town in 1956, Main Street became the direct route between the mines and the processing plant. By that time the movement of uranium was already at the center of Moab's existence.[54]

The URECO mill was dedicated in September 1957, eleven months after beginning operations. A number of dignitaries were present including Jesse C. Johnson, director of the AEC's Division of Raw Materials; Utah governor George Clyde; Utah senator Howard Young; and Charlie Steen. Johnson explained that the new mill was the largest in the country, and Senator Young talked about the impact the new mill would have on jobs in the state, but Steen stole the show.[55] In his address Steen noted that "this URECO coffee grinder symbolizes many things to different people," including a continued flow of yellowcake to the AEC, return on investment to financiers, and "stable employment and a large payroll" to local merchants and citizens. Steen presented Johnson with the honorary degree Doctor of Uranium.[56]

Hidden Splendor Ore arrives at URECO mill, c. 1960. This view shows a truckload of uranium ore on its way to the Uranium Reduction Company (later Atlas) mill north of Moab. With most of the mines to the south of town and the mill to the north, trucks like this were a common site in Moab during the uranium boom. Courtesy, Dan O'Laurie Canyon Country Museum, Pictorial Review of Hidden Splendor Mine Collection, Moab, Utah.

Samuel Taylor, editor of the Moab *Times-Independent,* also reflected on the impact of the new mill on Utah and Moab. In an editorial titled "A Pause for Appreciation," Taylor conclusively noted Moab's new status as a yellowcake community:

> Uranium Reduction company has brought Moab its first large steady payroll, which means prosperity for almost every business in town; and employment for many local people who would have had to look elsewhere for a livelihood had not the mill been built here. The size of the operation, ranking it among the largest uranium ore mills in the world, has brought Moab into its own as a major uranium milling center. And not to be forgotten are the many new people that have come to Moab to operate the mill. They have shown pride in their community and a willingness to help in promoting the area.

To Charles A. Steen; to all the officials, directors and employees of Uranium Reduction company—a tribute. To you a grateful community gives its thanks.[57]

As Taylor clearly noted, the most important player in Moab's transformation to a yellowcake community was Charlie Steen. Not only did he initiate the rush with his pitchblende discovery in 1952, he also became Moab's biggest booster, developer, builder, and leader. Just a few months after his discovery, the local paper was following Steen's every move with headlines such as "C A Steen Goes on Television, Boosts Section," "Utex Produces Million in Ore—Charles A. Steen's Claim Proved True—Big New Find," and "The Story of Charles A. Steen Featured in *Mining and Engineering Journal* for Sept."[58]

Once boomtown conditions prevailed, Steen responded. He purchased a motel to house company personnel and bought land and started the "Steenville" subdivision. He provided land, at no personal profit, for the Harriet Knight elementary school; gave lots for churches; and donated money for a new hospital. He served on the school board and constructed the town's largest employer, the URECO mill.[59]

In addition to these economic and civic benefits, Steen symbolically brought uranium and Moab together with his annual company picnics to which the entire town was invited. Noted by nearly all observers as one of the biggest events of the year, the annual festivity was held on 6 June—the day of Steen's famous discovery. The annual party not only provided Moabites with free food and entertainment but also demonstrated the increasing importance of uranium to the community. Indeed, the mill, its sustained employment, and the annual open house all signified Moab's growing uranium dependence.[60]

Moab's civic leaders also contributed to the town's success. Men like Mayor J. W. Corbin, newspaper editors L. L. and Samuel Taylor, and the Moab city council helped boost the town and identified problems and discovered innovative means to combat them. At the beginning of the boom in the fall of 1953, L. L. Taylor described Moab's new role:

The sky is the limit, as we enter the Atomic Age. Moab is in the very middle of the activity, with its importance increasing from day to day as the known size of the deposits of fissionable material are more carefully explored and evaluated.

We are pilgrims on an uncharted sea of the future and it remains to be seen whether we will yield to fear and be swallowed-up in oblivion or whether we will, with prayer, choose right from wrong and lead the world

Aerial view of Moab's West Side after the first uranium boom, c. 1960s. This view clearly shows the transformation of the town's landscape as fruit orchards gave way to the new hospital, a few homes, and a trailer park. Courtesy, Dan O'Laurie Canyon Country Museum, *Times-Independent* Collection, Moab, Utah

> into a tomorrow of possibilities unlimited—a future so rosy with promise that one contemplating it is lost in wonder.
>
> Do we have the intestinal fortitude—guts, if you want plain talk, to forget partisan politics—walking down the middle of the road—working for the good of ALL—not any selfish group or body? I repeat, do we have the courage?[61]

Mayor Corbin and the town council issued their "Official Outlook" in January 1954 identifying specific problems and asking for the public's patience as they tried to solve them. Over the next two years the mayor and council adopted creative new methods of raising money, greatly increased the size of local government, and modernized Moab. This transformation is best illustrated by a comparison.

In 1952, to meet the needs of its 1,300 inhabitants, the city council budget provided a general fund totaling $10,890. This included $4,100 for administrative expenses, $2,470 for police, $760 for the fire department, $2,210 for the street department, and $1,350 for the municipal swimming pool. In addition, the council budgeted $8,640 for sewer and water department operations and $3,265 for depreciation, $9,285 for revenue bond interest and retirement, and $3,387 for general obligation bond interest and retirement.[62]

To pay for municipal projects that had been needed since the Depression, the City of Moab bonded itself to the legal limit of $58,000 and sold another $95,000 in revenue bonds. These funds were used to pay for a new sewage treatment plant, water supply development, and water and sewer line extensions. At the time, city officials felt these projects were more than adequate for Moab's needs. The city tax levy was just 16 mills on an assessed valuation of less than $500,000.[63]

Moab's city payroll was also small. The police department consisted of just one man—the city marshal. Other employees included the water master, city recorder, a sexton, and a justice of the peace. The council consisted of a mayor and five councilmen. Most of these jobs were part-time.[64]

By 1956, the transformation was amazing. The comprehensive city council budget had increased to $124,000, including 600 percent growth in administrative costs, a 1,200 percent increase in public safety allocations, and a 1,300 percent increase in street funds. The sewer and water budget had grown to $38,500. Moab's assessed valuation had quadrupled to over $2 million. In addition to the positions mentioned earlier, the city added a planner and four police officers.[65]

In general terms, Moab accomplished this growth by passing new ordinances and creating a new infrastructure and bureaucracies. Some of the new laws involved trailer court and subdivision organization, garbage removal, building and zoning codes, plus revised water and sewer regulations. In addition, the city created new government agencies to address boom conditions, including a board of health, a new police department, and a planning commission.[66]

To fund these projects, the Moab city council increased the mill levy from 16 mills to 24.75 mills, and the boom brought added funds from new businesses and increased revenues. Still, the income was insufficient to keep pace. Because the town had reached its legal limit of indebtedness, no bonds could be issued until tax assessments went up. Two solutions were tried: new tax sources and federal aid.[67]

In July 1954 Moab enacted a business license tax of one-tenth of 1 percent (increased to 1 percent in 1955) on all retail sales in the city. Although the tax brought some criticism, the town gained $56,000 during the first twelve months. This stopgap measure helped pay police salaries, begin sidewalk and curb placement, construct a new fire station, and pull several city services out of debt until tax assessments increased and the city's bondedness increased to $200,000. By 1955, federal money arrived in the form of a $113,000 grant and a $49,000 loan to pay for new water and sewer operations.[68]

Although most Moabites liked and encouraged their town's growth, former resident Mardy Thomson attacked the transformation in a paper for a college writing class. According to an article in the *Times-Independent,* the story created "quite a stir." Thomson began by describing how Moab had once been a slow, wholesome little town located among marvelous scenery. The town produced breathtaking fruit and good people. Although it got busy on Saturday nights, church attendance on Sunday was always strong. Then, Thomson wrote,

> A ragged, underfed little man known as "Hot Rock Charley" stumbled onto a large deposit of high grade uranium ore near Moab. This started it all. Moab was invaded by Texans, and they took over the place without firing a shot.
>
> The sweet smelling fruit orchards have been converted into trailer courts. The beautiful scenery now includes tents and one room shanties with a Cadillac parked in front. Old homesteads have been sold and in their place now stand a new service station or motel. Real estate flourishes and uranium claims are sold on every street corner, while claim jumpers play hop-scotch on staked territories. Ore trucks and Jeeps along with fat men in fine cars make safe driving another thing of the past. A new police force was obtained to strengthen the old western style sheriff system. Bad checks bounce in and out of the business houses to the bank. People have forgotten the beautiful scenery and the La Sal Mountains, and spend all their time with Geiger counters, jaunting miles in search of a hot spot to get rich quick.
>
> The old dance hall has been converted into a modern furniture store and uranium offices. Moab patrons dance in a garage where they should have a gas mask to keep from being suffocated by dust. The general appearance is that of an old folks' party. This is because dust has greyed hair, eyelashes, and settled a ghastly look upon smiling faces.
>
> Moab is widely known throughout the United States. Prominent magazines have featured articles on the "Uranium Center of the World," and papers have run continued stories on the fabulous UTEX Mine. Though Moab may be known as "Little Texas" or "Steenville," true Moabites will always love Moab, and down deep the memories are ever lasting.[69]

Apparently, Thomson's attitude changed, for the next year she was a candidate for Miss Atomic Age.[70]

By 1957 Moab had been transformed from a boomtown into a true yellowcake community. In a revealing editorial, *Times-Independent* editor Samuel J. Taylor admitted that Moab was now indisputably tied to the uranium industry:

> Let there be no mistake. Moab has grown to five times its size in 1950 — and this growth has been brought about by the uranium industry and nothing else. A good percentage of the local population is now directly associated with the industry, and another large portion is dependent upon uranium-associated people for a livelihood through service industries. There is hardly a person in the entire community that is not touched by the uranium economy in one way or another.[71]

As a one-industry town, Taylor noted that Moab either had a bright future or no future, depending on the fortunes of the uranium industry.

Because uranium was totally regulated by the federal government, Taylor could have noted that Moab was now tied to the federal government as well. Already, the town's status within national defense had provided federal grants and loans for school construction and municipal services. The federal bond was strengthened with the completion of the URECO mill where the AEC exchanged yellowcake for salaries. In short, the federal government was indirectly responsible for Moab's uranium boom and its urban transformation. Moab's new status as a yellowcake community was ensured until the end of the government buying program in 1966. The future of the community after that would be subject to the uranium industry, the Atomic Energy Commission, and the federal government.[72]

Notes

1. "Atomic Bomb Element Produced Here," Moab *Times-Independent,* 16 August 1945, 1.
2. "Vanadium Probe Starts," Moab *Times-Independent,* 1 November 1945.
3. "Prospectors Needed to Discover Uranium Ore for Atomic Age," Moab *Times-Independent,* 28 February 1946; "To Urge Office at Moab," Moab *Times-Independent,* 31 October 1946.
4. Faun McConkie Tanner, *The Far Country: A Regional History of Moab and La Sal, Utah,* 2d ed. (Salt Lake City: Olympus, 1976).
5. Writer's Program of the Work Projects Administration in the State of Utah, *Utah: A Guide to the State* (New York: Hastings House, 1941), 426.
6. See three articles in the Moab *Times-Independent:* "Great Future for Uranium District Forecast," 15 September 1949; "New Uranium Mill at Moab

Planned by Salt Lake Group," 29 September 1949; "1950 Census Figures Now Give Moab Population of 1272," 24 August 1950.

7. "Red Rock Roundup Queen Contest Ends With Street Fete and Dance Saturday," Moab *Times-Independent,* 29 September 1949; "New Picture Set for Spring," Moab *Times-Independent,* 26 January 1950. The article "Coast-to-Coast Broadcast Originates at Moab" reported that the Sons of the Pioneers, on location for the filming of the John Ford western *Rio Bravo,* performed to a crowd at the Moab high school auditorium. In addition to the quartet, several guest stars from the movie attended the show including John Ford, John Wayne, Maureen O'Hara, Chill Wills, Ben Johnson, and Harry Carey Jr.

8. Ramona W. Cannon, "Community Was Once Gateway to This Area," unknown paper (probably Salt Lake *Tribune* or *Deseret News*), 6 February 1949, Moab file, Utah Historical Society, Salt Lake City.

9. "Zone Map of Moab, Utah: May 1954," Moab *Times-Independent,* 27 May 1954.

10. See three articles in the Moab *Times-Independent:* "Hopes Brighten for Activity in Uranium," 1 January 1948; "Vast Uranium Activity Seen," 22 January 1948; "Rich Carnotite District Described by Eminent Mining Engineer," 19 February 1948. The latter reported that "hundreds of new claims have been filed for record in the county recorder's office at Moab."

11. "Atomic Commission Announces Increase in Uranium Price," Moab *Times-Independent,* 13 May 1948; "Much Assessment Work Underway in Carnotite Properties Through District," Moab *Times-Independent,* 20 May 1948.

12. See five articles in the Moab *Times-Independent:* "Local Area Is 2nd Biggest Producer," 22 March 1951; "Uranium Hunt Rivals Gold Rush of Old," 29 November 1951; "Hunt for Uranium Promises to Dwarf Old Time Gold Rush," 8 May 1952; "Geologist Reports Pitchblende Find," 4 September 1952; "Assay Reports Good," 4 December 1952.

13. Daniel Albert Keeler, "Town on a Powder Keg: A Video Tape Production on the Industrial Emergence of Moab, Utah," unpublished M.A. thesis, University of Utah, 1966, 75.

14. "The Official Outlook," Moab *Times-Independent,* 21 January 1954.

15. T. Dee Tranter, interview by Steve Guttman, 11 August 1970, interview no. 35, transcript, UUOHP.

16. "U-Boom Woes Studied by Moab Council," Salt Lake City *Tribune,* 22 July 1954; M. Demar Teuscher, "Water, Schools, Mail: Big Problems Beset Moab as Result of A-Ore Boom," *Deseret News,* 9 July 1954.

17. "$80,000 Sewage Treatment Plant Has Been City's Big Headache for 1957," Moab *Times-Independent,* 28 November 1957.

18. "Building Boom Hits Moab as Spring Nears—Race to Be Ready for Influx," Moab *Times-Independent,* 14 January 1954.

19. "C of C Board Checks Housing Needs in City," Moab *Times-Independent*, 28 January 1954.

20. "Utex Purchases Starbuck Motel for Own Use," Moab *Times-Independent*, 20 August 1953, quoted Steen as saying, "Contrary to rumor, we are not trying to buy all of Moab."

21. "Utex Corporation to Build Ten New Modern Homes at Once—Salt Lake Firm in Charge of Job," Moab *Times-Independent*, 14 January 1954.

22. "Building Hits Fast Pace in Boom City," Salt Lake *Tribune*, 22 July 1954; "Moab Goes Modern . . . With a Rash of Home Building," Salt Lake *Tribune*, 18 July 1954.

23. Beverly Spencer, "Housing Remains Moab's No. 1 Problem," Moab *Times-Independent*, 10 June 1954. The following articles all appeared in the 1 July 1954 edition of the Moab *Times-Independent*: "Twenty-Eight New Homes for Moab—Work Begins Soon," "60 Unit Modern Motel to Go up at Once," "Balsley-Hines Apts. to Be Completed End of Next Week."

24. See the Ken Garff Sales, Inc., ad, 27 May 1954, and the R & W Trailer Sales ad, 4 March 1954, in the Moab *Times-Independent*. Charlie Steen and his wife, M. L., relate the importance of trailers to his 1952 pitchblende discovery in Dora Tennyson, "The Trailer That Led to Millions," *Trailer Life* (April 1954). This clipping was found in the Charlie Steen Scrapbook, Western History Department, Denver Public Library.

25. "Moab's Last Four Years: Boom Problems Really Piled up on City in '54, but Most Have Been Solved Now," Moab *Times-Independent*, 14 June 1956.

26. "Moab's Last Four Years: School Growth, Improvements Since Start of Boom Exemplify Community Progress," Moab *Times-Independent*, 27 September 1956.

27. Winford Bunce, interview by Steve Guttman and John Donnely, 29 July 1970, interview no. 29, transcript, UUOHP.

28. Ibid.

29. "Schools So Overcrowded Pupils Sit in Windows—Class Out of Doors," Moab *Times-Independent*, 2 September 1954.

30. "Moab's Last Four Years: Walker School Addition to Solve Elementary Problem, but High School Needs More Space," Moab *Times-Independent*, 4 October 1956.

31. Ibid.

32. "Moab's Last Four Years: Boom Brings Progress, Growth—and Also Lots of Headaches—to Local Businesses," Moab *Times-Independent*, 5 July 1956.

33. The telephone crisis can be traced in front pages of the *Moab Times-Independent* from 4 February to 18 November 1954. See also J. Wallace Corbin, interview by Steve Guttman, 23 July 1970, interview no. 30, transcript, UUOHP.

34. "Moab's Last Four Years: Boom Brings Progress."

35. Don Robinson, "Water Situation Improved Over Last Report in Early June," Moab *Times-Independent*, 28 November 1957.

36. "New Law Passed as Moab Water Dwindles," Moab *Times-Independent,* 10 July 1958; "City Officials Lift Water Restrictions," Moab *Times-Independent,* 28 August 1958.

37. E. R. Carter, interview by Steve Guttman, 22 July 1970, interview no. 33, transcript, UUOHP; see four articles in the Moab *Times-Independent*: "New Boxes a Big Help at Post Office," 8 July 1954; "Post Office Service Improved by Adding Boxes and Clerks," 29 July 1954; "New Post Office to Be Ready in Late Summer," 10 February 1955; "Post Office Building Goes up on Schedule; Opens in August," 23 June 1955.

38. "Moab's Last Four Years: Boom Brings Progress."

39. Ibid. Nearly every issue of the *Times-Independent* in 1954 carried a story relating to a new business opening.

40. Samuel Taylor, interview by Steve Guttman, 23 July 1970, interview no. 56, transcript, UUOHP.

41. See three articles in the Moab *Times-Independent*: "Moab Hires Extra Cop for Week-Ends," 25 March 1954; "Chief of Police Warns to Lock Homes and Cars — Many Petty Thefts," 10 June 1954; "Moab City to Get New Patrol Car," 24 June 1954.

42. "Moab Police Force Geared to City's Needs," Moab *Times-Independent,* 1 July 1954; "County Hires Deputy for Sheriff," Moab *Times-Independent,* 9 December 1954.

43. "Curfew Edict Passed Tuesday Night by Moab City Council," Moab *Times-Independent,* 19 April 1956.

44. See three articles in the Moab *Times-Independent*: "Holiday Sees Series of Break-ins," 5 January 1956; "Sheriff Writes Rules Asked for Operations of Jail House," 10 May 1956; Samuel J. Taylor, "Get Them Before They Get You," 3 March 1957. The lack of adequate jail space is discussed in "Sheriff John Stocks Looks Back Over Decade of Enforcement Work," Moab *Times-Independent,* 4 December 1962.

45. Bureau of the Census, *U.S. Census of Population: 1950,* Vol. 2, *Characteristics of the Population,* Part 44, Utah (Washington, D.C.: Government Printing Office [GPO], 1952); Bureau of the Census, *U.S. Census of Population: 1960,* Vol. 1, *Characteristics of the Population,* Part 46, Utah (Washington, D.C.: GPO, 1963).

46. "Man in Search of Million: Negro Prospector Seeks Fortune in Uranium Boom," *Ebony* (February 1955): 16–22.

47. The first four headlines are from the Moab *Times-Independent,* 24 September 1953, 16 September 1954, 11 March 1954, and 8 July 1954. The last is from the *Deseret News,* 9 June 1954.

48. "Ann West Named Queen; Alice-Jo, Hidden Splendor, County, Parade Winners for U-Days," Moab *Times-Independent,* 12 September 1957.

49. The Moab *Times-Independent* included the nickname "Uranium Center of the World" in its masthead from late March through 16 June 1955. Only after

the Uranium Capital rodeo debuted in late May did the nickname change to Uranium Capital of the World.

50. "Utex Considers Mill—AEC and Co. Investigate," Moab *Times-Independent,* 27 August 1953.

51. Robert W. Bernick, "$4 Million Uranium Mill Set for Moab," Salt Lake City *Tribune,* 13 April 1954; Mitchell Melich, "An Historic Look Back: How the Uranium Reduction Company Got Its Start," *Annual Report of the Uranium Reduction Company,* in Moab file, Museum of Western Colorado, Grand Junction.

52. Holger Albrethsen and Frank E. McGinley, *Summary History of Domestic Uranium Procurement Under U.S. Atomic Energy Commission Contracts: Final Report* (Grand Junction, Colo.: U.S. Department of Energy, 1982), A86–A88; Frank Hewlett, "Dream Ends: Rite 'Starts' Moab U-Mill," Salt Lake City *Tribune,* 15 September 1957.

53. "Utex Exploration Company Ad," San Juan *Record,* 7 April 1953.

54. See three articles in the Moab *Times-Independent*: "To Consider Parking Meters at Monday Meeting," 15 July 1954; "No Meters for Moab for Now," 22 July 1954; "What About the Parking Meters," 2 May 1957. In a related story, Charlie Steen noted that "the shopping district is about two blocks long and while Moab may have some problems, downtown parking isn't one of them." See Dan Valentine, "Parking Meter Court Is Hinted Here," Salt Lake *Tribune,* clipping in Charlie Steen Scrapbook, Denver Public Library.

55. Hewlett, "Dream Ends." Growth attributed to the mill is also discussed in Jack E. Jarrard, "Speaking of Business: U-Mill Points Growth of Moab, Ex-Cowtown," *Deseret News,* 16 September 1957.

56. Hewlett, "Dreams Ends"; Raye C. Ringholz, *Uranium Frenzy: Boom and Bust on the Colorado Plateau* (New York: W. W. Norton, 1989), 160–164.

57. Samuel Taylor, "A Pause for Appreciation," Moab *Times-Independent,* 12 September 1957.

58. See the Moab *Times-Independent,* 2 April, 13 August, and 24 September 1953.

59. Norman Boyd, interview by Steve Guttman and John Donnely, 4 August 1970, interview no. 28, UUOHP. The article "Charles Steen, Atom Age Pioneer, Brought Many Changes to Moab," Moab *Times-Independent,* 29 April 1955, also credits Steen as indirectly contributing to the building of a new bridge on the Colorado, the remodeling of the downtown business district, and the construction of hundreds of new homes.

60. Early descriptions of the growth of this party can be found in three *Times-Independent* stories: "Citizens of Moab Will Be Guests of Utex Exploration Open House June 6 at Arches," 21 May 1953; "Utex Party Last Saturday Was Huge Success," 11 June 1953; "YOU ARE INVITED TO UTEX PARTY AT AIRPORT THIS SATURDAY—FUN FOR ALL," 3 June 1954. Steen's efforts to provide a variety of

entertainment—including a noted Denver singer, a roller skating trio, a dog act, a juggler, and a chorus line of girls, all doing two shows—are described in "Utex Discovery Party at Airport Saturday Night," Moab *Times-Independent,* 2 June 1955. An excellent photograph of one of the parties is in Maxine Newell, "The Scrapbook," in *Canyon Legacy: Journal of the Dan O'Laurie Museum, Moab, Utah* 14 (summer 1992): 16–17.

61. "The Sky Is the Limit," Moab *Times-Independent,* 1 October 1953.

62. "The Last Four Years: Growing Pains Born of Boom Are Easing, but They've Been Costly to City's Purse," Moab *Times-Independent,* 7 June 1956.

63. Ibid.

64. Ibid.

65. Ibid.

66. Ibid.

67. Ibid.

68. Ibid.

69. Mardy Thomson, "Moab Then and Now," Moab *Times-Independent,* 4 March 1955.

70. "Three Local Girls Enter G. J. Contest," Moab *Times-Independent,* 10 May 1956.

71. Samuel J. Taylor, "Bright Future or No Future," Moab *Times-Independent,* 24 October 1957.

72. Arthur R. Gomez. *Quest for the Golden Circle: The Four Corners and the Metropolitan West, 1945–1970* (Albuquerque: University of New Mexico Press, 1994), 47–52.

Chapter 5

The Uranium Capital
of the World II:
Grants

UNLIKE MOAB, the small village of Grants, New Mexico, had neither a history of uranium mining nor a part in making atomic bombs. But after two major discoveries, it became the center of the largest uranium rush of the 1950s and home to five yellowcake-processing mills. Grants is located in the western part of the state about halfway between Albuquerque and Gallup. In 1945 the town's 2,500 residents earned their living from agriculture, stock grazing, or tourists who passed through on Highway 66. In fact, most of the town's businesses were not located in a traditional square or "T" pattern but instead hugged the highway for 3 miles, spreading perpendicular to it for only a few blocks.

Situated between the shadows of 11,000 foot Mt. Taylor to the northeast and an ancient lava flow called the Malpais to the south, the area now known as Grants was started in 1872 when Don Jesus Blea settled near a spring among the lava and called his home Alamitos (little cottonwoods). The following year Don Ramon Baca brought his family to Alamitos. When the Atchison, Topeka, and Santa Fe Railway built a line through the area around 1880, Alamitos became a coaling station, and its name was changed to honor the Grant brothers who constructed the road.[1]

Over the next half century Grant's Station grew to include a central shipping point for area ranchers, several mercantiles, a small lumber company, and a minor pumice mining industry. In 1927 the completion of the Bluewater Reservoir 8 miles west of Grants spawned the development of commercial agriculture in the area. Two years later a newspaper, the Grants *Review,* began publication and announced the opening of Grants Union High School. By 1930 the community boasted a population of about 600, a water system and lighting plant, and a small telephone exchange.[2]

Grants took another big leap forward in 1939 when the water from nearby Bluewater Reservoir, combined with underground water pumped to the surface, was first used to irrigate an experimental vegetable farm. When it was discovered that carrots grew exceptionally well in the volcanic soil, Grants was on its way. The new industry made Grants the carrot capital and brought growing prosperity. In 1940 a local newspaper, the *Beacon,* replaced the *Review,* and the following year the town was incorporated. By 1947 local businessmen started the Grants State Bank to serve the growing community. In 1950 the census showed a 270 percent population increase over the last decade, making Grants one of New Mexico's fastest-growing communities. The discovery of uranium would amplify this trend and change the community forever.[3]

The transformation of Grants began in late spring of 1950 when a local Navajo sheepherder named Paddy Martinez discovered uranium-bearing rocks on nearby Haystack Mountain. Although the find was on land owned by the Atchison, Topeka, and Santa Fe Railway, prospectors soon swarmed into the area to stake claims on adjacent properties.[4] By December of that year, the Grants *Beacon* announced that the Santa Fe was going to develop its property and that "uranium ore, like the gasoline buggy, is here to stay."[5] The following week the paper noted the effect the discovery would have on the community:

> While no great boom is due here in the immediate future, a definite and orderly expansion and growth in population is practically certain for this town of 2,281 residents. . . . While no great boom is being experienced, a number of new faces and cars, jeeps, and pickups are evident on Grants' streets. Prospectors have arrived from California, Wyoming, and Texas. . . . One Grants businessman expressed the thoughts of most of the people in

this locality when he said, "We don't want a boom and bust affair. Let's have orderly growth."[6]

Although most people may not have wanted a "boom and bust affair" to strike their community, that is exactly what happened. Over the next decade, uranium transformed Grants from the carrot capital to the self-proclaimed uranium capital. The booms caused shortages of housing and classrooms while increasing employment, commerce, and crime.

The rush unfolded in two distinct phases. The first period followed Martinez's discovery in 1950 to the building of the area's first uranium-processing mill in 1953. Although Grants was already a yellowcake community, it experienced a second, even larger boom during the last half of the decade when another major uranium discovery was made at nearby Ambrosia Lake in 1955. From that date to the completion of four more mills in 1958, Grants truly became the uranium capital.

The first uranium boom could be called the "Anaconda boom," for the large, long-standing mining corporation had brought the initial expansion to Grants. As the Santa Fe began to ship ore from its New Mexico mine to the AEC mill at Monticello, Utah, in early January 1951, it also began a wide-ranging exploration project known as "Operation Haystack."[7] At the same time, the Santa Fe negotiated with the Anaconda Copper Mining Company for the purchase and processing of its ore. Anaconda quickly assembled exploration parties in Grants, and in July 1951 the mining giant made a large strike near the Laguna Pueblo east of town. With these significant discoveries, the Santa Fe Railway, Anaconda, and the community of Grants were well on their way toward uranium dependence.[8]

The Laguna strike brought a new twist to the uranium story. Instead of involving public or corporate lands, the Laguna discovery was located on lands held in trust by the pueblo. Before any mining could be done, Anaconda needed to reach an agreement with the pueblo. In essence, the question of whether the Lagunas would comply constituted a classic pattern in Native American history. Until a precious commodity was discovered on the lands, the government considered most native lands worthless. But when uranium was discovered, the country's national defense was suddenly at stake. In a bold editorial entitled "A Patriotic Obligation," Grants *Beacon* editor Wayne Winters wrote: "If the Laguna Tribal Council is sincere and loyal to the United States they will place no stumbling blocks in the way of the mining of any uranium which is to be found on their reservation. . . . Now is the time for another show of patriotism by selling their atomic ore to the United States government."[9]

After signing a contract with the Lagunas, Anaconda had two major prospects and began negotiating with the Atomic Energy Commission to build its own processing mill. To stimulate further exploration and ore production, the AEC contracted with Anaconda to operate an ore-buying station for the area. Over the next six years Anaconda received, sampled, and stockpiled over 320,000 tons of area ore at this facility. Of this amount, the company purchased and processed just over 180,000 tons, with the rest going to other mill operators.[10]

As Anaconda became entrenched, a steady stream of private prospectors and businessmen began trickling into Grants. After the usual winter business slump in 1950–1951, commerce began to increase the following spring. The local paper began printing ads for Geiger counters, along with pictures and news stories of uranium prospectors.[11] In 1951 the city approved plans for a new airport and a new sewage disposal plant. Still, a new $500,000 ice plant showed that Grants had not outgrown its carrot industry. The *Beacon* attested to this continued allegiance when it reported that the discovery of uranium had "given the town the biggest shot in the arm since the advent of the carrot industry some years back."[12]

The year 1952 dawned bright for Grants. Just five days earlier, Anaconda had reached an agreement with the AEC to build and operate an ore-buying station and processing mill at Bluewater, 11 miles northwest of Grants. The mill would process company ores from Anaconda's mines northwest of Grants and at Laguna, plus those purchased from the Santa Fe Railway and independent miners. With this knowledge secure, the *Beacon* began a drive to get local citizens to think about their community and its future. On December 27 the editor wrote a column suggesting that the uranium industry would soon burden the school system.[13] Less than a month later the paper again warned its readers that the town was at a critical point and that if it expected continued growth, the community had to address some of its major problems. In this no-holds-barred editorial, the *Beacon* submitted:

> We cannot expect the hundreds of people who will come here from modern cities to want to live amidst mud streets, the filth of open privies and the lack of other civic improvements. . . . If Grants does not get down to business and pave the streets, force sewer connections, and provide at least a city park and a full-time public library we're going to awaken one of these mornings to find an entirely new town somewhere to the west of here, complete with stores, theater, newspaper, and many attractive homes. . . . All of this belongs here with Grants, where a fine start of a darned good

little city already is located, but newcomers are not going to stand for the present situation.

Remember, Grants is either going to go forward or drop backward. . . . It cannot and will not stay just as it is.[14]

In April 1952 a reform-minded group of politicians, led by Mayor-Elect George Dannenbaum, swept into office proclaiming they would modernize Grants for the uranium boom. In his published remembrance, Dannenbaum recalled that in 1952 Grants had few paved streets and inadequate sewage facilities, water tanks, fire and police departments, and phone and power systems. Additionally, the town had overstretched itself in bonded indebtedness and was practically broke. As one of his first acts, Dannenbaum pushed for a street-paving program, arguing that the town must look as though it was ready to accept newcomers.[15]

Over the next three years, Anaconda's development continued to spur the area's uranium industry. Employment levels continued to rise as would-be prospectors and miners continually arrived and established companies while prospective merchants and service people came to mine the miners. Although official population records are not available, the Grants *Beacon* reported that the community was the fastest-growing town in the United States during these years, as its population increased from 2,500 in 1950 to an estimated 6,000 in 1955.[16]

School enrollment figures reflect the population growth in Grants. Every fall between 1952 and 1955, the newspaper reported that school enrollment had reached an all-time high.[17] To combat this unexpected growth, the school district attempted to add classrooms the first year, but by the fall of 1954 it was apparent that more drastic measures were needed. In the spring of 1954 local voters solidly carried a new bond issue to replace the twenty-five-year-old Grants Union High School.[18] A month later the booming community learned that it qualified to receive government grants because of its role in national defense. Still, students crowded the classrooms until the necessary buildings were completed. One teacher recalled: "My classroom was so crowded, like sardines, that when a child wanted to leave the room, he had to back up to the front blackboard, pushing through the mass until he reached the little clear area up front, where he could then turn and walk out of the room."[19]

Besides the government funds and local bond issues, the Grants school district also received money from a growing tax assessment. From 1954 to 1955, district tax valuations climbed over $2.6 million, with the largest share going to the schools. This increase was the result of uranium mining and milling construction outside of town, not of structures within the city.[20]

Although the tax base increased mainly because of uranium industry construction, there was a notable increase in houses built within the community. Less than six months after it signed the AEC mill contract, Anaconda decided that adequate housing was not available and began constructing its own. In May 1952 the mining company announced plans to erect 28 new homes near its Bluewater mill.[21] Within a year, independent entrepreneurs began a new 100-home subdivision in east Grants.[22] As mill construction progressed, the housing situation grew worse. To alleviate the "deplorable" situation, Anaconda bought 27 lots in one of the new eastside subdivisions to house 25 new prefabricated homes.[23] In 1955 the company constructed 40 or so new houses at Bluewater and over a hundred in various new subdivisions in Grants.[24] In addition to the permanent housing, newcomers brought so many trailers into the community that by Christmas 1954 the city was forced to pass a law governing the location and construction of new trailer parks.[25]

As housing expanded, developers added to the built environment in other ways. Between December 1952 and December 1954, entrepreneurs constructed a new office building, clothing store, supermarket, and library in the community. Because of the area's topography, most new construction developed to the north and east of the original city further and further from the mill. The town's streets were paved, enabling home postal delivery. In 1954 the government announced that it would rebuild Highway 66 through the town. Thus by 1955 the landscape of Grants was beginning to show signs of improvement thanks to the developing uranium industry.[26]

Similar progress occurred in public utilities. In 1952 townspeople relied mostly on propane for heat. In 1954 the Southern Union Gas Company contracted to provide natural gas service to the city. The number of gas meters jumped from zero in 1953 to 279 in 1954, almost doubling to 517 by the end of 1955.[27]

The city's telephone system experienced similar growth. Before the uranium boom, Grants relied on an old-fashioned operator-controlled phone system. The number of phones in Grants had expanded from 105 in 1943 to 580 ten years later. Over the next two years the telephone company installed a new dial system and added additional long-distance cables. Nearly 900 phones were in operation by June 1955.[28]

With the growth of the population and the building boom came an increase in crime. Although the boomtown social malaise of elevated drunkenness, depression, delinquency, and divorce would not be labeled the

"Gillette Syndrome" until the 1970s, the uranium boom brought these conditions to Grants in the early 1950s.[29] According to George Dannenbaum, life in Grants during the boom was one big party. The center of the activity was a two-block stretch of Santa Fe Avenue, where no fewer than seven bars were located.[30] After numerous gambling and liquor-related troubles, the Grants police force stopped protecting bars in December 1954.[31] Similarly, increasing marijuana and alcohol use by juveniles forced Grants officers to initiate a curfew in 1953 that kept everyone under age sixteen off the streets after 9 P.M. and all those under eighteen off the streets by 11 P.M.[32]

By the summer of 1955 Grants was firmly entrenched as a yellowcake community. The most visible evidence was the completion of the Anaconda mill in November 1953. With 169 employees and an AEC contract through 1962, the mill marked the beginning of uranium dependence.[33] Changes were also present in town, including freshly paved streets, new water and sewer facilities, and a modern high school. Houses were going up all over town. New stores opened every year, and local businessmen reorganized the chamber of commerce.[34]

The town's image and psyche were clearly turning toward uranium. One story related that band leader Guy Lombardo visited the city to examine a uranium mine in which he owned stock. Another said local ranchers were complaining that the increased number of prospectors was hurting the area's rangelands. In April 1955 local uranium operators chose Anaconda employee Lavon Caldwell to represent them in a Uranium Queen contest where the winner received 10 tons of uranium ore.[35] Finally, one report from the spring of 1953 described a situation in which miners thought they had discovered ore in the very heart of the city. On April 23 Geiger counters began going off all over Grants. It seemed the town was sitting on high-grade ore. After checking with scientists at Los Alamos, Grants citizens were somewhat disappointed to learn that they may have been dusted with radioactive fallout from a nuclear test upwind in Nevada.[36]

A formal transformation to yellowcake status was taking place in the town's paper. In January 1955 the *Beacon* changed its banner's subtitle from "New Mexico's Picture Newspaper" to "Valencia County's Only Weekly Newspaper Published in the Uranium Capital of the World." A new paper, *Uranium City News,* began publication in 1955. By early 1955 the carrot capital had become the uranium capital.[37]

The transformation of Grants into a yellowcake community had come at a price. In late August 1955 the *Beacon* reported that the Valencia County Court was penniless and that the city of Grants might go bankrupt. Three

Miss Atomic Energy receives her prize, a truckload of uranium ore, May 1955, Grand Junction, Colorado. Several yellowcake towns participated in atomic beauty contests. This contest was sponsored by the Uranium Ore Producers Association and the Grand Junction Chamber of Commerce. Note the atomic crown in the winner's left hand. Courtesy, Department of Energy Collection, Loyd Files Research Library, Museum of Western Colorado, #163, Grand Junction.

weeks later a group of Texas businessmen announced that they were willing to purchase the town. At about the same time, a wildcat prospector from Houston named Louis Lothman discovered a new uranium body 20 miles northwest of Grants at Ambrosia Lake. A new boom was on.[38]

Over the next four years the new strike developed into a giant uranium district that eventually produced almost one-fifth of the nation's ore and caused the AEC to change its buying program. If the period 1950–1955 can be called the "Anaconda boom," the interval 1955–1959 is best described as the "Ambrosia Lake boom."[39]

Ambrosia Lake was a small, dry lake originally called La Laguna del Defunto Ambrosio because a man named Ambrosio was found dead floating in the lake. Early settlers anglicized the name to Ambrosia. By the early 1900s, area ranchers and Navajos used the sagebrush valley solely as pasture. Then, during the national oil boom of the 1920s, a young wildcatter named Stella Dysart purchased large tracts of Ambrosia Lake land in hopes of striking crude.[40]

Beginning in the mid-1920s, Dysart established a ranch house in the area and began drilling test holes around Ambrosia Lake. To encourage investors, Dysart presented sales talks, made motion pictures of her properties, and produced a 1931 promotional handout about Grants called *Black Gold*. When this proved ineffective during the Depression, Dysart decided to subdivide her holdings into small lots for sale to modest investors. She whittled some of those tracts down to as small as one-sixteenth of an acre and sold them for as little as $18 each. Over the next twenty years Dysart's oil misfortunes continued, but she persisted in selling lots, paying taxes, and stockpiling unsuccessful drilling logs.[41]

Paddy Martinez's uranium discovery on nearby Haystack Mountain in 1950 brought hordes of uranium prospectors to the nearby hills, but few were interested in Ambrosia Lake. In 1952 extensive drillings were made for gas and oil, but to no avail. Then in early 1955 Louis Lothman met with Dysart and made plans to drill for uranium. After several unsuccessful tries, Lothman struck atomic ore at 292 feet. By mid-March 1955 a new boom was on.[42]

Like Charlie Steen's discovery, Lothman's strike was in an area not usually considered uranium country. Further, the land situation was unlike any previously encountered. Instead of simply staking claims on government land, prospectors had to deal with a mosaic of landowners. About half of the odd-numbered sections belonged to the Santa Fe Railway, with the rest constituting patented homesteads. Public domain lands and homesteads equally divided the even sections. Two of Dysart's subdivided tracts contained between 4,000 and 7,000 landowners on just over 4,000 acres of land. To further complicate the situation, many survey markers disappeared as the rush ensued, so clear property lines could not be established.[43]

Despite the confusion, Lothman used forty drill rigs to continue to explore Dysart's lands and set out the area's ore body. In May 1955 Rio De Oro Uranium Mines sank the Dysart No. 1 mine shaft to a depth of 396 feet. In December, the company hauled out its first load of ore and sent 1,500 tons to the AEC's Grand Junction plant for testing. When the AEC established that the uranium could be processed economically, the government established an ore-buying station west of Grants the following year.[44]

Because the individuals and small companies that made the first Ambrosia Lake discoveries lacked both the land holdings and the capital to develop mines and construct mills, large mining and energy companies including Kerr-McGee, American Metal Company, Phillips Petroleum, and Homestake Mining Company came in to develop the area. Anaconda, already the operator of the area's first mill at nearby Bluewater, chose not to participate in the Ambrosia Lake development. Nevertheless, this move toward bigness set the Ambrosia Lake discoveries apart from others in the 1950s and foreshadowed developments in the uranium boom of the 1970s.[45]

Over the next three years Kerr-McGee, Phillips, American Metal, and Homestake worked with smaller companies to dig mines and build mills to process Ambrosia Lake uranium. The first company to complete this task was Homestake–New Mexico Partners (H-NMP). Formed in late 1956 by the merger of the large South Dakota mining company with six local firms, H-NMP signed the first AEC mill contract in December 1956. Construction on the mill, located 7 miles north of Grants on State Highway 53 en route to Ambrosia Lake, began the following spring. When completed in February 1958, the H-NMP mill processed 750 tons of ore per day and employed 94 people.

In late 1956 Homestake also became involved with the Sabre-Pinon Corporation. Sabre-Pinon had formed earlier that year when two small companies, Sabre Uranium and Pinon Uranium, had merged. The evolving company, Homestake-Sapin Partners, signed a separate AEC contract in April 1957 to supply uranium from its ore bodies. This second Ambrosia Lake mill, employing 121 persons, was constructed next to the H-NMP mill.[46]

Another corporation that came to Ambrosia Lake was the Oklahoma-based Kerr-McGee Oil Industries. To mine Ambrosia Lake uranium, Kerr-McGee formed a partnership with two smaller companies in August 1956. This new company, Kermac Nuclear Fuels, reached an agreement with the AEC in May 1957. Ore reserves were estimated to constitute 23 million tons at 0.32 percent U_3O_8 grade, so the company began construction of a large mill in the heart of the Ambrosia Lake district, 23 miles north of Grants. Unlike the two Homestake mills, Kermac located its operation in neighboring McKinley County. Grants and Valencia County felt the impact, but McKinley received the property tax revenue. When completed in November 1958, the Kermac mill employed 126 workers and had a capacity of 3,360 tons of ore per day. It was the largest uranium plant in the nation.[47]

The last company to utilize Ambrosia Lake uranium was Phillips Petroleum. Like Kerr-McGee, Phillips was an oil company seeking to expand into uranium. The company signed its AEC contract in September 1957 and began operation of its mill, 20 miles north of Grants and 3 miles east of Kermac, in June 1958. The mill, also located in McKinley County, employed 150 people and had a capacity of 1,750 tons per day.[48]

Quivira mill, Ambrosia Lake, New Mexico. The mill, built by Kerr McGee in 1957, processed more uranium than any other conventional mill in the United States and produced the largest tailings pile. As of summer 2001 the mill, although not in production, was one of only six operational processing plants in the country. Photo by Michael Amundson, 2001.

By the summer of 1958, just three years after Lothman's discovery, Ambrosia Lake had been transformed from pasture to pay dirt. Where a few homesteads had once stood, headframes dotted the landscape. Where cattle and sheep had once grazed, over 400 people were now employed. The Ambrosia Lake landscape had been changed forever. As humans and machines poured into Ambrosia Lake, the community of Grants faced the same boomtown problems it had experienced with Anaconda except increased fourfold. Further, the growing number of uranium mills and the community's increasing uranium economy and image cemented the town's fate to the atomic industry and the federal government.

Population figures for Grants are difficult to ascertain after the Ambrosia Lake strike. What is certain is that the population of Grants expanded greatly after 1955, and both the population estimates and the number of forecasts continued to rise during this second boom. In 1950 the federal census reported that Grants had a population of 2,251. By the summer of 1955, just before the Ambrosia Lake discovery, the population had reached around 6,000. In March 1957 the Grants Chamber of Commerce calculated that the population had reached 6,500 and was expected to be 16,000 by 1959.[49] In June 1957 the Grants *Beacon* suggested that the area's population would soon increase by 150 percent and warned that for every 100 uranium workers the city should plan for 700 other residents.[50] As of October 1957, the paper gauged the city had added 1,500 persons for a total of 8,000.[51] By the end of the year, new predictions proposed an additional 4,000–5,000 newcomers for 1958 when the four new Ambrosia Lake uranium mills would be completed. Projections in 1958 suggested 15,000 people by the end of the decade, 39,000 by 1965, and 60,000 soon after.[52]

In his 1957 year-end review, the *Beacon* editor predicted that 1958 would be a banner year for the community:

> This is the year when Grants truly becomes the uranium capital of America. Four new uranium mills will be completed and go into operation in 1958.
>
> This is the year in which the long years of exploration and development of the vast uranium deposits begin to pay off.
>
> This is the year of production. It will also be the year of vast problems. This is the year in which the population growth . . . will become explosive. This is the year in which the pressure for new housing will double and triple. This is the year in which the schools will be crowded almost to the bursting point. This is the year when a new hospital will become an emergency need.
>
> This also will be a year of great development. It will be a year when the municipal school plan will be virtually doubled, we predict. It will be a year in which the town of Grants will build its long-awaited new sewage disposal plant. We'll embark on a vast street paving effort. We'll probably build a new runway at the municipal airport. We'll perhaps start work on a new municipal building. . . . It will be another record year for retail businessmen in Grants. A record on top of their 1957 record. The population growth will bring many new customers to retailers. It will probably also bring many new stores to Grants, bring new competition, and mean more hustle and bustle among retailers. This is going to be a year when it will be fun to live in Grants, see the struggle as a town becomes a city. Welcome 1958.[53]

Regardless of whether citizens of Grants found fun in the ensuing struggle to provide homes, schools, water, sewage disposal, telephones, and other services for the many newcomers, they did begin to see their town not only become a city but also validate its claim as the nation's uranium center.

The massive influx of people wreaked havoc on the housing situation. Already overcome by the growth resulting from the Anaconda boom in the early 1950s, Grants was crippled by the Ambrosia Lake boom beginning in late 1955. Over the next four years, housing shortages were the talk of the town, the subject of continual editorials by local editors and politicians, and a recurring nightmare for uranium companies looking to expand into Grants. An example from this period is a *Beacon* story dated 29 January 1957: "Our problems are just starting. We need roads and need them bad. We're having housing troubles. There is nothing to rent."[54] Six months later the problem continued. In a June editorial the *Beacon* editor suggested: "Housing—or more properly, the lack of it—is the No. 1 topic of conversation around Grants. The problem is going to be solved. The houses will be built. We just hope the situation comes soon. We suspect, however, that things are going to get even worse before they begin to improve."[55]

By fall, stories were circulating that new teachers could not find housing. Again, the *Beacon* suggested that if one were to ask 100 people on the street what the community's biggest problem was, 99 would "promptly answer housing."[56] A *U.S. News and World Report* article on Ambrosia Lake quoted someone as saying it was "easier to get a job than a place to stay."[57]

By the summer of 1958 almost 500 new homes had been built, with hundreds of others either planned or already under construction. Grants was beginning to take on a more permanent look. The *Beacon* suggested that

> The home building activity means even more. It means that Grants is becoming a town of homes and families, a stable, prosperous community, ready to settle down and mill and process uranium for the nation's needs for many years to come.
>
> Many have viewed Grants with skepticism as a flash in the uranium pan, as a boom and bust proposition. They ought to take a look at all those brand new houses. We are beginning to turn into a fine new city.[58]

A little over a month later the editor continued to downplay Grants' boomtown aura and defend the problems as temporary. On 30 August he wrote:

> The newcomer finds housing ranging from the difficult to the impossible. . . . It isn't a pretty town—yet. It has a raw, being-built look.
>
> All these liabilities are a passing phase. Those of us who have been here long enough to escape the title of newcomers can look back only a year and measure the enormous strides the Grants area has made in a single year. Yes, the newcomers should have been here a year or so ago, if they think things are tough now.

It should be remembered that Grants [and its surroundings] are trying to compress in a year or two the progress most towns took 50 years to do—the growing from a village into a city.[59]

Like Moab, Grants experienced the boomtown problem of great building expansion that never meets demand. In Grants, the construction increase came from company-built housing and subdivisions, entrepreneurial building, trailers, and the creation of Milan, a new community a few miles to the west.

The four big uranium companies were the most conspicuous house builders during the Ambrosia Lake boom. Concerned that private housing was not being constructed rapidly enough, the firms purchased land and erected their own homes, recreation centers, and subdivisions. A year after the Ambrosia Lake discovery, Anaconda was already completing its first 100 homes when Kermac began building a 150-unit subdivision. Promising that the area would not be a "company camp," Kermac opened its neighborhood to noncompany personnel. As their mills neared completion in the summer of 1957, Homestake and Phillips also contracted to build homes and, in the case of Homestake, several 48-man dormitories.[60]

Private individuals also planned and constructed new housing divisions and trailer parks in Grants during the late 1950s. From 1956 to 1958, the *Beacon* was filled with stories of plans for new housing projects, apartments, and at least three new subdivisions.[61] Besides the housing boom, Grants also endured a trailer explosion. From 500 in the spring of 1956, the number of trailers grew to over 2,500 two years later and 3,500 by late 1959. New courts were built in town and along the road to Ambrosia Lake. Although one story related how much a family of five enjoyed trailer life, city officials worried about the threat of fires and floods to the densely packed prefabricated homes.[62]

The most obvious manifestation of the housing crunch during the Ambrosia Lake boom was the creation and expansion of a new community, Milan. Located on what had been a carrot field owned by businessman Salvador Milan, the new townsite was formed during the housing shortage in early autumn 1956. An article in the *Beacon* described it this way:

Another indication that Grants is bursting at the seams is Salvador Milan's announcement that 410 lots have been sold in the Milan townsite west of Town. The townsite, which is incorporated under the names of Mr. and Mrs. Salvador Milan, covers about 600 acres in a strip of land running along 66. . . . The final townsite will have 15 streets.[63]

The following year Milan residents incorporated as a village, elected Salvador Milan as their first mayor, and adopted the carrot, not uranium, as the town's symbol.[64]

Almost immediately, Milan's creation brought resentment from Grants. Located closer to the Ambrosia Lake mines and mills, Milan's existence suggested that Grants was not capable of handling the boom. In effect, Milan seemed to be the proof of the *Beacon's* 1952 admonition that a new community might replace Grants' role as uranium town.[65] From its inception, Milan faced challenges over its status as a separate village and from uranium company leaders who urged the two communities not to compete.[66]

Despite the objections, Milan continued to plan new lots and build new houses. By the summer of 1957 there were twenty-five businesses skirting Highway 66 and two model homes in place. The town boasted its own Elks Lodge and country club and had been approved as the site of a new elementary school. By the end of the year, Milan's 2,000 residents made it the third-largest community in Valencia County.[67]

The Ambrosia Lake boom also caused more problems for the Grants school district in the form of increasing enrollments, teacher shortages, and inadequate facilities. Unfortunately, these troubles began just as the city was catching up with the difficulties caused by the first growth spurt. Beginning in the fall of 1955, six months after the Lothman discovery, enrollment figures began to climb. From a record 2,160 students that October, enrollment figures grew to 2,600 in 1956, over 3,000 the following year, and more than 4,000 by the fall of 1958.[68] As expected, the number of teachers also increased during this time, although shortages occurred in 1957. Moreover, new teachers found Grants' high cost of living and housing shortage to be additional problems.[69]

Inevitably, such substantial growth in so little time created immediate facility problems for the growing number of students. Although a new high school had just been completed in response to the Anaconda boom, the new growth forced Grants to experiment with half-day sessions and to hold classes in makeshift rooms.[70] Grants was further hindered by the loss of potential property taxes when the new Kermac mill was constructed in neighboring McKinley County, although most of its workers lived in Valencia and sent their children to a Grants school. To alleviate possible busing problems for children living in one of the Ambrosia Lake trailer camps, area uranium companies chipped in to build a new school there.[71] Still, Grants was forced to turn to federal funding and new bond elections to construct needed schools. With this money the district was able to build a new junior high and four new elementary schools and to remodel several other buildings.[72]

Despite nearly 8,000 new residents between 1950 and 1960, the uranium rush did not change the overall ethnic makeup of Grants. In 1950 the census reported that whites composed 97 percent of the town's 2,251 residents. Ten years later the population had more than quadrupled, but whites still composed 97 percent of the 10,274 inhabitants.[73] Although the local paper commented that children of "three different tribes, Blacks, Anglos, and Spanish" were learning side by side in Grants, evidence suggests that racism still existed.[74]

In addition to the many new houses and schools, a number of businesses opened their doors during the Ambrosia Lake boom, including three new motels, a men's store, a drugstore, barber shop/beauty salon, and a new shopping center. Grants State Bank reported that it had grown 900 percent in the period 1947–1958. Additionally, several new public buildings were erected during this time, including a post office, five churches, and a hospital.[75]

The flood of people also overwhelmed the already problematic sewer, water, and telephone services. Still recovering from the first boom, Grants began 1955 with unsafe water caused by overflowing sewage lines. Over the next four years the community refinanced its water and sewer bonds and sought loans to build new lines.[76] Problems persisted to the point that Kermac threatened to house its workers elsewhere unless the sewage problem was corrected.[77] Finally, by 1959 new bonds, government loans, and a slowdown in construction allowed Grants' $1.5 million effort to catch up with expansion.[78]

The Grants telephone system was inadequate as soon as the Ambrosia boom erupted. In the summer of 1956, 400 new customers asked for service. In 1957, 800 new lines were added. The following year continued expansion brought 900 new phones into service. In addition, Grants added nine new trunk lines for long-distance connections to Albuquerque.[79]

Crime multiplied from 1955 to 1959. Part of the concern was that the town had three different police chiefs between 1953 and 1956. Another seemed to be the manifestation of the old adage that miners work hard and play harder. In his remembrances, George Dannenbaum relished stories of Grants as "one big party" and tales of how the social life revolved around the seven saloons in the so-called bar center.[80] Some townspeople believed city officials were not doing enough. In an editorial critical of Dannenbaum, the *Beacon* wrote:

Has the Old West returned to this uranium boom town? Numerous people are asking themselves this question. The evident laxiveness of law enforcement during the past ten days, an obvious result of conditions known to the most naive for months, has become apparent to all. Only those directly most concerned will not admit the severity of the condition. Some of the more worried adults are seriously talking of forming a vigilante committee. There are reports of some carrying their own protection—a loaded side arm. The mayor and acting police chief admit that they have done the best job they can. The job they have done is not good enough.[81]

Over the next three years, complaints continued that the police force was not large enough to handle the city's problems. Others protested the sale of alcohol to youths or the advent of prostitution in the bars or at a brothel called the Rockhouse in nearby San Rafael.[82]

Although not all of its boomtown problems had been solved by 1959, Grants was well on its way. From a town of 2,000 hugging Highway 66, the population had quadrupled and was spreading to the north and east with new subdivisions, schools, and businesses. Moreover, by the end of the 1950s, the federal government's uranium program had transformed Grants into the most dedicated yellowcake community in the nation. This transformation, from carrot capital to uranium capital in just one decade, is evident from a number of factors at work in the community.[83]

One of the most conspicuous determinants of Grants' uranium capital status was funding. Although the citizens of Grants deserve credit for overwhelmingly passing new bond issues in 1957 and 1958 to pay for the construction of new schools and for supporting a city sales tax to fund smaller projects, the other two major sources of income were increased property taxes—from the uranium companies—and federal loans.[84] Thus the burdensome conditions wrought directly by the uranium companies and indirectly by the federal government forced Grants to seek help from those causing the difficulties. In doing so, Grants voluntarily linked itself to both the uranium industry and the federal government in a type of corporate and governmental colonialism.

With the support of the reorganized chamber of commerce and the voice of the *Beacon*,[85] Grants also strengthened its symbolic tie to yellowcake. In 1956, it held a citywide festival in which a local miner was named Uranium Prospector of the Year and a beauty pageant named a Miss Atomic Age.[86] That same year the Uranium Cafe opened for business on Route 66 in the heart of town. The high school band marched in parades carrying a banner that read "Uranium Capital." Another story suggested that a local

Uranium Cafe, Grants, New Mexico. The Uranium Cafe, opened as a Chinese restaurant in 1956, still operates on Route 66 in downtown Grants. The original neon sign represented an exploding mushroom cloud. Customers today can enjoy a plate of "yellowcakes" (pancakes) or a "Uranium burger." Photo by Michael Amundson, 2001.

class was pushing to have a nuclear-powered ship named for Grants.[87] The following year little jars of Grants yellowcake became marketing souvenirs when they were handed out at the state fair and by Miss New Mexico at the Miss America pageant in Atlantic City.[88]

Finally, although the *Beacon* was clearly a booster, the newspaper was also one of the community's most vigilant observers of the growing dependence on the uranium industry and the federal government. In a probing commentary, editor James B. Barber both cautioned his fellow townspeople of this development and justified the community's need for federal assistance. In an editorial entitled "Uncle Sam's Creature" he wrote:

> Grants, if it develops as it appears almost certain to do so, is going to be a creature of Uncle Sam. . . . We are not attempting to make a judgement in this particular piece on whether it is good or bad to lean so heavily on the federal government. We merely call your attention that it is so.
>
> Of course—and this is where Grants is different—if Uncle Sam weren't up to his ears in the deadly international game of atomic energy, Grants wouldn't need all this federal help. It is, after all, uranium for federal government use that has bulged this community at the seams. We have here, at least, more reason to call on the federal government for aid than most communities.[89]

Like Uravan, Jeffrey City, and Moab, by 1958 Grants had been transformed to a yellowcake community by the government's uranium procurement program. As in the other communities, uranium was directly responsible for the growth of the town's landscape, local government, schools, utilities, and housing. Uranium also recast the town's image and self-identity into what could be called an atomic subculture. Like most people in the United States at that time, especially those in the nation's other atomic communities of Oak Ridge, Tennessee, and the tri-cities of Washington state, the citizens of the yellowcake communities saw the great future potential for nuclear power. Moreover, residents of these communities understood their economic tie to this new military-industrial complex and its effect on their new image. They wanted to see it continue, but forces were already at work to change the government's policy and therefore affect the uranium industry and the yellowcake communities.[90]

Notes

1. Writer's Program of the Work Projects Administration of the State of New Mexico, *New Mexico: A Guide to the Colorful State* (New York: Hastings House, 1940), 320.

2. Sue Winsor, "Centennial 1882–1982: Grants Station, New Mexico Territory, to Grants, New Mexico," *Grants Centennial Edition,* Grants *Daily Beacon,* 30 April 1982, 7–21; Curn C. Harvey, "Grants, New Mexico: The Uranium Capital," paper prepared for the U.S. Navy Department, History file no. 26, State Research Center and Archives, Santa Fe, New Mexico.

3. Winsor, "Centennial," 27.

4. Although often abbreviated ATS&F, the Atchison, Topeka, and Santa Fe Railway was almost always referred to as the Santa Fe in Grants.

5. "Uranium Ore Is Here to Stay," Grants *Daily Beacon,* 14 December 1950.

6. "Orderly Growth Expected Here," Grants *Daily Beacon,* 21 December 1950.

7. "First Load," Grants *Daily Beacon,* 4 January 1951.

8. "Uranium Pioneer," souvenir booklet, Uranium file, Mother Whiteside Memorial Library, Grants, New Mexico; "Laguna Uranium Find Will Extend Field Over 35 Miles," Grants *Daily Beacon,* 9 August 1951.

9. Wayne Winters, "A Patriotic Obligation," Grants *Daily Beacon,* 10 August 1951.

10. "A-Ore Buying to Begin Shortly," Grants *Daily Beacon,* 1 November 1951; Holger Albrethsen and Frank E. McGinley, *Summary History of Domestic Uranium Procurement Under U.S. Atomic Energy Commission Contracts: Final Report* (Grand Junction, Colo.: U.S. Department of Energy, 1982), A-53.

11. One story told of a local prospector who taped a sheet of film onto his dog's nose, then taught the dog to run around in a large grid pattern. The dog "prospected" the locale until the master removed the film, developed it, and looked for exposed areas. Any lit areas meant the film had been radiated. See "Uranium Hounds," Grants *Daily Beacon,* 19 July 1951.

12. Wayne Winters, "Uranium Boom at Grants," *New Mexico* (March 1951): 13–15, 52; "Grants Is Coming Into Its Own," Grants *Daily Beacon,* 25 October 1951.

13. "Let's Think About Our Schools," Grants *Daily Beacon,* 27 December 1951.

14. "Anaconda's Announcing Plans Spotlight Grants," Grants *Daily Beacon,* 24 January 1952.

15. George Dannenbaum, *Boom to Bust: Remembrances of the Grants, New Mexico, Uranium Boom* (Albuquerque: Creative Designs, 1994), 26–27, 92.

16. "High-Powered Rush for Uranium Claims," *Life* (17 September 1956): 57–62; "Grants, Fastest Growing Town in United States," Grants *Daily Beacon,* 17 March 1955.

17. See four articles in the Grants *Daily Beacon*: "Largest Enrollment in History of Grants School," 11 September 1952; "804 Students Enrolled at School on First Day," 10 September 1953; "Enrollment in Grants School Well Over That of Last Year," 26 August 1954; "School Enrollment Climbs to Record 2,160," 13 October 1955.

18. "School Bond Issue Carries by Large Majority," Grants *Daily Beacon,* 11 March 1954.

19. Gertrude Crume, quoted in Dannenbaum, *Boom to Bust,* 117.

20. University of New Mexico, Department of Educational and Administrative Services, *Grants Is Growing! School Facilities Survey Report* (Albuquerque: University of New Mexico, 1960), 17.

21. "More Uranium Activities Rumored for Near Future," Grants *Daily Beacon,* 15 May 1952.

22. "New Housing Project Proposed for Grants," Grants *Daily Beacon,* 23 May 1952; "Million Dollar Housing Project Here: George Rutherford to Build 100 New Homes in East Part of Grants," Grants *Daily Beacon,* 19 March 1953.

23. "Anaconda to Build 25 New Homes in East Part of Grants," Grants *Daily Beacon,* 5 August 1954.

24. See four stories in the Grants *Daily Beacon:* "Anaconda to Build 86 New Homes," 31 March 1955; "117 Homes to Be Built in Grants, Starting Today," 2 June 1955; "Anaconda to Continue Uranium Depot Indefinitely," 3 November 1955; "Anaconda Will Build 100 Homes in City of Grants," 8 December 1955.

25. "Trailer Law Now in Effect," Grants *Daily Beacon,* 23 December 1954.

26. See four stories in the Grants *Daily Beacon:* "Another Step Forward in the Growth of Grants," 18 December 1952; "Gladin's Super-Market Opened Today in Grants," 20 July 1953; "200 Attend Dedication of New Library Here," and "Highway to Go Through," 25 November 1954.

27. Dannenbaum, *Boom to Bust,* 27; "Natural Gas Comes to Grants," Grants *Daily Beacon,* 20 May 1954; "Southern Union News Tells Grants U Boom," Grants *Daily Beacon,* 29 July 1955; "Bright Future Predicted for Grants," Grants *Daily Beacon,* 29 December 1955.

28. Dannenbaum, *Boom to Bust,* 27; "Promise Additional Phone Service for East Part of Grants," Grants *Daily Beacon,* 28 May 1953; "Grants to Get Dial Phones," Grants *Daily Beacon,* 16 June 1955; Mickey Toppino, "Installation of New Telephone System Goes Into Second Phase," Grants *Daily Beacon,* 22 September 1955.

29. Robert W. Righter, *The Making of a Town: Wright, Wyoming* (Boulder: Roberts Rinehart, 1985), 4.

30. Dannenbaum, *Boom to Bust,* 95.

31. Grants *Daily Beacon,* 10 March 1955.

32. In a 1956 article, a local judge observed a "notable" increase in the use of intoxicating beverages, marijuana, and pornography by Grants' youths in 1953. See "Judge Points to More Marijuana Use, Drinking by Juvenile Delinquents," Grants *Daily Beacon,* 5 April 1956; "Police to Crack Down on Grants Curfew Violators," Grants *Daily Beacon,* 2 December 1954.

33. Albrethsen and McGinley, *Summary History,* A-52.

34. "Grants C of C Is Reorganized," Grants *Daily Beacon,* 24 March 1955.

35. See three articles in the Grants *Daily Beacon:* "Band Leader Lombardo Inspects Holly U-Mines," 10 March 1955; "F. Lee Says U-Ore Men Hurting

Range Land," 14 April 1955; "Independent Miners Choose Uranium Queen," 28 April 1955.

36. "Geiger Counters Act Haywire," Grants *Daily Beacon,* 23 April 1953. The story reported that Geiger counters were going haywire all over town even when they were placed near other people. Apparently, the fallout originated in a series of eleven nuclear shots beginning 17 March and ending 4 June 1953 at the Nevada test site. Code named "Upshot-Knothole," the demonstrations are known to have released high levels of radioactive fallout over southern Utah. See A. Constadina Titus, *Bombs in the Backyard: Atomic Testing and American Politics* (Reno: University of Nevada Press, 1986), 64–65.

37. Grants *Daily Beacon,* 27 January 1955.

38. Three *Daily Beacon* stories describe the town's financial situation in 1955: "Grants May Go Bankrupt" and "Valencia Dist. Court Penniless," 25 August 1955; "Texans Consider Buying Grants," 15 September 1955. The Ambrosia Lake strike first appears in "Found Where Experts Said NO: Uranium 'Strike of the Year' Is North of Here," Grants *Daily Beacon,* 11 August 1955.

39. The developing Lothman story was reported in three issues of the *Daily Beacon:* "Uranium Strike," 22 September 1955; "Ambrosia Strikes Add to Grants Ore Problem," 17 November 1955; "U-Ore Tonnage at Ambrosia Lake Near 4,500,000," 8 December 1955. Later stories extolling Ambrosia Lake in national magazines include "Pay-offs for Many in Giant Uranium Jackpot," *Life* 41 (10 December 1956): 133–134; "Atomic Energy: Uranium Jackpot," *Time* (30 September 1957): 89–90; "Boom That Gives U.S. Top Spot in Uranium," *U.S. News and World Report* (16 August 1957): 120–121.

40. Merle Armitage, *Stella Dysart of Ambrosia Lake* (New York: Duell, Sloan, and Pearce, 1959).

41. Ibid., 61–69.

42. Lothman retells his own story in ibid., 75–77. See also, William L. Chenoweth, "Ambrosia Lake, New Mexico — A Giant Uranium District," *New Mexico Geological Society Guidebook,* 40th Field Conference, Southeastern Colorado Plateau, 1989.

43. "Ambrosia Lake Land Has 7,000 Owners," Grants *Daily Beacon,* 31 May 1956; Armitage, *Dysart,* 95–100; Chenoweth, "Ambrosia Lake," 298–299.

44. Chenoweth, "Ambrosia Lake," 299.

45. Ibid.

46. Ibid.; Albrethsen and McGinley, *Summary History,* A-59–A-63; Office of the State Inspector of Mines, *Forty-Seventh Annual Report by the State Inspector of Mines to the Governor of the State of New Mexico, 1959* (Albuquerque: Office of the State Inspector of Mines, 1959), 31.

47. Albrethsen and McGinley, *Summary History,* A-45–A-48; Chenoweth, "Ambrosia Lake," 299; Office of the State Inspector of Mines, *Forty-Eighth Annual Report by the State Inspector of Mines to the Governor of the State of*

New Mexico, 1960 (Albuquerque: Office of the State Inspector of Mines, 1960), 36.

48. Albrethsen and McGinley, *Summary History*, A-49–A-50; Office of the State Inspector of Mines, *Forty-Ninth Annual Report by the State Inspector of Mines to the Governor of the State of New Mexico, 1961* (Albuquerque: Office of the State Inspector of Mines, 1961), 40.

49. "C of C Sees 10,000 More People Here in 2 Years," Grants *Daily Beacon*, 28 March 1957.

50. "150% Population Jump Forecast," Grants *Daily Beacon*, 18 June 1957; "Just Watch Our Smoke," Grants *Daily Beacon*, 4 June 1957.

51. "8,000 Population Estimate Given," Grants *Daily Beacon*, 3 October 1957.

52. See three articles in the Grants *Daily Beacon*: James M. Barber, "Best Year Yet Expected in Grants Area in 1958," 31 December 1957; "Population May Even Be 15,000," 26 April 1958; "Mayor Predicts 60,000 People," 19 June 1958. See also *Grants Is Growing! School Facilities Survey Report* (February 1960), 6.

53. Barber, "Best Year Yet."

54. "Kermac Looking at Local Project From 45 Year Viewpoint," Grants *Daily Beacon*, 29 January 1957.

55. "We Need Those Houses," Grants *Daily Beacon*, 8 June 1957.

56. "'Real Crisis' City in Teacher Housing," Grants *Daily Beacon*, 27 August 1957; "Housing No Better," Grants *Daily Beacon*, 5 September 1957.

57. "Top Spot in Uranium," *U.S. News and World Report*, 120–121.

58. "Heartening Development," Grants *Daily Beacon*, 3 July 1958.

59. "Welcome Newcomers," Grants *Daily Beacon*, 30 August 1958.

60. "Anaconda Will Build 100 Homes," Grants *Daily Beacon*. The story "Anaconda Employees to Get 100 New Homes," Grants *Daily Beacon*, 8 March 1956, reported that 79 of the 100 homes were under construction. The Kermac development first appears in "Kermac Looks Over Sites for Possible 150 Houses," Grants *Daily Beacon*, July 1956, and "Kermac Contracts Stagner to Construct 25 Homes Here," Grants *Daily Beacon*, 7 May 1957, describes the subdivision as not a "company camp." Homestake's progress is described in *Daily Beacon* articles "Homestake Signs 12 Homes in Grants," 25 June 1957, and "Homestake Building Dormitories," 15 October 1957. The Phillips article is "900 New Houses to Be Built," Grants *Daily Beacon*, 30 January 1958.

61. Several *Daily Beacon* stories cover the growth of private housing: "Carder-Eden Plan 100 New Homes for Addition," 23 February 1956; "New Housing Project Plans Spacious Homes," 29 November 1956; "Hawkinson Sells 150 Acres for a 600 Home Site," 28 February 1957; "Will Build 12 Unit, $40,000 Apartment House," 9 April 1957; "FHA OKs 60 House Project Here," and "Homes to Be Built at Once in Sierra Heights," 19 September 1957; "37 More Houses for Grants," 26 September 1957; "30 Unit Apartment Project Going

up on Second Street," 15 October 1957; "900 New Houses to Be Built," 30 January 1958.

62. The growth of trailers is traced in several *Daily Beacon* stories: "Grants Family of Five Enjoys Living in Trailer Home," 28 June 1956; "105 Unit Trailer Court Will Be Built Here Soon," 25 July 1957; "Another New Trailer Court," 1 August 1957; "Board, Commission Worries Over Pre-fab Housing," 9 August 1957. The 2,500-trailer count is in "Population May Even Be 15,000," 26 April 1958. See also, Petty and Ryan, *Grants Is Growing!*, 6.

63. "Grants Still Bursting at Seams as 410 Milan Townsite Lots Are Sold," Grants *Daily Beacon,* 11 October 1956.

64. See three Grants *Daily Beacon* articles: "'Village of Milan' Seeks to Incorporate," 5 February 1957; "Village Elects Milan for Its First Mayor," 19 March 1957; "Carrot Appropriately Made Symbol on Seal," 25 June 1957.

65. "Anaconda's Announcing Plans," Grants *Daily Beacon.*

66. "Village of Milan 'Infant' Already Faces Stormy Future," Grants *Daily Beacon,* 28 February 1957; "Build One Strong Town at Grants Says McGee," Grants *Daily Beacon,* 27 September 1958.

67. The growth of Milan is described in several editions of the Grants *Daily Beacon*: "Model Homes Started in West Milan Village," 30 April 1957; Walt McKinstry, "Milan Is Growing Up," 18 June 1957; "Elks Charter Sought for Grants, Milan," 12 September 1957; "Board Gives Green Light for New School in Milan," 15 May 1958; "Milan Now Third Largest Town in County," 30 December 1958.

68. See these *Daily Beacon* stories: "School Enrollment Climbs to Record 2,160," 13 October 1955; "School Enrollment Here May Climb to 2,600 Mark," 23 August 1956; "Enrollment Tops 3,000 in School," 26 September 1957; "Enrollment in Schools Goes Over 4,000," 4 September 1958.

69. See these stories in the *Daily Beacon*: "Grants to Hire 16 New School Teachers," 19 April 1956; "'Real Crisis' Cited in Teacher Housing," 27 August 1957; "Costs 68.4% More to Live in Grants Than Belen, Board Told," 13 March 1958. The article "School Enrollment Jumps 24 Percent," 5 September 1957, states that the district was 13 teachers short.

70. See these stories in the *Daily Beacon*: "Half-Day Elementary School Session Planned Next Week," 2 April 1957; "More Classrooms a Must!" 16 April 1957.

71. "Ambrosia Mill Might Present School Tax Problem for District," Grants *Daily Beacon,* 22 November 1956; "'Lake' People Plan School," Grants *Daily Beacon,* 20 August 1957.

72. Dannenbaum, *Boom to Bust,* 118; Petty and Ryan, *Grants Is Growing!,* 32–42. See also these *Daily Beacon* articles: "Grants Schools Seek 1.5 Million in Federal Funds," 6 December 1956; "Record Bond Issue Sails Through 5–1," 20 February 1958; "$389,000 in Federal Funds Asked for New Grade School," 13 November 1958.

73. U.S. Bureau of the Census, *U.S. Census of Population: 1950,* Vol. 2, *Character-istics of the Population,* Part 31, New Mexico (Washington, D.C.: Government Printing Office [GPO], 1952); U.S. Bureau of the Census, *U.S. Census of Population: 1960,* Vol. 1, *Characteristics of the Population,* Part 33, New Mexico (Washington, D.C.: GPO, 1963).

74. The editorial "We'll Take Grants" in the Grants *Daily Beacon,* 7 October 1958, was commenting on the integration of Little Rock High School. A discussion of the ethnic makeup is in Petty and Ryan, *Grants Is Growing!* 5–6. For how an Acoma Pueblo man viewed the uranium rush, see Simon Ortiz, *Woven Stone* (Tucson: University of Arizona Press, 1992).

75. See these stories from the *Daily Beacon:* "Building Boom Starts," 5 January 1956; "Grants to Have New Post Office," 15 March 1956; "New Men's Store Opens," 19 April 1956; "Newest Motel Is Desert Sun," 31 May 1956; "CHURCH GROWTH SETS RECORD," 18 October 1956; "Chemical Plant, New Drug Store, Post Office Due," 20 December 1956; "Business Men See Tremendous Growth Ahead," 27 December 1956; "$500,000 Shop Center Planned," 2 July 1957; "Construction Started on $350,000 80 Room Motel for East Grants," 23 January 1958; "Beauty Parlor and Barber Shop Open in New Uranium Building," 30 September 1958; "Grants State Bank Grows 900% in 11 Years," 20 November 1958.

76. See these articles on water and sewer problems from the Grants *Daily Beacon:* "Grants Water Declared Unsafe to Drink," "Department Ignores Reports," and "Sewage Flowing in Grants River," 14 July 1955; "City Considering Refinancing to Meet Growth," 9 February 1956; "Path Clearing for Grants to Issue $150,000 in Water and Sewer Bonds," 28 June 1956; "Immediate Work Needed on Water, Sewer System," 15 November 1957; "Water Problem called 'Serious,'" 27 June 1957.

77. "Kermac Says Sewage Situation Threatens Grants," Grants *Daily Beacon,* 18 April 1957.

78. See three articles in the Grants *Daily Beacon:* "Sewage Disposal Funds Approved," 2 July 1957; "Town's Future at Stake," 27 March 1958; "Lucky You," 30 December 1958.

79. See these *Daily Beacon* articles: "Phone Company to Add Five Trunk Lines, Double Equipment in Grants," 24 May 1956; "New Phone Books Show 400 New Customers," 8 November 1956; "$100,000 Telephone Expansion, Post Office to Start 1957 Off Fast," 10 January 1957; "Relief on Way to Ease Jammed Phone Circuits," 4 December 1958; "Lucky You," 30 December 1958; "Telephone Company's Growth Here Described as Phenomenal," 31 March 1959.

80. Dannenbaum, *Boom to Bust,* 91–95.

81. "What About Our Law Enforcement," Grants *Daily Beacon,* 31 May 1956.

82. See these stories in the *Daily Beacon:* "Police Force Only Half Large Enough," 1 August 1957; "Legion Asks Crackdown on Booze Sales to Kids," 11 February

1958; "Board Approves New Misdemeanor Code," 19 July 1958. Tales of prostitution and the Rockhouse are in Dannenbaum, *Boom to Bust,* 98–102, 111–115.

83. The demise of the area's carrot industry can be linked directly to the growth of uranium as housing developments overtook carrot fields, field-workers found higher-paying mining jobs, and industry water requirements replaced irrigation. This symbolic collapse during the Ambrosia Lake boom can be traced through these issues of the *Daily Beacon*: "Carrot Industry on Upswing Here," 15 September 1955; "Carrot Raising Loses Ground to Uranium Growth," 10 May 1956; "Farmers Protest Grant of Water Rights to Uranium Company," 11 October 1956; "Carrot Yield Drops as Uranium Takes Water," 6 December 1956; "Carrot Industry Here Falls to 400 Acres," 5 June 1958.

84. The Grants *Daily Beacon* traced these local developments. The bond story is analyzed in "Voters OK $700,000 Bond Issue 4 To 1 In Favor Of New School Buildings," 25 April 1957; "Record Bond Issue Sails Through 5–1," 20 February 1958. The evolution of county property tax valuations is found in "County Valuations Jump $5 Million," 14 June 1956; "Anaconda Uranium Operation Becomes Valencia County's Leading Taxpayer," 14 June 1956; "Valuations Jump $17 Million," 27 June 1957; "Anaconda Assessment $24 Million," and "Uranium Firm to Pay Half of County's Property Tax Bill," 9 September 1957. The local sales tax history is in "Sales Tax OKd by Vote of 2–1," 22 August 1957, and "Town's Future at Stake," 27 March 1958. Finally, the search for federal funding for schools, water, and sewage plants can be traced in "City Considering Refinancing to Meet Growth," 9 February 1956; "Grants Schools Seek $1.5 Million in Federal Funds," 6 December 1956; "$500,000 in U.S. Loans, Gifts Made Available for New Plant," 2 July 1957; "$389,000 in Federal Funds Asked for New Grade School," 13 November 1958.

85. See "Chamber of Commerce Encourages Uranium Industry," Grants *Daily Beacon,* 23 February 1956. The 4 June 1957 *Daily Beacon* editorial "Just Watch Our Smoke" explains that the *Beacon* had absorbed Grants' other paper, the *Uranium City News,* and that the paper would now be a "highly partisan newspaper — partisan toward Grants, Western Valencia County, and the Uranium Industry."

86. "Grants 3-Day Uranium Fete to Start Friday," Denver *Post,* 25 January 1956.

87. "Atomic Banner Will Accompany Band," Grants *Daily Beacon,* 22 November 1956; "Still Hope That Atomic Ship Will Be USS Grants," Grants *Daily Beacon,* 27 December 1956.

88. The 3 October 1957 issue of the *Daily Beacon* shows a woman holding a jar of yellowcake at the New Mexico state fair. The distribution of free samples at the Miss USA pageant is described in "Uranium Ore From Grants to Be Used by Miss New Mexico," Grants *Daily Beacon,* 11 July 1957.

89. James B. Barber, "Uncle Sam's Creature," Grants *Daily Beacon,* 21 November 1957.

90. Arthur R. Gomez, *Quest for the Golden Circle: The Four Corners and the Metropolitan West 1945–1970* (Albuquerque: University of New Mexico Press, 1994), 50.

Chapter
6

Allocation, Protectionism,

and Subsistence:

Changing Federal Policies

to Preserve

Domestic Producers,

1958–1970

By 1958 the Atomic Energy Commission's (AEC) uranium procurement program was a tremendous success. Thanks to the price schedules and incentives offered through the AEC Circulars, uranium companies had been extremely successful with prospecting for new ores, mining, and building processing mills. In 1948 two mills produced just over 100 tons of uranium oxide in yellowcake. By 1958, 23 mills produced over 12,000 tons. But there was a problem. Although the supply of uranium had increased greatly, demand was stagnating.[1]

In the 1950s, AEC demand came from military weapons and peaceful uses. Although news reports suggested that atomic-powered generating plants, airplanes, trains, ships, and even cars were soon to be commonplace, the technological development of such applications lagged. As for weapons, the increasing uranium stockpile combined with an international test ban movement drastically reduced the government's requirements. Until private demand increased, many officials suggested limiting the number of uranium producers. Over the next dozen years, the government's uranium policy changed from one of developing new resources and industries to one of providing the allocations and protectionism necessary to keep a glutted but needed industry alive. By 1970 the once booming uranium industry was barely surviving on what one reporter called "starvation rations."[2]

The inception of the change in policy began with the adoption of a new AEC program in 1956 under which only processed yellowcake would be purchased from mills instead of both yellowcake and raw ore being purchased from miners. The new policy would be in effect from 1 April 1962 (the end of the price schedules in Circular 5 revised) to 31 December 1966. AEC officials believed this move would standardize purchasing and assist U.S. mining and milling companies with planning for a transition into future commercial uranium markets.[3]

By late 1957 the potential of the new discoveries in the Ambrosia Lake region of New Mexico and the Gas Hills of Wyoming kindled talk that perhaps the AEC should also curtail production. Indeed, uranium ore reserves continued to increase even as production levels grew. In 1947, uranium production had been practically nil, with 2,200 tons of ore in reserve. By 1956, annual production had reached 8,400 tons of uranium oxide, with 120,200 tons in reserve. In 1957 production increased to 9,800 tons while reserves grew to 166,300 tons of uranium oxide. A year later production had swelled to 14,000 tons of U_3O_8, but reserves also grew to 181,800 tons.[4]

As supplies increased, slow-moving private and leveling military demand called for a change in the procurement program. Although President Dwight D. Eisenhower had requested nonmilitary use of atomic energy in 1953 in his "Atoms for Peace" speech at the United Nations, nuclear technology was not developing as fast as many had believed it would. The potential growth of domestic reserves was becoming apparent at the same time the United States and the Soviet Union were negotiating the first test ban treaties on nuclear weapons. Because Congress was not willing to continue to stockpile uranium, some government officials began calling for a revision of the domestic uranium procurement program.[5]

In response to this growing divergence between uranium supply and demand, the AEC began to make moves to corral the domestic uranium procurement program. The first official word about a change in policy came when Jesse C. Johnson, director of the AEC's Raw Materials Division, speaking at the Fourth Annual Conference of the Atomic Industrial Forum on 28 October 1957, announced that "it no longer is in the interest of the Government to expand production of uranium concentrate."[6]

The following spring the AEC put teeth into Johnson's announcement by altering its 1956 procurement program for the years 1962–1966 to prevent further expansion in the domestic uranium industry. On 24 November 1958 the AEC announced that it would purchase for that period only "appropriate quantities of concentrate derived from ore reserves developed prior to 24 November 1958." The AEC maintained aspects of the 1956 plan by only buying concentrates, setting the price for those concentrates at eight dollars per pound, and refusing to guarantee ore prices or purchase unprocessed uranium ores.[7]

The announcement sent shock waves through the uranium industry. Exploration ended almost overnight.[8] Some miners said the government was pulling the rug out from under domestic producers by withdrawing from a market it had created. Henry W. Hough, editor of *Uranium* magazine, argued that the federal government's new policy deceived U.S. uranium companies and was the worst case of government deception since the government went off the gold standard in 1933.[9] Later that year, a still bitter Hough printed a jingle that explained how quickly the market had changed: " '57—you're in heaven! '58—you're too late!"[10] Charlie Steen also lamented the AEC's new policy, saying "anybody who goes out and prospects for uranium now is a damned fool."[11]

The new program marked a major transition in the domestic uranium program from development to allotment. Uranium companies with AEC contracts were "in," and those without contracts were "out." Over the next four years, AEC geologists poured over exploration records to determine which had been developed before 24 November 1958 and thus were market eligible. For companies with AEC contracts already in hand, the new policy often meant restructured buying programs and bigger production contracts for some mills. Some independent producers that had not blocked out ores prior to the date were given allocations based on their historical production.[12]

Although the uranium exploration rush was over by 1958, ore shipments to mills continued to increase into the early 1960s. In 1958, 5.178 million tons of ore were shipped to U.S. mills. That amount grew to 6.935 million tons in 1959, to 7.97 million tons in 1960, and peaked at 8.041 million tons of ore in 1961.[13] New mills were also coming into service. After the 24 November 1958 announcement, four new mills opened with a total processing capacity of 1,800 tons of ore per day. With the completion of the Petrotomics Company mill at Shirley Basin, Wyoming, there were twenty-six plants in operation, processing more than 30,000 tons of uranium ore each day.[14]

As mill capacity continued to increase, the AEC issued a new program on 8 May 1958 allowing uranium companies to sell their products to AEC-licensed private parties for peaceful uses only. Although the new program did not start for eight more years, this early announcement indicates that the commission was beginning to look toward a future break with the industry.[15]

As the allocation process began to certify qualified domestic ore reserves for continued purchase, the AEC made a second significant policy change when it announced on 9 November 1959 that it would stop purchasing uranium from foreign countries when their contracts expired in 1962. This protectionist measure created a major stir in Canada, where uranium mining had grown into the country's fourth-largest industry and employed 14,000 workers nationwide. When Canadian firms realized the potential impact of the new AEC policy, they negotiated a deal with the U.S. government to extend sales in the United States until 1966.[16]

The final policy modification came in 1962 when the AEC realized that the private market for uranium would not sustain domestic producers by the conclusion of AEC contracts in 1966. Therefore, on 17 November 1962 the AEC announced a new "stretch-out" program allowing milling companies to defer part of their 1963–1966 obligation voluntarily until 1967–1968. In return, the AEC promised to purchase an additional amount of yellowcake, equal to the deferred amount, in 1969 and 1970. This move was intended to keep the domestic uranium industry alive until private power could increase demand.[17]

By 1962, the government-aided exploration and development of the 1950s had been replaced by a new system of allocation, protectionism, and subsistence. The new policies reflected the government's effort to wean domestic milling companies from federal purchases while realizing that private sales were not yet capable of supporting the AEC's baby. Over the next eight years, the AEC focus shifted from creating a U.S. uranium industry to keeping its once thriving creation from collapse. This change was accomplished in two ways: by making it easier for private companies to own and operate nuclear power materials and by protecting U.S. producers from foreign competition.

To understand the intricacies of these policies, it is important to examine the process by which uranium ore becomes nuclear fuel. The natural uranium mined in the United States during the 1950s was approximately 0.25–0.30 percent uranium oxide. In other words, for every ton of ore, milling companies could produce 5 to 6 pounds of uranium oxide (U_3O_8), or yellowcake. Of this amount, only 0.7 percent was the fissionable isotope U-235. For the natural uranium to be used in most nuclear reactors, scientists purified the material to around 3 percent. This process, called enrichment, was very costly and potentially dangerous since highly enriched uranium could be used for nuclear weapons. Because of these factors, the only enrichment facilities outside the Soviet Union during the 1960s were owned and operated by the U.S. government. During the 1950s the U.S. Atomic Energy Commission maintained both a monopsony on purchasing uranium ore and a monopoly on providing enrichment services. When licensed private companies began building power plants, they had to lease their fuel from the AEC monopoly.[18]

From the time of the 8 May 1958 announcement that AEC-licensed private companies could begin to purchase uranium concentrates for peaceful use, the government continued to pass laws easing regulations on corporations to own and operate nuclear reactors. In August 1964 Congress modified the Atomic Energy Act of 1954 by allowing private utilities to purchase uranium directly from mining and milling companies. This statute, called the Private Ownership of Special Nuclear Materials Act, provided a shortcut to the government's enrichment monopoly by allowing private companies to purchase ore from millers and have the AEC enrich it on a toll basis.[19]

In effect, the new law allowed private utilities to purchase uranium ore from any producer and then contract to enrich it at government plants. Potentially, this meant such companies—unlike the AEC—could also purchase yellowcake from foreign producers. It seemed ironic that while the AEC was trying to protect U.S. producers by banning new purchases from foreign companies as of 1959, it would allow private companies to do so. Because of this possibility, in 1963 the AEC considered banning the enrichment of foreign uranium intended for sale in the United States. In hearings before the congressional Joint Committee on Atomic Energy during 1963–1964, Congress moved to extend the protection of domestic producers by restricting toll enrichment of imported yellowcake until 1975.[20] As amended in Section 161(v) of the 1954 Atomic Energy Act, the commission, "to the extent necessary to assure the maintenance of a viable domestic uranium industry, shall not offer such services for source or special nuclear materials of foreign origin intended for use in a utilization facility within or under the jurisdiction of the United States."[21] Subsequent congressional action detailed the embargo by stating that from time to time the AEC would review the status of the domestic uranium industry to "determine the need for continuing this restriction."[22]

With the allocation system protecting long-standing mining and milling operations, the AEC ban on foreign yellowcake purchases and enrichment services, and the stretch-out contracts all in place by 1966, U.S. producers had to continue to wait for private utility companies constructing nuclear power plants to begin buying U.S. yellowcake. It was a long delay because of the persistent holdup in nuclear power plant construction. Although the first commercial plant had started operating in 1957, continuing techno-logical, engineering, and licensing costs made nuclear power too expen-sive to compete with conventional electrical plants. By 1965 only seven nuclear stations were in operation, and early projections seemed overly optimistic.[23]

The delay created even more problems for the domestic uranium in-dustry. Despite government protectionism, the lack of new demand forced many companies to reassess their situations. For many domestic producers the best option was to complete their AEC contracts on time and hope that a commercial market would quickly develop at home or abroad.[24] Alterna-tively, companies could sign stretch-out contracts with the AEC and pro-duce the same amount of yellowcake over a longer period. The former choice could mean temporary plant shutdowns and layoffs. The latter would mean continued existence but at reduced annual profits. In either case, companies wanting to move into the commercial market would have to begin new exploration to ensure adequate future supplies while strug-gling to stay alive in the interim.[25] Higher exploration and production costs with increasingly lower profits would be the rule until commercial de-mand increased.[26]

Given these choices, a number of uranium companies opted for the stretch-out program. Beginning in December 1963, eleven U.S. uranium producers extended their existing milling contracts under the new pro-gram. In Grants, four companies—Anaconda, Kerr-McGee, Homestake-Sapin Partners, and United Nuclear[27]—decided to stretch out. In Jeffrey City, Western Nuclear signed its new contract in March 1964. Moab's Atlas mill enlisted in the program in December 1964. Uravan's Union Carbide became one of the last milling companies to sign on when it did so in October 1965. All told, the AEC announced that the eleven stretch-out contracts deferred over 15,300 tons of yellowcake from the 1962–1966 pe-riod for delivery in 1967 and 1968 at $8.00 per pound. In addition, the AEC agreed to purchase an additional 15,300 tons in 1969 and 1970 at a price not to exceed $6.70 per pound.[28]

A number of other companies chose not to stretch out but instead pre-pared for the commercial market as their AEC contracts expired on the last day of 1966. For these companies the lack of AEC purchases meant com-peting in a free market for the first time. Moreover, with delays in nuclear power plants keeping commercial demand to a minimum, these mills found themselves on the "deathbed" of a "sick" and "depressed" industry.[29]

Uranium milling companies were in the ever-tightening bind of having to conduct costly new exploration as profits slowly dwindled. The answer to the dilemma for many was to close the mill and quit the field or merge with another company to ride out the recession.[30]

From the end of the original AEC contracts in 1966 to the last days of the government buying program in 1970, closure and consolidation dominated the uranium field. In 1961, 24 companies operated 26 mills in the United States; by the end of the stretch-out period in 1970, 13 companies operated 17 U.S. mills. Some small, independent producers that could not stay afloat during the stretch-out period were forced to sell out to bigger, more diversified companies. During the late 1960s, oil companies such as Kerr-McGee, Gulf Oil, Continental Oil, Getty Oil, and Exxon became "energy" companies as they expanded their uranium purchases and exploration. Indeed, only these diversified companies could afford to explore during the dismal stretch-out period. Finally, the delay in commercial power demand caused some companies to overextend themselves in the exploration boom of the late 1960s. This increased the pattern of closure and consolidation as the oil and mining companies gained a tighter hold on the domestic market.[31]

During the exploration upswing in the late 1960s, Congress passed one more piece of legislation that would ultimately play a large role in the U.S. uranium industry: the 1969 National Environmental Policy Act. Under this federal law, environmentalists could delay mining, milling, and nuclear power plant construction until a detailed report—called an environmental impact statement—had been written describing the effect of new construction on the land and ecosystem. This new directive eventually played a major role in the U.S. uranium industry by increasing the cost of domestic production.[32]

As the Atomic Energy Commission's procurement program ended in 1970, the AEC could look back on its role in the domestic uranium industry with a feeling of success. Over the two and a half decades since the end of World War II, the AEC had created a domestic uranium industry where virtually none had previously existed. The government supplied more than enough nuclear material for the nation's defense, provided incentives and jobs for entrepreneurs throughout the West, and helped modernize some of the country's remotest areas.[33] Then, when its creation grew too large, the AEC figured out ways to keep the domestic uranium industry alive until commercial nuclear power plants could take over demand from the federal government. By 1970, although direct federal purchases in the uranium market had ended, the federal government continued to influence the industry through international trade agreements, enrichment services, and increasing environmental regulation.

Notes

1. Holger Albrethsen and Frank E. McGinley, *Summary History of Domestic Uranium Procurement Under U.S. Atomic Energy Commission Contracts: Final Report* (Grand Junction, Colo.: U.S. Department of Energy, 1982), B-7; U.S. Energy Research and Development Administration, *Statistical Data of the Uranium Industry* (Grand Junction, Colo.: Government Printing Office, 1976), 12 (hereafter USERDA, *Statistical Data*).

2. The term *starvation rations* is from Glynn Mapes, "Off the Deathbed: Nuclear Power Plant Needs Begin to Revive Sick Uranium Industry," *Wall Street Journal* (1 August 1966): 1; Anthony David Owen, *The Economics of Uranium* (New York: Praeger, 1985), 36–44.

3. Prior to this revision, the AEC individually negotiated uranium concentrate prices with each mining producer. The 24 May 1956 announcement ensured each mill $8 per pound of uranium oxide in concentrate while offering independent miners a "reasonable" price for their ores based on the new standardized price. See Albrethsen and McGinley, *Summary History,* 9.

4. USERDA, *Statistical Data,* 19.

5. Arthur R. Gomez, *Quest for the Golden Circle: The Four Corners and the Metropolitan West* (Albuquerque: University of New Mexico Press, 1994), 51–54.

6. Johnson cited in Albrethsen and McGinley, *Summary History,* 5.

7. Ibid.; U.S. Atomic Energy Commission, Grand Junction Operations Office, press release no. 220, 24 November 1958; Raye C. Ringholz, *Uranium Frenzy: Boom and Bust on the Colorado Plateau* (New York: W. W. Norton, 1989), 207–208.

8. "Freeze on Uranium," *Time* (11 November 1957): 114–115; "With Nowhere to Go, Uranium Sits It Out," *Business Week* (30 November 1957): 116–117.

9. Henry W. Hough, "Starvation in the Midst of Plenty," *Uranium* (February 1958): 4–5.

10. "Top of the News," *Uranium* (July-August 1958): 6.

11. Charles A. Steen, "A Timely Statement From Charles A. Steen," *Uranium* (February 1958): 14.

12. William L. Chenoweth, "Ambrosia Lake, New Mexico—A Giant Uranium District," *New Mexico Geological Society Guidebook,* 40th Field Conference, Southeastern Colorado Plateau (1989): 300; Albrethsen and McGinley, *Summary History,* 10.

13. USERDA, *Statistical Data,* 10.

14. June H. Taylor and Michael D. Yokell, *Yellowcake: The International Uranium Cartel* (New York: Pergamon, 1979), 33. For individual contracts and mill capacities, see Albrethsen and McGinley, *Summary History,* A-78–A-80, A-101–A-106, A-115–A-117.

15. U.S. Atomic Energy Commission, Grand Junction Operations Office (USAEC, GJO), "AEC to Permit Private Sales of Uranium to Foreign and Domestic Buyers," press release no. 213, 8 May 1958.

16. Taylor and Yokell, *Yellowcake,* 31; Earle Gray, *The Great Uranium Cartel* (Toronto: McClelland and Stewart, 1982), 65.

17. Albrethsen and McGinley, *Summary History,* 5.

18. Atomic Energy Act of 1954, *Statutes at Large* 68 (1954): 919–961; USAEC, GJO, press release no. 213; Gray, *Uranium Cartel,* 80.

19. Private Ownership of Special Nuclear Materials Act, *Statutes at Large* 78 (1964): 602–607; Gray, *Uranium Cartel,* 80.

20. U.S. Congress, Joint Committee on Atomic Energy, *Atomic Energy Commission Authorizing Legislation Fiscal Year 1965: Hearings Before the Joint Committee on Atomic Energy,* 88th Cong., 2d sess. (Washington, D.C.: Government Printing Office, 3 February 1964), 215–216.

21. Private Ownership of Special Nuclear Materials Act.

22. Gray, *Uranium Cartel,* 81. Details of this action were outlined in "Atomic Energy Commission, Uranium Enrichment Services, Criteria," notice, *Federal Register* 31, no. 248 (23 December 1966): 16479.

23. Owen, *Economics of Uranium,* 45; Gary Lee Shumway, "A History of the Uranium Industry on the Colorado Plateau," Ph.D. diss., University of Southern California, 1970, 208–219.

24. Indeed, some of the first commercial contracts were with foreign power companies. See Mapes, "Off the Deathbed," *Wall Street Journal.*

25. In an AEC press release dated 1 July 1966, the AEC Grand Junction Office reported that it had been receiving an "increasing number of inquiries about uranium prospecting and marketing" as a result of increased discussions of nuclear power. See USAEC, GJO, "Inquiries About Uranium," press release, 1 July 1966.

26. Michael A. Amundson, "Home on the Range No More: The Boom and Bust of a Wyoming Uranium Mining Town, 1957–1988," *Western Historical Quarterly* 26 (winter 1995): 492.

27. The creation of United Nuclear Corporation from three previous companies is discussed in Chapter 7.

28. Nielson B. O'Rear, *Summary and Chronology of the Domestic Uranium Program* (August 1966), report prepared for USAEC, GJO (Grand Junction, Colo.: Government Printing Office, 1966), Chronology 15–16; Albrethsen and McGinley, *Summary History,* 11.

29. Mapes, "Off the Deathbed," *Wall Street Journal.*
30. Ibid.
31. The concern over consolidation during the stretch-out period had been raised before the program was ever implemented. See U.S. Congress, Joint Committee on Atomic Energy, Subcommittee on Raw Materials, *AEC Uranium Procurement Program: Hearings Before the Subcommittee on Raw Materials of the Joint Committee on Atomic Energy,* 87th Cong., 2d sess. (Washington, D.C.: Government Printing Office, 18–19 June 1962), 72–73; Taylor and Yokell, *Yellowcake,* 34, 44–46.
32. National Environmental Policy Act of 1969, *Statutes at Large* 83 (1970): 852–856; Taylor and Yokell, *Yellowcake,* 34.
33. Shumway, "History," 222–224.

Chapter 7

Creatures of Uncle Sam: Yellowcake Communities During the Allocation and Stretch-out Periods

BY 1958 URANIUM HAD TRANSFORMED URAVAN, Moab, Grants, and Jeffrey City into yellowcake communities in terms of their economy, landscape, and image. Just as the Atomic Energy Commission (AEC) maintained strict control over the domestic industry, the futures of these towns and their citizens were intricately tied to the federal government. Grants *Daily Beacon* editor James B. Barber could have been speaking for any of the communities when he commented in 1957 that his city was now "Uncle Sam's Creature." Because nearly everyone in the community was dependent on either the uranium industry or a uranium-associated business, Barber suggested that his town's future lay almost beyond local authority.[1] Up to 1957, this growing dependence had meant unexpected growth. But as the industry matured and the government programs shifted from increased production to allocation and protection, this dependency redefined the yellowcake communities by first stabilizing their growth and then stopping it. By 1970 the federal government's shifting policies had turned the boom to bust.

In short, AEC policies during the period 1958–1970 recognized the fact that the government's procurement program had been so successful that domestic supply was rapidly outgrowing both military demand and slowly developing commercial power plant needs. Therefore, identifying the government's responsibility to assist the domestic industry it had created, the AEC took measures to limit the production of uranium while keeping many producers and the yellowcake towns alive until commercial demand increased. These measures were intended to stabilize supply, decrease foreign purchases and competition, and increase demand.

Beginning with the allocation program's intent to buy only ore developed prior to 24 November 1958 and continuing through the stretch-out program's goal to redistribute those purchases over a longer time period, the AEC sought to steady domestic uranium production. Additionally, starting with its 1959 ban on the purchase of foreign ore and continuing to the 1964 embargo on the enrichment of foreign yellowcake for use in U.S. reactors, the AEC moved to decrease foreign competition. Finally, deregulation of fissionable materials through the Private Ownership of Nuclear Fuels Act in 1964 sought to increase potential markets by making it easier for commercial nuclear power plants to purchase uranium.

These policy shifts directly impacted the yellowcake communities. Although the protectionist measures banning sales of foreign uranium in the United States ruined several Canadian communities such as Uranium City, Saskatchewan,[2] the decrease in competition barely affected U.S. suppliers because of the depressed market. Likewise, the passage of new environmental regulations in 1969 came so late in the federal program that it had little effect. Nevertheless, continued dependence on uranium and the government market shaped the yellowcake communities until the federal program ended in 1970.

Because of their common connection to uranium, the four yellowcake communities reacted similarly to the changing federal programs. First, the new allocation program benefited them all by slowing the boom and allowing each community to catch up with boomtown problems. Further, the program provided new milling schedules for many processors, thus strengthening their tie to the government. Second, when the government moved to sustain the industry through its stretch-out program, mills in each of the four towns signed new agreements that kept their business alive at reduced levels. For the most part, the curtailed production schedules forced layoffs, closings, and a general bust in uranium-dependent communities. Third, when the AEC eased the purchase of yellowcake by private power companies and a new exploration boom began around 1965, all four towns noted the beginning of a second commercial boom. Finally, when delays in power plant construction and the end of the government market in 1970 brought home the reality that new demand would not support the level of production already present, the yellowcake communities experienced more layoffs, closings, and consolidations.

The degree to which the four communities shared these common problems depended on the diversification of their economies. Obviously, the changing federal policies were most observable in the one-industry towns of Uravan and Jeffrey City. Grants, although not a company town, experienced similar problems because its five uranium mills composed such a large part of its economy. Moab, however, was different. Because of its location in the canyon country of eastern Utah, tourism had always been part of Moab's economic base. As uranium waned in the late 1960s, Moab increasingly diversified its economy. By 1970, visitation to the area had gained enough momentum that the once uranium capital had been transformed into a tourist center.

Although the uranium mines and mills in Grants, Uravan, and Jeffrey City were located in three different states, operated by different companies, and governed by different people, their strong tie to the burgeoning uranium industry made the communities kin in the late 1950s and the 1960s. Beginning with the allocation program in 1958, all three towns reacted similarly to the government's slowing uranium-buying program and the transition to a commercial market.

In Grants, the 24 November 1958 announcement of the new allocation program came at a time of prosperity. Thanks to the Ambrosia Lake discoveries, the area was making the switch from exploration and construction to the operation of new mines and mills. Almost 600 new homes and 13 business buildings had been built. School enrollment had increased by over 1,300 students during the past twelve months. Grants had the third-highest number of building permits in New Mexico for the year. Despite the caution warranted by the new program, Grants continued to exude confidence. The *Daily Beacon* wrote that the slowdown expected as a result of the new allocation program "hardly more than raised an eyebrow." In fact, the paper noted proudly that the overproduction was probably a result of the Ambrosia Lake discovery.[3]

Grants continued to expand in 1959 even as the new allocation program slowed exploration throughout the Colorado Plateau. Construction passed the $3.3 million mark as the new Cibola General Hospital, two schools, new churches, and a new water plant were completed. Symbolic of its progress, the town was chosen one of twenty-two finalists in the All-

America City contest conducted by *Look* magazine and the National Municipal League. Optimism continued as the *Beacon* became a daily paper and efforts were made to move the Valencia County seat to Grants.[4]

A few subtle signs, however, suggested that Grants was affected by the changing uranium market. In April 1959, Anaconda announced that it planned to close two of its mines and part of its mill.[5] Later that year a brief strike at the Phillips mill and the threat of another at Kermac caused uneasiness. Changes in the housing market were indicated when a trailer merchant reduced his prices on mobile homes. By the end of the year, the *Beacon* noted that "residential building had slowed greatly."[6]

Over the next three years, the expansion and optimism of the uranium boom were replaced by the stability of the allocation program. Population and school enrollment began to level off or even decline. Construction, although still positive, fell from $7 million in 1959 to less than $1 million in 1960. The housing shortage declined as three developers worked to complete new homes in the area.[7]

Although uranium employment also leveled off, community leaders suggested that the industry was healthy and that the decline was merely a result of the shift from construction to operation. The *Beacon* bravely stated that the uranium industry appeared to be "in the soundest health since Paddy Martinez picked up the yellowish sandstone [limestone] at Haystack Mountain in 1950. The miners have discovered how to get the ore out safely and economically, [and] the mills are running on 21 jewel bearings."[8] Nevertheless, employment continued to drop, and by 1963 the sense of security faltered as questions surfaced regarding the end of the AEC buying program in 1966.[9]

The allocation program brought a similar stability to Jeffrey City. Because Western Nuclear, like the Ambrosia Lake companies, had obtained its mill late in the 1950s boom, Jeffrey City was still expanding when the new quota system was established. From the single store and post office called Home on the Range, Western Nuclear built a town of 900 people in a few short years. Residents were housed in a conglomeration of 26 houses, 145 trailers, and a dormitory. Instead of a traditional main street, Jeffrey City's business district consisted of a restaurant/bar plus a huge Quonset hut that served as company offices, a school, a meeting house, and an entertainment facility. Western Nuclear also installed and maintained the town's water and sewage system.[10]

Instead of hindering the company, Western Nuclear's 1959 allocation contract extended the firm's contract from 1962 to 1966. Although the new agreement established mill quotas, the extra four years increased total production. With an agreed sale of 12,970,012 pounds of yellowcake over the next seven years at $8 per pound, Western Nuclear stood to gross over $103 million.[11]

The allocation deal also stabilized growth in Jeffrey City. Western Nuclear continued to improve its company town by constructing a community church and a swimming pool. The 220-person workforce used some of its $145,000 monthly payroll to finance bonds to build a new elementary school.[12]

Uravan's expansion also slowed after the allocation announcement. With most of its infrastructure already in place, Union Carbide sought to secure a new AEC contract to extend production to 1966.[13] In addition, the company signed a new labor agreement in 1959 assuring its workers of a small raise. The continued market and secure labor helped bring stability to the community.[14]

With its new allocation contract in place, Union Carbide slowed its building program to match its expected growth. Having completed its last residential construction in 1956, the company did not expand permanent housing during the 1960s. Instead, new work focused on improving the mill's efficiency and building a new swimming pool on the northwest end of town.[15]

By 1960 Uravan had several attributes uncommon for a town its size at the time. In addition to the new pool, the town boasted its own doctor, volunteer fire crew, community library, gym, and movie theater. A number of service organizations and clubs met regularly.[16] When Dr. Leroy Edward Ellinwood was offered a job as company physician in the fall of 1958, he looked at other Western Slope communities and decided that Uravan had the most to offer. In addition to the promise of a steady job, Ellinwood cited the town's kindergarten, ball team, and scouting programs as reasons for relocating in Uravan.[17]

Uravan's population reflected the change in the community following the allocation contract. From a peak of about 2,000 during the boom, Uravan dwindled to about 850 inhabitants by 1970. Although one story suggests a high rate of job turnover, a core population began to make Uravan its home.[18] The economic slowdown can also be detected in the number of grade school children. From a peak of just over 400 at the end of the boom in 1958, enrollment continually declined to just over 150 by 1970. Although these numbers show a marked reduction in new arrivals, they also depict a maturing population base.[19]

Despite the cutbacks and stability created by the allocation program, the AEC's uranium procurement program continued to grow. To further slow the boom, on 17 November 1962 the AEC announced a new stretch-out program designed to lengthen producers' contracts to allow for a longer transition to private power demand. Basically, the new policy would allow milling companies to voluntarily defer part of their 1963–1966 obligation until 1967–1968. In return, the AEC promised to purchase an additional amount of yellowcake, equal to the quantity deferred, at reduced prices in 1969 and 1970.[20]

The stretch-out program impacted the domestic uranium industry in several ways. First, existing producers now had a choice: they could simply finish their government contracts on time and hope that a new market would arise, or they could stretch out and process the same amount of ore over a longer period, reducing annual profits. Second, the end of the federal market and beginning of private ownership meant companies now had to operate in a competitive marketplace. Third, in anticipation of competition, producers began new exploration projects so they would have an adequate supply of U_3O_8 to offer. These new factors meant existing mills faced higher production costs amid lower and lower profits.

For the yellowcake communities these choices produced a variety of slumps depending on the strength of the paternal uranium companies and the economic diversity of the community. In Uravan, Union Carbide's corporate power helped to offset the community's one-industry dependence. Jeffrey City's one company, however, was only involved in uranium, making it exceedingly vulnerable to changes in the nuclear market. The existence of five uranium mills made Grants subject to changes in the uranium trade and also at the mercy of five different corporate reactions. In all of the towns, the stretch-out program's "starvation rations" usually produced a closing, consolidation, or combination of the two.[21]

Although the new program was announced in 1962, Union Carbide of Uravan was the tenth of eleven U.S. producers to sign a stretch-out contract in October 1965. The decline in demand forced many of the small independent producers out of business. But Uravan was able to survive the downturn in its economy thanks to Union Carbide's diversification, especially in vanadium production, and the belief that the company would prosper in the ensuing commercial market.[22]

Environmental concerns also played an increasingly important role in Uravan in the 1960s. After nearly five decades of processing radium, vanadium, and uranium, Union Carbide became more concerned about tailings. In 1959 the company began a discharge and river water monitoring system. Four years later new settling ponds were built at Club Ranch to treat mill tailings. But these evaporation ponds needed level ground, which was hard to come by in San Miguel Canyon, so in 1967 the company added a neutralization step to its processing to moderate the acidity of releases into the river.[23] In 1968 the Colorado Health Department took over environmental licensing of the mill. Although these moves seemed insignificant at the time, environmental and health concerns escalated in Uravan over the next two decades.[24]

Although Jeffrey City, like Uravan, had never diversified beyond its uranium dependency, the town did not have the power of Union Carbide behind it. Jeffrey City's corporate parent, Western Nuclear, was a one-industry company. Therefore the transition from allocation to stretch out created a state of decline for both Western Nuclear and the town. Although in its stretch-out contract in March 1964 Western Nuclear agreed to postpone the delivery of approximately 2.5 million pounds of yellowcake, the finite mill schedule, reduced prices, and growing exploration costs forced the company to make some hard decisions. The company's annual net income fell drastically by the end of the 1960s. Even the signing of several multimillion dollar contracts with private utilities could not bring Western Nuclear out of its slump.[25]

On 1 September 1967 company president Bob Adams described the predicament in a letter to Western Nuclear employees. In 1965, he wrote, the company had decided to strengthen its competitive position by increasing its properties and expanding its exploration to Washington state and Australia. Because such activities produced no new income, the company's profits had fallen by 30 percent while exploration and development costs had increased almost 50 percent. To augment the profit margin, Adams asked employees to become more efficient, cost-conscious, and disciplined. In 1968 Western Nuclear profits increased 46 percent, but the reduced profits of the stretch-out period caught up the following year when the company actually lost money.[26]

Adams finally developed a solution that is symbolic of the competitive marketplace boom in the 1970s. Lacking the capital resources to survive on its own, Western Nuclear decided to consolidate. In 1970 Adams sold a minority interest in Western Nuclear to the international copper firm Phelps-Dodge. Two years later the two companies merged, and Western Nuclear became a wholly owned subsidiary of Phelps-Dodge.[27] The new company's resources and experience became readily apparent. Phelps-Dodge created new trailer lots, constructed new houses, and built another dormitory. The company even took trees uprooted by mining activity and replanted them in town.[28]

Because of the number of mines and mills with different owners nearby, Grants faced a more complex situation than the two uranium company

Jay's Liquors Welcomes You to Uranium Country, near Ambrosia Lake, New Mexico.
Photo by Michael Amundson, 2001.

towns. Instead of simply staying with one company or merging with another during hard times, Grants was subject to a combination of closings and consolidations during the stretch-out period.

The first major consequence of the slowing uranium industry was consolidation. In a somewhat confusing evolution beginning in 1961, the adjacent Homestake mills were combined into one corporation and then merged with a third to form yet another company. The specifics are as follows. In November 1961 Homestake-Sapin Partners acquired Homestake–New Mexico Partners (H-NMP), and the H-NMP mill closed. The following spring a third company, United Nuclear Corporation, procured the Sabre-Pinon Corporation, which was in partnership with Homestake. The resulting company was known as United Nuclear Corporation (UNC) until 1968, when it became known as United Nuclear Homestake Partners (UNHP).[29]

Having consolidated its resources, in 1963 UNC added closure to its stretch-out strategy. In February 1963 United Nuclear purchased yet another Ambrosia Lake operation, Phillips Petroleum. After merging that company's mines, mill, and AEC contract into the corporation, UNC closed

122

the Phillips mill and arranged to process the additional ore at the partnership plant (UNHP).[30]

The remaining uranium mills in the Grants area chose to sign stretch-out contracts. The district's first company, Anaconda, became the first area mill to accept a stretch-out contract in late December 1963. The following summer Kermac signed the nation's fifth stretch-out contract. Finally, after consolidation and closure stabilized its position, United Nuclear accepted an extension in the summer of 1965.[31]

The net effect of these mergers, closures, and new contracts was a marked downturn in the community's economy. At first the Grants *Daily Beacon* attempted to cloak its worries in optimism by stating that the "economy of the Grants-Milan area, heavily dependent on uranium payrolls, will do no worse than remain at its present level for the next seven years."[32] Over the next four years, however, that optimism turned sour. The consolidation and closing of mills forced many mines to close, and employment in others dropped 50–75 percent. Overall, uranium mining employment in the Grants area fell sharply from a high of 2,700 in 1961 to 1,100 four years later.[33] The housing market, which had experienced great shortages in the 1950s, turned completely around as hundreds of homes stood vacant. Mining company homes, built to ensure adequate housing during the boom, now stood empty despite 40 percent cuts in rent.[34] Further, school enrollment fell from its 1961 peak.[35]

As the uranium industry declined, local leaders attempted to diversify Grants' economy. Beginning in 1963 the *Beacon* advocated a platform that included routing the new Interstate 40 through town, implementing an urban renewal program, building a new ski resort and paved highway on nearby Mt. Taylor, and developing neighboring lava beds into a national park.[36] These programs do not appear to have succeeded because in 1965 a million dollar municipal water and sewer refunding bond received no bids, "apparently due to uneasiness about the town's uranium-based economy."[37]

The situation had improved slightly by 1970, thanks to an increase in uranium exploration. But Grants was still significantly tied to uranium. In an end-of-the-decade editorial, Barber, who recall had labeled his fellow residents "creatures of Uncle Sam" back in 1957, wrote:

> If this area has learned anything, it is that a one-industry community is the greatest kind of folly. When the uranium mining and milling industry shudders, we all shake, whether school teacher, miner, or shoe clerk.
>
> Diversification—spreading our economic eggs in more nests—is an absolute must. Uranium employment will still be the king for a long time to come, but we must develop some jacks and tens to fall back on.[38]

Unfortunately, those cards had not materialized by the end of the government procurement program.

By 1970 Uravan, Jeffrey City, and Grants were still yellowcake communities. Just as the government's uranium procurement program had caused the towns to boom in the 1950s, the allocation and stretch-out programs had strung them along in the 1960s. The towns were also beginning to understand that in addition to the government, reliance on an illusory private market made them increasingly dependent on consolidated energy companies. Colonialism, whether federal or corporate, still meant community well-being was beyond local control. Without economic diversification, the yellowcake communities could be creatures of Adam Smith as easily as they had been creatures of Uncle Sam.

By 1958, Moab was also a yellowcake community. The town's economy, landscape, and image had been changed by uranium. In addition to the 200 workers at the new Uranium Reduction Company mill, nearly every citizen benefited from the presence of the many miners and mill workers in the self-proclaimed uranium capital of the world. Like the other uranium towns, Moab was tied to the federal government's ongoing uranium procurement program. As this policy began to change, Moab changed too.[39]

Although the allocation and stretch-out programs in the 1960s created stabilization and then consolidation conditions in Moab, the growth of other industries—especially potash and tourism—diversified the town's economy and lessened uranium's impact. By 1970 uranium was still a major player in the economy, but it was no longer the sole basis for economic success. Indeed, by the end of the government program, Moab was no longer solely dependent on uranium.

Moab's boom peaked with the dedication of the Uranium Reduction Company's (URECO) mill in the fall of 1957, and the town experienced an economic afterglow that continued over the next few years. As local industry officials waited for details of the post-1962 government purchasing program, Moab faced shortages of water and classroom space as construction of new houses, schools, and businesses continued. Reports predicted that the county would continue to grow, perhaps doubling its population by 1975.[40]

This optimism was shared by uranium company officials. To process its ores more efficiently, the URECO mill announced plans in June 1958 to add a $3 million refining method to its Moab facility.[41] Then in August 1959 URECO signed a new allocation contract through 1966 that certified the sale of over 27 million pounds of yellowcake to the government for almost $300 million.[42]

The new contract promised to bolster Moab's economy by offering the "hidden blessings" of a continued guaranteed market.[43] With this assurance, the city council passed the biggest budget in the town's history.[44] But over the next two years, the stabilizing influence of the allocation program made uranium take a back seat as the developing potash and tourist industries gained footholds in the town's economy and image.

The development of a marketable potash industry helped to diversify Moab's economy and stabilize its boom growth. The potash interest had begun in 1953 when exploration began about 10 miles downstream from Moab. Strikes were made in 1955, and shafts were sunk the following year. The project culminated in 1960 with the announcement that Texas Gulf Sulphur Company would build a $25 million mine and processing mill near Moab. Community leaders immediately recognized the potential of this new industry to offset possible setbacks in uranium. A contemporary story noted that the "potash industry has been regarded as insurance against the possible end of the uranium industry."[45]

In addition to Moab's economic diversification, the town's reliance on Charlie Steen also diffused in the half decade following completion of the URECO mill. In the summer of 1958 Steen ran for a state senate seat representing southeastern Utah. He won, thanks largely to his generous civic contributions including the annual company picnic, donations of land for schools and churches, and his name recognition.[46]

In office, Steen supported bills at odds with the traditional conservatism of Mormon Utah, including selling liquor by the drink, lowering the legal age to purchase cigarettes, and legalizing pari-mutuel horse racing. Steen resigned from the senate during the last year of his term in March 1961 and announced plans to move his family to Nevada.[47] *Times-Independent* editor Sam Taylor praised Steen's many contributions to Moab:

> In respects, the name "Moab" has been synonymous with Charles A. Steen in area-boosting publicity all across the nation. . . . Further, contributions to civic and government organizations and projects by Steen-controlled operations have made possible the growth and development of even more community assets.[48]

Less than six weeks later, reports surfaced that Steen was thinking about selling his interest in the URECO mill and his Mi Vida mine. The following May the Atlas Corporation of New York announced that it had purchased the mine and the mill for $25 million.[49] From that point on, Charlie Steen was no longer a part of the business or the town he had made famous.[50]

Although the reasons for consolidation were different in Moab than in the other yellowcake communities, Steen's sale of the URECO mill to Atlas demonstrates the integration of independent uranium companies into larger corporate structures. As occurred in Jeffrey City later, corporate consolidation helped restore uranium confidence within the community.[51]

With the uranium boom and its symbol gone and potash just developing, Moab increasingly turned to tourism to stabilize the local economy. Because of its beautiful setting and moderate climate, tourism had always been a factor in Moab's economy, although it slowed during the frenzy of the uranium rush.

With the completion of the URECO mill in 1958 and the move from promotion to production, Moab began to shift toward tourism for continued growth.[52] Thanks to the AEC's road-building program that had opened up the backcountry, plus a growing local effort to accommodate tourists, a new highway in Arches National Monument, and a movement to beautify the city, the community successfully broke free from its yellowcake dependence.[53] This effort was symbolized in 1962 when the annual rodeo and town festival, originally called the Red Rock Round-Up before being changed to the Uranium Days Round-Up during the boom years, became the Canyonlands Festival.[54] The following year a chamber of commerce contest chose "Heart of the Canyonlands" to replace "Uranium Capital of the World" as Moab's motto. Although the *Times-Independent* kept the uranium symbol atop its banner, the aphorism "Uranium Capital of the World" was replaced with the new slogan.[55]

The change in the newspaper was symbolic of the transformation occurring in the community. With the uranium industry slowing and tourism and potash growing, Moab was no longer the boomtown of the 1950s. This combination of new development and stability brought a balance not felt in Moab since the uranium expansion. In a 1962 editorial, editor Samuel Taylor remarked that although more homes had been built in Moab than in any previous year, "an entirely new atmosphere became evident." Despite the completion of a new high school, a new water and sewer system, a courthouse expansion, and new businesses, Taylor asserted that Moab had reached stabilization: "Moab is no longer a boom-town. It is no longer a town where quick riches are to be had by those wishing to stay only long enough to 'get well.'"[56] Taylor concluded that stability had also produced a decline in business and employment compared to the boom days.[57]

The transition from uranium boomtown became more pronounced over the next three years as the stretch-out program impacted Moab. The new policy had been greeted with pessimism because producers predicted it would bring lower prices.[58] When Atlas purchased the small uranium mill at Mexican Hat, Utah, in 1963, the company suggested it would help Moab by assuring that its mill would participate in the new stretch-out program.[59] A year later Atlas laid off 25 percent of its workers at the Moab mill after announcing its intention to sign a stretch-out contract.[60] Downtown businesses closed, school enrollment fell, and uranium employment dropped significantly for the first time in years.[61] When Atlas finally signed its stretch-out contract in December 1964, the impact had already been felt.[62]

From that point to the end of the decade, Moab continued to push tourism as a means of diversifying its economy. This effort was aided by the creation of Canyonlands National Park southwest of Moab in 1964 and the founding of a local action group, dubbed "Operation Tourism," the following year.[63] The organization, composed of local business and community leaders, worked with the Moab Chamber of Commerce to inform outsiders about Moab's scenery and accommodations, build a visitor's center, and publicize Moab's tourist industry.[64] The results were gratifying. Record numbers of travelers visited neighboring parks in 1965, with nearly 20,000 at Canyonlands and over 143,000 at Arches a mile north of Moab. Officials predicted that over a million tourists would visit the parks by 1970.[65]

By the late 1960s tourism had become so imbedded in Moab's economy that many people wondered whether mining and industrial activity was needed. In a frank editorial that noted the competing values of aesthetic preservation and resource development, *Times-Independent* editor Sam Taylor argued that Moab needed both mining and tourism:

> All efforts should be made to bring about the progressive development of all segments of the economy in the future, with maximum utilization and protection of the public domain.
>
> Minerals resource people should be thankful for the broadened tax base brought about by the construction of motels, restaurants, service stations, and other facilities which serve primarily the tourist industry. They should be in the front ranks of those who would promote the scenic attractions of Southeastern Utah.
>
> On the other hand, those who view the aesthetic values of Canyon Country as the ONLY real values of the land should be realistic enough to know that the above-mentioned industries gave us the standard of living which included sufficient leisure to enjoy the aesthetics; and that people who have carved out an existence here for three-quarters of a century have a certain right to remain in that self-sufficient existence.[66]

Then, in a tone reminiscent of the uranium boom, Taylor commented:

> Whether or not we like it, minerals are going to be developed in Southeastern Utah in the future as they have been in the past. And whether or not we like it, hordes of people are going to continue to come to this area to view the scenic wonders that have made residents of so many of us in the past.[67]

This concern for balance hints at tourism's growth and also at a recovering uranium industry.

The revival of uranium began around 1965 after the AEC had made it legal for uranium companies to sell yellowcake directly to power plant customers. Exploration, which had practically stopped during the allocation period, started up again in 1965 and soon outdistanced the original boom records.[68] This time, however, the lone prospector equipped with a Geiger counter had been replaced by energy companies doing deep drilling.[69]

Atlas was one of the companies making the transition from government to the commercial market. As with other firms at the time, though, future expansion had to begin during an economically depressed market. Despite the fact that Atlas was operating with only half of its mill workers and less than a quarter of its miners, in 1966 the company began a major exploration program. To add milling capacity, Atlas then purchased the AEC contracts of another Utah mill.[70] Finally, in 1967 Atlas announced that it had begun selling uranium to private power companies.[71] These plans were slowed, however, when a December 1968 fire closed the plant for six months. When the mill reopened, the company made efforts to assure Moab of its continued uranium future.[72]

In addition to Atlas, the Canadian uranium firm Rio Algom Mines began constructing a mine and mill complex south of Moab at La Sal. Designed to allow the company into the embargoed U.S. market, the new plant was the first non-AEC mill in Utah. With contracts to feed U.S. power plants and enough ore under its own control, Rio Algom brought more jobs to the area.[73]

The renewed uranium interest led to the familiar boomtown conditions Moab residents had come to expect. During the period 1965–1970, the community experienced another round of increased home sales and rentals, rising school enrollment, expanded postal traffic, zoning problems, increased business, and more crime.[74] The newspaper declared that Moab's outlook was bright and cautioned its readers to be prepared for uranium's new challenge in the postgovernment market.[75] The *Times-Independent* printed more and more stories supporting nuclear energy.[76]

Although uranium continued to play a significant role in Moab's economy, the town was no longer yellowcake dependent. Economic diversification had helped Moab to break free of uranium's bonds. The town again experienced the pains uranium expansion wrought but did not suffer as it had in the 1950s. When Sam Taylor called the cessation of the government procurement program the "end of an era," he was referring to the end of federal subsidy. But by 1970 the end of the era also referred to Moab's break from single-industry colonial control.[77]

By 1970 one thing was certain in the yellowcake communities: the federal uranium-buying program had ended. As historians scoured the Colorado Plateau interviewing those associated with uranium, it was evident that an important transition was taking place.[78] The government buying program had been a tremendous success. It had brought good jobs, new schools, and a general prosperity to places normally suspicious of government activity.[79] In return, these communities had adopted uranium not only in their pocketbooks but in their hearts as well. By 1970 these creatures of Uncle Sam were beginning to think government control had ended. Little did they know, however, that federal power would continue to be dominant in the supposedly free market. As long as they failed to diversify their economies and remained tied to uranium, the yellowcake communities would still be subject to outside control. By 1970 these communities had learned that such domination could be both good and bad. Over the next twenty years they would learn that the commercial market was the same.

Notes

1. James B. Barber, "Uncle Sam's Creature," Grants *Daily Beacon,* 21 November 1957. A similar editorial is Samuel J. Taylor, "Bright Future or No Future," Moab *Times-Independent,* 24 October 1957.
2. Ben McIntyre, *Uranium City: The Last Boom Town* (Mill Bay, B.C.: Driftwood, 1993).
3. "AEC Slowdown Order on U-Ore Expected to Benefit Grants Area," and "We're in Good Shape," Grants *Daily Beacon,* 25 November 1958.
4. These stories appeared in the *Daily Beacon*: "They've Got Gripes," 22 January 1959; "Beacon Starts Daily Publication Today," 31 March 1959; "Grants Construction During 1959 Passes $3,300,000," and "Grants Merchants Report 1959 Was Excellent Business Year," 31 December 1959.
5. In May 1959 Anaconda closed the 1,200-ton-per-day carbonate leach mill that had processed Todilto Limestone ores since 1950. The 2,000-ton-per-day acid leach, resin-in-pulp mill that had processed ores from the Jackpile mine since 1955 remained in operation. See "Anaconda Company Plans to Close Two Mines, Mill in Curtailment Move," Grants *Daily Beacon,* 24 April 1959;

Holger Albrethsen Jr. and Frank McGinley, *Summary History of Domestic Uranium Procurement Under U.S. Atomic Energy Commission Contract: Final Report* (Grand Junction, Colo.: U.S. Department of Energy, 1982), A-52–A-53.

6. "Goss Slashes Prices," advertisement, Grants *Daily Beacon,* 19 February 1959; "1959 Good, 1960 Better," Grants *Daily Beacon,* 31 December 1959.

7. "Looks Good for the Future," Grants *Daily Beacon,* 30 December 1960.

8. Ibid.

9. "West Valencia Looks Ahead," Grants *Daily Beacon,* 31 December 1962.

10. Dorsey Woodson, "Frontier Town—Atomic Age Style," Denver *Post Empire* magazine (5 February 1961): 6–7.

11. Albrethsen and McGinley, *Summary History,* A-118; "Top of the News," *Uranium* (November-December 1958): 6.

12. Woodson, "Frontier Town"; James E. Quinn, *Western Nuclear, Inc., Uranium Mill* (Denver: Denver Equipment Company, [1960]), 2. This report was found in the private collection of Richard Fairservis, former Jeffrey City townsite manager, Riverton, Wyoming.

13. Albrethsen and McGinley, *Summary History,* A-38; Nielson B. O'Rear, *Summary and Chronology of the Domestic Uranium Program (August 1966),* report prepared for the U.S. Atomic Energy Commission, Grand Junction Office (Grand Junction, Colo.: Government Printing Office, 1966), 14.

14. "Negotiations Completed," *UCN Photo News* 41 (1st quarter 1959).

15. "New Uravan Pool," *UCN Photo News* 47 (3rd quarter 1960); J. F. Frost, "Historical Overview: Uravan Milling Operations 1913–1985," Uravan file, Umetco Minerals, Grand Junction, Colorado.

16. "The Uravan USV Community Center," *USV Photo News* 20 (April-May 1955); "Community Workers at Uravan," *UCN Photo News* 46 (2nd quarter 1960).

17. Dr. and Mrs. Leroy Edward Ellinwood, interview by Clare Engle, 23 July 1970, no. 178, Utah Uranium Oral History Project, Marriott Library, University of Utah, Salt Lake City (hereafter UUOHP).

18. Ellinwood suggested that from 1946 to 1966, over 5,000 people worked in Uravan despite the fact that the town's population never exceeded 2,200 at one time. Ibid.

19. Estalee Silver, telephone interview with author, 12 June 1996.

20. Albrethsen and McGinley, *Summary History,* 5.

21. The term *starvation rations* to describe the stretch-out period is from Glynn Mapes, "Off the Deathbed: Nuclear Power Plant Needs Begin to Revive Sick Uranium Industry," *Wall Street Journal,* 1 August 1966, 1.

22. Albrethsen and McGinley, *Summary History,* A-38; Ellinwood interview, UUOHP; William L. Chenoweth, letter to author, 29 June 1996.

23. The effluent was neutralized for the removal of acid, dissolved solids, and metals. It was then treated with barium chloride to remove radium and clari-

fied to remove remaining solids. The material was then monitored before being discharged into the river.

24. Frost, "Uravan Milling Operations"; Colorado Department of Health, Radiation Control Division, *Preliminary Executive Licensing Review Summary for the Uravan Uranium Mill* (Grand Junction, Colo.: 1984).

25. O'Rear, *Summary and Chronology,* 16. Data on Western Nuclear's financial status are derived from the *Wall Street Journal Index,* 1959–1970; "Western Nuclear Gets $14 Million of Orders for Uranium Concentrate," *Wall Street Journal,* 22 December 1966, 16; "Western Nuclear Contracts: Correction," *Wall Street Journal,* 23 December 1966, 11.

26. Robert Adams to fellow employees, 1 September 1967. The letter is owned by Dick Fairservis, former Jeffrey City townsite manager, Riverton, Wyoming. Still, the profit of $1.671 million for 1968 was lower than the $2.3 million margin anticipated by Adams in the letter.

27. John R. Adams and Muril D. Vincelette, interview by author, 20 May 1992. Although it had merged with Phelps-Dodge in 1972, Western Nuclear maintained its name and stature in Jeffrey City. After three years as president of Western Nuclear under Phelps-Dodge, Bob Adams broke away from his original company and started a new energy firm in 1974 that was staffed by many original Western Nuclear people. Adams soon built the new company, Energy Fuels Nuclear, into a major uranium firm. A view from the Phelps-Dodge side of the merger is Carlos A. Schwantes, *Vision and Enterprise: Exploring the History of Phelps-Dodge Corporation* (Tucson: University of Arizona Press, 2000), 261–264.

28. Richard Fairservis, interview by author, 22 September 1993.

29. Albrethsen and McGinley, *Summary History,* A-59.

30. Ibid., A-55–A-63. The Grants *Daily Beacon* called the sale of Phillips a "severe economic blow—perhaps the worst it has ever gone through." See "Prospects Bright for 1964," Grants *Daily Beacon,* 31 December 1964.

31. United Nuclear's subsidiary, Homestake Partners, also signed a stretch-out agreement. Albrethsen and McGinley, *Summary History,* A-55.

32. "Prospects Bright for 1964," Grants *Daily Beacon.*

33. Office of the State Inspector of Mines, *Annual Report of the State Inspector of Mines to the Governor of the State of New Mexico 1958–1970* (Albuquerque: Office of the State Inspector of Mines, 1958–1970).

34. Roger W. Benedict, "Atomic Reaction: Uranium Boom Fades as Demand for Metal Trails Expectations," *Wall Street Journal,* 15 August 1963.

35. Office of the Associate Superintendent for Curriculum and Accountability, "History of Enrollment for the Past 38 Years at the 180th School Day," in *Cibola County Schools 1991–92 Accountability Report,* on file at Cibola County Schools Main Office, Grants, New Mexico.

36. "Our Platform," Grants *Daily Beacon,* 31 December 1963.

37. "Town's Bonds Get No Bids; Will Uranium Bubble Pop?" *Wall Street Journal,* 10 September 1965.

38. James B. Barber, "Editorial," Grants *Daily Beacon,* 31 December 1969.

39. Samuel J. Taylor, "Bright Future or No Future," Moab *Times-Independent,* 24 October 1957.

40. These stories are from the Moab *Times-Independent*: "Research Bureau Predicts Population of 10,900 for Grand in Next 17 Years," 29 February 1958; "Filling the Gaps," 27 March 1958; "Grand County Leads State in Population Jump Since 1950," 10 April 1958; "New Law Passed as Moab Water Dwindles," 10 July 1958; "County Valuation Goes Over $12 Million Mark for 1958," 24 July 1958; "School Enrollment Breaks Previous Records for Moab," 4 September 1958.

41. "URC Plans Expansion for Big Moab Mill," Moab *Times-Independent,* 26 June 1958.

42. "Mill Extension Will Bolster Economy," Moab *Times-Independent,* 6 August 1959.

43. "AEC Alters Ore Buying Program Hidden Blessings May Result," Moab *Times-Independent,* 27 November 1958.

44. "Moab's Biggest Budget Passed After Hearing," Moab *Times-Independent,* 24 December 1959.

45. "Optimism Soars for Future in Moab After Announcement," Moab *Times-Independent,* 4 May 1960; "Texas Gulf Sulphur Announces Start of $25 Million Potash Project Near Here," Moab *Times-Independent,* 3 November 1960. The quote is from "Eight Years' Wait May Be Ending," Moab *Times-Independent,* 4 May 1960.

46. Steen's story is in Raye C. Ringholz, *Uranium Frenzy: Boom and Bust on the Colorado Plateau* (New York: W. W. Norton, 1989), 254–269.

47. Ibid., 261.

48. "A Change for the Area," Moab *Times-Independent,* 16 March 1961.

49. "Utah Uranium King Sells Mines for $25 Million," Ogden *Standard-Examiner,* 4 June 1962.

50. Ringholz, *Frenzy,* 264.

51. Atlas president David A. Stretch assured Moabites that Atlas "had every intention of remaining in the uranium mining and milling business following 1966." See "Atlas President Lists Aug. 1 as URECO Takeover Date," Moab *Times-Independent,* 12 July 1962.

52. Robert W. Bernick, "Utah Uranium—Production Replaces Promotion: Moab Readjusts Sights in U-Boom Wake," Salt Lake City *Tribune,* 10 May 1956, 21. The tourist industry is examined in Hal Rothman, *Devil's Bargains: Tourism in the Twentieth Century American West* (Lawrence: University Press of Kansas, 1998).

53. These stories are from the Moab *Times-Independent*: "Committee Named to Inform Tourists of Accommodations," 7 June 1956; "Dedication Ceremony

Opens New Paved Arches Highway," 28 August 1958; "Residents Go All-Out to Clean up City, Seek to Win Nation-wide Contest," 21 March 1963; "City Plans Improvement Project for Entire Town," 13 June 1963.

54. "Canyonlands Festival Promises to Be Best Ever for Moab," Moab *Times-Independent*, 23 August 1962.

55. "HEART OF CANYONLANDS C of C Choice—Selected From Hundreds of Entries," Moab *Times-Independent*, 7 March 1963.

56. Samuel Taylor, "1962—Year of Stabilization," Moab *Times-Independent*, 27 December 1962.

57. Ibid.

58. "Industry Reaction Varies on AEC Extension," Moab *Times-Independent*, 22 November 1962.

59. "Atlas Buys Mexican Hat Uranium Mill," Moab *Times-Independent*, 30 July 1963.

60. "Atlas Cuts Work Force for Stretch-out Program," Moab *Times-Independent*, 25 June 1964.

61. See three articles in the Moab *Times-Independent*: Don Robinson, "Closures Change Face of Moab Main Street," 16 July 1964; "School Census Takes Big Drop," 27 August 1964; "Hopes for Improved Economy Rise Here With Narrowing of Employment Gap," 8 October 1964. The last article noted that some of the men released by uranium firms found jobs in other area industries.

62. "New Atlas Contract Assures Moab Mill Operation to at Least 1970," Moab *Times-Independent*, 17 December 1964.

63. For a discussion of the evolution of Canyonlands National Park, see Arthur R. Gomez, *Quest for the Golden Circle: The Four Corners and the Metropolitan West 1945–1970* (Albuquerque: University of New Mexico Press, 1994), 140–146. See also, "Operation Tourism Draws Crowd," Moab *Times-Independent*, 15 April 1965.

64. "Operation Tourism Draws Crowd," Moab *Times-Independent*; "Background Report: Moab Builder Is a Local Authority on Travel Industry Motivations," Moab *Times-Independent*, 13 October 1966.

65. "Record Travel Listed at Local Parks," Moab *Times-Independent*, 6 January 1966. See also these stories by *Deseret News* associate business editor William A. Dunn: "Things Look up in Moab," 19 March 1966; "Moab, 'Boom or Bust' Town: Tourists $$ May Aid Economy," 27 March 1966; "Growing West: Moab— Well on the Road," 7 December 1966.

66. Samuel L. Taylor, "Needed: A Diversified Base," Moab *Times-Independent*, 22 May 1969.

67. Ibid.

68. "1967 Breaks All Prior Records for Uranium Ore Drilling," Moab *Times-Independent*, 25 January 1968.

69. Maxine Newell, "Uranium Industry Being Quietly Rejuvenated in the Moab Area," Moab *Times-Independent,* 23 February 1967.

70. See three articles in the Moab *Times-Independent*: Don Robinson, "Atlas Minerals President Optimistic About Future of Uranium Industry," 7 April 1966; "Atlas Minerals Outlines Exploration Plans," 4 August 1966; "Versatile Atlas Prepares for Future," 27 June 1968.

71. "Atlas Will Sell Uranium to General Electric," Moab *Times-Independent,* 16 March 1967.

72. "Fire Causes Big Damage at Atlas Minerals Moab Mill," Moab *Times-Independent,* 26 December 1968; "Atlas Inks New Uranium Sales Contract, Plans Reopening of Moab Mill," Moab *Times-Independent,* 3 April 1969.

73. Two stories from the 24 October 1968 edition of the Moab *Times-Independent* relay the Rio Algom story: "Rio Algom Announces Humeaca Mine Start Soon," and Samuel Taylor, "Long-Awaited Announcement."

74. See these articles from the Moab *Times-Independent*: "Combination of Things Brings Optimism Here," 1 September 1966; "Moab Restaurant Owner Too Busy Working to Get Into Uranium Boom," 24 November 1966; "New Year Brings Moab Promise of Renewed Industrial Activity," and "Moab Has Weathered Many a Rugged Storm; Keeps Growing Despite Temporary Setbacks," 29 December 1966; "Postmaster Has Seen 1000 Per Cent Increase in Traffic at Local Postoffice," 12 January 1967; "Drug Problems Increasing Here, Chief Tells Service Club," 23 April 1970.

75. Samuel Taylor, "The Future Is Bright," Moab *Times-Independent,* 23 March 1967.

76. Richard A. Firmage, *A History of Grand County,* Utah Centennial County History Series (Salt Lake City: Utah State Historical Society, 1996), 353.

77. Samuel Taylor, "End of an Era," Moab *Times-Independent,* 24 December 1970.

78. "16 Member Student Team Compiles History of Uranium Industry," Moab *Times-Independent,* 16 July 1970.

79. Gary Lee Shumway, "A History of the Uranium Industry on the Colorado Plateau," Ph.D. diss., University of Southern California, 1970, 207.

Chapter 8

The Commercial
Boom and Bust:
Federal Policies
and the Free Market,
1970–1988

WHEN THE GOVERNMENT-SPONSORED uranium procurement program ended in 1970, the domestic industry appeared bleak. Twenty-two years of federal incentives and guaranteed markets had created an industry too big for its own needs. Since the 1958 allocation announcement, the government had been trying to wean U.S. producers and milling companies from federal dependence, but nuclear power plants were not seeking uranium at levels to match production capabilities. Thus with supply exceeding demand, the few buyers in the market were driving down the price of uranium.

The uranium industry rebounded magnificently, creating typical boomtown problems for the yellowcake communities. Reminiscent of the government expansion in the 1950s, the commercial boom of the 1970s returned prosperity to all four towns. Jeffrey City and Grants became boomtowns, whereas Moab's economic diversification buffered it against the extremes. Uravan grew but was increasingly affected by government health regulations. To understand how the commercial market affected the communities, it is necessary to examine the complexities of the new market.

The setting U.S. uranium companies faced in 1970 was far different and more complicated than that in previous years. First, the federal government's role had shifted from purchasing agent and industry booster to regulatory agency. Increasingly, federal and even state officials regulated the health and environmental impacts of uranium mining and milling. Second, although the government no longer procured uranium, it remained influential in the new commercial market through its enrichment monopoly. The Atomic Energy Commission (AEC) affected uranium demand because until 1974 it had total control over how much yellowcake could be made into nuclear fuel.[1]

The federal government also established several programs to aid the industry in the transition to a commercial market. First, as part of the Private Ownership of Special Nuclear Materials Act of 1964, the government ended its uranium monopsony by allowing private utilities to purchase uranium directly from licensed producers. The act also amended the Atomic Energy Act of 1954 by providing a statutory basis for protecting the domestic industry from foreign imports. To maintain a viable domestic industry during this time of limited demand and excess foreign supply, the government placed limitations on the enrichment of foreign uranium for use in U.S. power reactors. This embargo began in 1966 and would continue until the AEC deemed that increased demand called for a change in the ban.[2]

Additionally, since the "starvation rations" of the stretch-out period, U.S. uranium companies had been consolidating with major mining and energy firms to outlast the recession. By 1970, oil companies controlled about 50 percent of the nation's best uranium reserves and over 70 percent of lower-cost reserves. Similarly, oil companies were either owners or partners in more than half of the fourteen remaining U.S. processing mills.[3] Initially, this increased capital allowed companies to survive the uranium depression, but some industry insiders worried that uranium expertise and experience had been lost when energy companies took over.[4]

The energy companies also faced a vastly different market from the one during the boom years of the 1950s. Instead of federal paternalism that assured companies of exploration services, haulage allowances, and guaranteed prices, the 1970s free market was subject to supply and demand. Initial excitement over the end of the government procurement program brought increased exploration between 1968 and 1970, but drilling fell in

1971 and 1972. Demand uncertainty dropped the price of uranium to its lowest point since 1948.[5]

The main reason for the depression was the continued delay in nuclear power plant starts. Although expected increases in electrical demand sparked expansion of the nuclear power industry beginning in 1965, the eight- to ten-year period between when a plant placed an order and when it began operations deferred uranium expansion until at least 1973. When increased environmental and regulatory licensing further delayed construction and rising inflation raised costs exponentially, the uranium industry suffered.[6]

In early 1974 the price of yellowcake began to rise, and a new uranium boom was on. Over the next three years the price of U_3O_8 climbed from the traditional eight dollars per pound to over forty dollars per pound.[7] The causes of this surge are complex. Although a number of unrelated factors combined to escalate the price, they can be categorized in three main areas: those that caused an increase in demand; those that caused a reduction in supply, each leading to a price increase; and those that impacted prices independent of supply and demand.[8]

Factors that caused changes in demand included the politics of reprocessing and enriching uranium, the oil crisis of the 1970s, and the operation of an international uranium cartel. Those forces that created a reduction in supply also included the uranium cartel, as well as delays in production from new uranium mines in Australia, the withdrawal of French uranium supplies in Africa, changes in Canadian export policies, the failure of the Westinghouse contract, and developing nonproliferation policies.[9]

The enrichment and reprocessing stories are complex. Naturally occurring uranium is composed of two isotopes, U-238 and U-235. Uranium 238 is not fissionable but constitutes 99.3 percent of natural uranium. The remaining 0.7 percent is the fissionable isotope U-235. Most nuclear power plants, including U.S. light-water reactors, require that the U-235 content be increased to 3 percent. This process, called enrichment, uses high amounts of electricity to extract the U-235 from the natural uranium.[10]

Until 1974, the U.S. government possessed a monopoly of enrichment services, called diffusion plants, in the Western world. Any noncommunist country that needed nuclear fuel had to contract with the government to have its yellowcake processed into enriched uranium. Since the earliest days of the AEC, these contracts had been flexible, short-term agreements that were advantageous to suppliers. Beginning in 1973, however, the government insisted on "fixed commitment contracts" that were more advantageous to the government. Designed to ease planning and assure that the existing capacity of the government's enrichment monopoly would not be overcome by increasing demand, the new compacts forced customers to schedule uranium commitments well into the future.[11] As utilities planned more nuclear reactors and demand for yellowcake increased, power companies began to sign new contracts to avoid possible shortages. Thus the government's new enrichment policy linked utilities to long-term yellowcake requirements, thereby increasing demand and contributing to a price rise.[12]

Beyond the long-term contracts, the AEC also made changes in its enrichment process to avoid shortages. This program, called "split tails," increased the processing capacity of U.S. enrichment plants by decreasing their efficiency. As a by-product of this move, however, an increase occurred in the amount of U-235 wastes, or "tails." Because of this increase, more yellowcake feed was needed to produce the same amount of enriched product. To offset this problem, the AEC offered to use uranium from its 50,000 ton stockpile left over from the military procurement program of the 1950s and 1960s. In effect, the plan would solve two problems: it would allow the government to dispose of its unwanted stockpile gradually, without upsetting the market, while allowing diffusion plants to process more uranium for the expanding nuclear power industry.[13]

Economists suggested that in the short term demand would drop because the government was fulfilling the gap between supply and demand from its own stock rather than from the open market. Critics also suggested that the complimentary consumption of over 100 million pounds of government uranium could cost the U.S. treasury millions and potentially handcuff the government's ability to respond to later market shortages.[14]

The government also affected the commercial market through reprocessing. Uranium used in a nuclear power plant can be remade to extract some unused uranium plus plutonium produced during the fission process. These materials can then be recycled into new fuel that can supply nearly one-third of nuclear power plant requirements. Although initial reports suggested that such technology would be available by the mid-1970s, difficulties postponed the introduction of reprocessing until the early 1980s. In addition, the recycling of weapons-grade plutonium into more plutonium set off fears regarding increased handling of this highly lethal substance. Finally, in April 1977 President Jimmy Carter postponed indefinitely both U.S. reprocessing and the export of such technologies. This change in the potential recycling of existing resources increased demand for new raw materials.[15]

The oil crisis of the 1970s also stimulated alternative energy demands and influenced yellowcake prices. When the Organization of Petroleum Exporting Countries (OPEC) began its U.S. oil embargo in 1973, the prices of all American fuels rose on a BTU equivalency basis.[16] As the price of oil quadrupled, new interest in nuclear energy developed, increasing demand and raising the price of uranium. Demand rose as confusion and insecurity about energy sources sparked utility companies' desire to negotiate long-term supply contracts and hoard their inventories.[17]

An international uranium cartel also influenced yellowcake demand. After the AEC imposed its embargo on foreign yellowcake in the United States, foreign producers found themselves shut out of the noncommunist world's largest market. Beginning in 1972 they apparently organized an international cartel to fix minimum prices, control production and distribution, and virtually end competition for yellowcake.[18] Within two years the free world's supply of uranium had been restricted, demand increased as buyers sought higher inventories, and the price of uranium increased.[19]

Just as the cartel impacted both supply and demand, several other demand factors also influenced the supply side of the uranium equation. The U.S. postponement of reprocessing spent nuclear fuel eliminated one potential fuel source, and the nonproliferation policies of the uranium-producing countries—the United States, Canada, and Australia—created a nuclear fuel shortage for Western Europe and Japan, especially in the late 1970s.[20]

More important, reductions in the supply of new uranium resources from Australian, French, and Canadian suppliers urged uranium prices upward. Although Australia had been considered one of the largest potential uranium suppliers after major discoveries in the early 1970s, the Labor Party froze the export of uranium in 1974. Similarly, the Canadian government, worried about the rising cost of energy after the OPEC embargo and conscious of its ability to supply the world's atomic demand, began limiting uranium exports in 1974. Finally, after making plans to implement the world's largest nuclear power program in 1974, France removed its uranium stockpile from the international supply.[21]

The final supply-side factor developed in September 1975 when Westinghouse, the giant electrical firm that had built and operated over half of the world's nuclear reactors and supplied them with uranium, announced that it could not deliver nuclear fuel it had promised. Although Westinghouse had contracted to supply about 80,000 pounds of uranium at roughly $10 per pound, it had not purchased the supplies before uranium prices rose.[22] With the market price of uranium at that time running about $25 per pound and with only 15,000 pounds on hand, the company stood to lose about $10 million on the deal. When uranium prices increased another $10 per pound during the next three months, the potential loss grew. At the peak price of $41 per pound, the company could lose around $2.5 billion—more than its stockholders' equity.[23]

This announcement had both positive and negative effects on uranium prices. At first, the increased demand caused by jilted utilities strengthened prices. Then, when it became apparent that the company was not going to purchase the uranium, the loss of such a sale weakened demand and hurt prices.[24]

Economists have noted that these various market factors created both real and psychological effects on uranium supply and demand. Real factors—like the delay in recycling uranium and plutonium, fixed enrichment contracts, and the loss of Australian, Canadian, and French supplies—tended to affect the short-term, or spot market, uranium price. Conversely, psychological factors such as split tails, the oil crisis, and nonproliferation policies affected expectations and, therefore, the futures market.[25]

In short, these components clearly indicate that during the commercial period uranium companies faced a much more complex market than the one that existed during the days when federal paternalism took care of the domestic industry. At the same time, the increasing power of continuing government enrichment and reprocessing policies suggested that the government still had a strong impact on the free market. In fact, one historian has suggested that the AEC was the primary contributor to the price rise.[26]

Others suggest that external factors were the greatest contributors to the price rise. In addition to the U.S. government, French, Canadian, and Australian national policies were increasingly important in the uranium market. Indeed, economists note that only two internal agents in the uranium equation—the operation of the cartel and the Westinghouse default—contributed to the price increase.[27]

As the price of uranium rose, U.S. producers realized that lower-grade reserves were becoming economically profitable. Companies opened new mines, constructed new mills, and increased employment. In 1980 uranium ore production reached its highest point since the height of the government procurement program in 1961. One factor in this increase was the development of solution mining in the late 1970s. In this method, solvents are pumped directly into the underground ore body in situ and are allowed to dissolve the uranium. The uranium is leached out and drawn to the surface, bypassing the costs of both mining and milling.[28]

As forecasts called for an expanded nuclear energy program, federal officials began to worry that the U.S. uranium industry might be inadequate to support the country's growing demand.[29] In September 1974 the congressional Joint Committee on Atomic Energy (JCAE) considered gradually ending the ban on the importation of foreign uranium for U.S. reactors. The committee planned to enlarge the foreign share of the market from no more than 10 percent in 1977 to 40 percent in 1981 and to create a free market by 1984.[30]

Reaction to the announcement was mixed. For the most part, utility companies welcomed the change, and domestic producers opposed it. The former agreed that opening the market was healthy and would ensure an adequate supply of uranium for years to come. The latter categorically rejected the proposal, suggesting that a free market would discourage new investment in domestic production and threaten the viability of the U.S. market. A few producers even argued that a totally free market might lead to a dependency on foreign uranium.[31]

Some U.S. companies recognized the need for imports yet worried about the possible problems they presented. Western Nuclear, a subsidiary of Phelps-Dodge, took a stance between most utilities and producers. Western Nuclear president Bob Adams argued that his company would support the JCAE proposal only if it strengthened the domestic industry. Although it was necessary to guarantee the utilities a supply of uranium, Adams suggested the AEC should ensure the viability of domestic production as well. Adams therefore proposed a compromise, opening the U.S. market to allow foreign companies to supply no more than one-third of the American market.[32] The JCAE rejected the plan, and gradual relaxation went into effect beginning in 1977.

As the boom progressed, the uranium industry continued to forecast expanded growth, especially in states like New Mexico and Wyoming that had large low-grade reserves. In 1978 the State of Wyoming Department of Economic Planning and Development predicted that yellowcake prices could rise to over $100 a pound by the late 1980s, thereby tripling Wyoming's production. In 1979 the New Mexico Energy and Minerals Department issued a report suggesting that New Mexico production might have to quadruple to meet demand.[33]

About the same time, the environmental journal *High Country News* devoted an entire issue to uranium. Beginning with its cover headline "The West Mines, Mills, and Worships Radioactive Fuel," the journal examined the booming uranium industry with stories that traced the history of uranium development in the West, the impact on communities including Jeffrey City, and the economics and politics of the commercial market. The publication described the impact of uranium growth on public lands and possible health concerns of workers and residents living near the growing uranium tailings piles throughout the West. A uranium-themed cartoon showed a man sitting at a bar talking to another fellow who seemed to be glowing. The caption read, "Been fooling with uranium tailings again, huh?"[34]

Then the uranium bubble burst. The first symptom of trouble appeared in the national reassessment of nuclear energy in the months following the Three Mile Island accident in March 1979.[35] As utility companies put plans for new plants on hold, the demand for yellowcake dropped. When these utilities abandoned their plans to build, some companies began to dump their stockpiled yellowcake back into the market at bargain costs. Uranium companies now found themselves not only competing against former buyers but also overstretched into expensive low-grade ore prospects. With this influx added to the already depressed market, the price of yellowcake fell further. From a high of nearly $50 a pound in 1977, yellowcake was selling for just $25 a pound by 1982.[36]

High Country News devoted a special issue to the growing bust. In the 10 August 1979 issue headlined "Uranium Industry's Expansion Prospects Bleak: Fallout From Three Mile Island Doesn't Help," Marjane Ambler reported that uranium faced "bleak prospects" that seriously threatened its continued growth. Ambler believed the boom had ended simply because uranium supply exceeded demand. Ambler noted that company officials blamed the problems on a number of issues including the bad publicity associated with Three Mile Island, the increasingly tough regulatory problems facing the uranium and nuclear power industries, burgeoning labor costs, and the threat of cheaper imports flooding the U.S. market.[37]

Although Three Mile Island became the easy scapegoat, the real causes of the slump ran much deeper. In the early 1950s and 1960s, as discussed previously, the federal government offered guaranteed markets, haulage allowances, the stretch-out program, and protectionism. In the 1970s and 1980s the international free market took control. The low-grade U.S. ore could compete internationally in a seller's market. But when the market reversed in the buyer's favor, domestic producers were in trouble.

Increasing environmental regulation also played a role in the uranium bust. In addition to delays in power plant construction caused by growing concerns over thermal pollution and nuclear waste, the health and safety of underground uranium miners came to the forefront in the late 1970s.[38] Further, as mines and mills came up for federal renewal licensing after 1970, they were required to provide environmental impact statements and meet expanding environmental guidelines.[39]

The most important of the new federal guidelines was the Uranium Mill Tailings Radiation Control Act of 1978. For the first time, mill tailings were placed under federal statutory control to neutralize wastes from inactive mills and subject current mills to Nuclear Regulatory Commission licensing. Under Title I of this legislation, all inactive uranium mills that had only sold yellowcake to the federal government would qualify as federally sponsored cleanup sites. Title II mills that continued to produce for the free market after 1970 would have to meet environmental standards on their own. Subsequently, the General Accounting Office advised Congress that the government had a "strong moral responsibility" to assist in the cleanup of the remaining active "commingled" tailings and mill sites. After more than a decade of debate, the National Energy Policy Act of 1992 established an annual congressional appropriation to help industry reclaim commingled sites.[40]

As the price of uranium fell, uranium companies were forced to close their mines and mills. From a peak of twenty-six mills in operation during the height of the commercial boom, by 1981 only twenty mills were working. The following year fourteen were active; two more closed in 1983, and by 1984 only eleven mills were operating.[41]

As the industry began to deteriorate, representatives from the uranium-producing states pushed for congressional guidelines for evaluating the status of the domestic industry.[42] They argued that federal law assured the maintenance of a viable domestic industry. Hearings before the Joint Committee on Atomic Energy and the Senate and House Committees on Energy and Natural Resources addressed both the demise of the domestic industry and the threat of growing dependence on ever increasing foreign sources. For the most part, these hearings produced the same reaction: it was the government's legal responsibility to protect the domestic uranium industry.[43]

The first attempt at fulfilling this duty on the national level occurred in January 1983 when Congress instructed Secretary of Energy Don Hodel to produce a comprehensive review of the domestic uranium mining and milling industry.[44] As part of this evaluation the secretary submitted to Congress a viability assessment of the domestic industry. In 1983 Hodel concluded that the industry remained viable in terms of resource, supply response, and financial capability and import commitment dependency. The following year, however, Hodel reversed his decision and determined that the domestic industry was no longer viable.[45]

With the collapse spreading throughout the uranium industry, domestic producers began to petition Congress and the Department of Energy (DOE) for action. By 1985, only four mills were operating whereas twenty-six had been working only a decade earlier.[46] As demand sank further, domestic producers argued that the share awarded to foreign producers was too large for the reduced market. U.S. companies asked the DOE to reimplement restrictions on foreign uranium as established by law. To their dismay, DOE established a new enrichment contract that made foreign purchases even easier. Irritated U.S. producers decided to take the matter to court.[47]

In 1987 Wyoming uranium producer Western Nuclear sued the Department of Energy and twenty-two electrical utilities. Joined by two other companies, Energy Fuels Nuclear and Uranium Resources, Western Nuclear argued that the DOE was "statutorily required to restrict enrichment of foreign uranium."[48] The states of Wyoming, New Mexico, Colorado, Utah, and Nevada filed friend-of-the-court briefs in favor of the company.[49]

The government countered that restrictions hurt U.S. utilities and consumers by making them pay higher prices. Further, DOE said such restrictions affected U.S. foreign policy by compromising trade agreements, nuclear cooperation, and nonproliferation policies. In support of the utilities, Canada and Australia—the two largest foreign producers—wrote briefs contending that such restrictions violated free trade.[50]

The legal battle hinged on the court's interpretation of the Atomic Energy Act of 1954. Western Nuclear argued that the act clearly stated that if the domestic industry was not viable, foreign yellowcake production would be restricted. DOE maintained that reimplementation of restrictions could not guarantee viability and that therefore the government should not establish such restraints. During the first round of hearings in Denver, U.S. District Court Judge James Carrigan sided with Western Nuclear and ordered the DOE to limit its enrichment of foreign uranium and to impose a total ban starting 1 January 1987. The DOE appealed the decision but lost when the Court of Appeals again sided with producers.[51] The DOE then appealed to the Supreme Court, which unanimously overturned the lower courts' decision on 15 June 1988. Justice Harry Blackmun wrote the decision, contending:

> The determination of the courts below that DOE was barred from enriching *any* foreign-source uranium rests on the assumption that the greater the restrictions, the more assured is the domestic industry's viability. This assumption cannot be grounded in the statutory language and, indeed, for the purpose of this case's summary judgement status, we must accept DOE's assertion that the assumption is false.[52]

In effect, this judgment ruled that the domestic market had dwindled to so little that even reinstituting restrictions could not guarantee that the U.S. industry would be viable.

By 1988 the U.S. uranium industry was at its lowest point ever. The promise of the commercial market had come, exceeded expectations, and gone. Unlike the end of the first uranium boom in the late 1950s, the government no longer offered allocations, stretch outs, or embargoes. Instead, growing environmental regulations, rising reclamation costs, and the free market meant another round of sellouts, layoffs, and consolidations for uranium companies.

Like the government-sponsored boom of the 1950s, the commercial boom and bust of the 1970s reverberated through the yellowcake communities. Both Grants and Jeffrey City experienced tremendous expansion similar to that which had created the first uranium towns twenty-five years earlier. Because Moab had diversified its economy, uranium-caused expansion in the 1970s, although strong, was less dominant than it once had been. Uravan's experience was similar, although it was increasingly affected by government health regulations.

The differences this time, however, were experienced in the aftermath of the bust. With no government protection and massive overproduction, the yellowcake communities were left wondering why the government no longer protected them. As the market collapsed, all four communities faced massive unemployment, depreciation of property values, and out-migration. The story of how the second uranium boom and bust affected the four yellowcake communities is told in Chapter 9.

Notes

1. During the commercial period the regulatory agency in charge of the uranium industry was reorganized twice. On 19 January 1975 the Atomic Energy Commission was divided into two separate units. The Nuclear Regulatory Commission (NRC) took over regulation of the industry, and the Energy Research and Development Administration (ERDA) handled development. ERDA was then reorganized into the cabinet-level Department of Energy (DOE) beginning 1 October 1977, whereas the NRC remained an independent commission. Despite the changing names, the federal group overseeing the uranium industry remained basically the same.

2. U.S. Department of Energy (USDOE), *Domestic Uranium Mining and Milling Industry: 1983 Viability Assessment* (Washington, D.C.: Government Printing Office [GPO], 1984), 1.

3. June H. Taylor and Michael D. Yokell, *Yellowcake: The International Uranium Cartel* (New York: Pergamon, 1979), 44–47.

4. Jack F. Frost, interview by author, 28 October 1993.

5. U.S. Energy Research and Development Administration (USERDA), *Statistical Data of the Uranium Industry* (Grand Junction, Colo.: GPO, 1976), 56.

6. Anthony David Owen, *The Economics of Uranium* (New York: Praeger, 1985), 45.
7. Yellowcake prices are from Taylor and Yokell, *Yellowcake,* 102.
8. A number of economic-based secondary sources discuss and debate the history, causes, and results of the 1970s commercial boom, especially how it related to the uranium cartel. See ibid., 57–119; Owen, *Economics,* 44–56; Marian Radetzki, *Uranium: A Strategic Source of Energy* (New York: St. Martin's, 1981), 47–148; Earle Gray, *The Great Uranium Cartel* (Toronto: McClelland and Stewart, 1982), 164–171.
9. Radetzki, *Uranium,* 137.
10. Gray, *Cartel,* 98.
11. Taylor and Yokell, *Yellowcake,* 102–103.
12. Radetzki, *Uranium,* 87–94.
13. Gray, *Cartel,* 98–99; ibid., 49–51; Taylor and Yokell, *Yellowcake,* 102–103.
14. Taylor and Yokell, *Yellowcake,* 102–103.
15. Ibid., 81–83.
16. "U$_3$O$_8$: Energy From Wyoming's Powerful Sand," *In Wyoming* (February-March 1980): 49.
17. Radetzki, *Uranium,* 97.
18. Works devoted entirely to the story of the uranium cartel include Taylor and Yokell, *Yellowcake,* and Gray, *Cartel.* A briefer study is in Norman Moss, *The Politics of Uranium* (New York: Universe, 1982), 106–119.
19. Radetzki, *Uranium,* 122.
20. Ibid., 131–132.
21. Loss of political control in its uranium-producing African colonies of Niger and Gabon that year contributed to this decision. See ibid., 129.
22. Gray, *Cartel,* 172–194; ibid., 129–131.
23. After the utilities filed suit against Westinghouse for failing to deliver its contracted uranium, Westinghouse filed antitrust litigation against twenty-nine uranium producers, saying they had participated in the illegal cartel to drive prices up.
24. Radetzki, *Uranium,* 130.
25. Ibid., 136–138.
26. Gray, *Cartel,* 165.
27. Radetzki, *Uranium,* 136–138.
28. Robert A. Meyers, ed., *Encyclopedia of Physical Science and Technology,* 2d ed. (San Diego: Academic, 1992), s.v. "Uranium," by William L. Chenoweth.
29. Radetzki, *Uranium,* 67–72.
30. U.S. Congress, Joint Committee on Atomic Energy (JCAE), *Proposed Modification of Restrictions on Enrichment of Foreign Uranium for Domestic Use: Hearings Before the Joint Committee on Atomic Energy,* 93rd Cong., 2d sess. (Washington, D.C.: GPO, 17–18 September 1974), 235–236.

31. Ibid., 223, 225. An interesting look at this issue from the Canadian perspective is Hugh C. McIntyre, *Uranium, Nuclear Power and Canada-U.S. Energy Relations* (Montreal and Washington, D.C.: C. D. Howe Research Institute [Canada] and National Planning Association [U.S.A.], 1978).

32. JCAE, *Restrictions on Enrichment*, 231.

33. New Mexico Energy and Minerals Department, *An Overview of the New Mexico Uranium Industry* (Santa Fe: New Mexico Energy and Minerals Department, 1979), 36; Quality Development Associates, *Wyoming's Uranium Industry — Status, Impacts, and Trends* (Cheyenne: State of Wyoming Department of Economic Planning and Development, Mineral Division, 1978). Even the conservative estimate suggested a leveling in the $55–$60/pound range.

34. Justas Bavarskis, "The West Mines, Mills, and Worships Radioactive Fuel: Uranium," *High Country News* 10, no. 5 (10 March 1978): 1.

35. On 28 March 1979 the Three Mile Island Unit 2 reactor near Harrisburg, Pennsylvania, overheated and released radiation into the plant. Later studies suggested that the accident came within sixty minutes of a meltdown. The incident was much publicized in the national press and was thoroughly investigated by the NRC. Although no one died as a result of the incident, Three Mile Island became a symbol for citizens opposed to the nuclear power industry. See Daniel Ford, *Meltdown: The Secret Papers of the Atomic Energy Commission* (New York: Simon and Schuster, 1986).

36. USDOE, *1983 Viability Assessment*, 10.

37. Marjane Ambler, "Uranium Industry's Expansion Prospects Bleak: Fallout From Three Mile Island Doesn't Help," *High Country News* 11, no. 16 (10 August 1979): 1. Related stories in the issue explained the self-imposed moratorium on nuclear power plant construction and the closing of a New Mexico uranium mill after its tailings dam broke and sent radioactive waste into the Rio Puerco.

38. Peter H. Eichstaedt, *If You Poison Us: Uranium and Native Americans* (Santa Fe: Red Crane, 1994).

39. By the late 1970s, uranium companies had to meet environmental requirements set forth under federal guidelines including the National Environmental Policy Act, the Clean Air Act, the Federal Water Pollution Control Act, the Solid Waste Disposal Act, and the Safe Drinking Water Act. See U.S. Department of the Interior, San Juan Basin Regional Uranium Study, *Uranium Development in the San Juan Region: A Report on Environmental Issues, Final Report* (Albuquerque: Bureau of Indian Affairs, 1980), XII-1–XII-15.

40. Uranium Mill Tailings Radiation Control Act of 1978, *Statutes at Large* 92, 3021; American Mining Congress, "Commingled Uranium Mill Tailings — A Historical Perspective," report, 4 March 1985; National Energy Policy Act of 1992.

41. USDOE, *1983 Viability Assessment*, 21.

42. U.S. Congress, Senate, Committee on Environment and Public Works, *Domestic Uranium Mining and Milling: Hearing Before the Subcommittee on Nuclear Regulation,* 97th Cong., 1st sess. (Washington, D.C.: GPO, 29 August 1983).

43. See U.S. Congress, Senate, Committee on Energy and Natural Resources, *Status of the Domestic Uranium Mining and Milling Industry: The Effects of Imports,* 97th Cong., 1st sess. (Washington, D.C.: GPO, 25 September 1981), and U.S. Congress, Senate, Committee on Energy and Natural Resources, *Review of the Status of the Domestic Uranium Mining and Milling Industry: Hearing Before the Subcommittee on Energy Research and Development,* 97th Cong., 2d sess. (Washington, D.C.: GPO, 12 September 1984).

44. U.S. Department of Energy, *United States Uranium Mining and Milling Industry: A Comprehensive Review* (Washington, D.C.: GPO, May 1984).

45. The criteria used for determining viability are in USDOE, *1983 Viability Assessment,* ix. A summary of the assessments for 1983–1985 is in U.S. Department of Energy, *Domestic Uranium Mining and Milling Industry: 1985 Viability Assessment* (Washington, D.C.: GPO, 1986), ix–x.

46. USDOE, *1985 Viability Assessment,* 17.

47. *Western Nuclear, Inc., v. Huffman,* 825 F 2d 1430, 1433 (10th Cir., 1987).

48. Ibid.

49. An article in the *Deseret News* on 10 April 1988 quoted Wyoming governor Mike Sullivan as saying he supported the mining companies and that if he were a Supreme Court Justice, he would "view this appeal by DOE as frivolous."

50. Robert H. Woody, "Uranium Industry Holds Breath as Court Weighs Restrictions," Salt Lake City *Tribune,* 13 January 1988.

51. *Western Nuclear, Inc., v. Huffman,* 1430.

52. *Huffman v. Western Nuclear, Inc.,* 108 S.Ct. 2087 (1988). See also Stuart Taylor Jr., "Uranium Industry Loses in High Court on Imports," *New York Times,* 16 June 1988, sec. 4, p. 2. An interesting reaction to this decision is Bill Payne, "Lights Dim for Domestic Uranium Producers," *Natural Resources Journal* 29, no. 4 (fall 1989): 1079–1091.

Chapter 9

Yellowcake Towns During the Commercial Boom and Bust, 1970–1988

IN THE EARLY 1980s, residents of America's oldest uranium town, Uravan, Colorado, could look back on their town's past and see the evolution of uranium in U.S. national security. After providing yellowcake for the Manhattan Project's first atomic bombs during World War II, the town had mirrored the boom and bust of the postwar uranium industry. During the glory days of the government's procurement program, the Union Carbide company town grew from a handful of workers to more than 1,000 residents. The mill operated around the clock to provide yellowcake for national defense. New houses were constructed and trailers were crammed into any available space in the narrow San Miguel River valley. The company provided a recreation hall, tennis courts, a library, and a store. A new school was constructed for the growing numbers of children, and the company operated a small medical clinic for the town. Union Carbide converted the cooling reservoir at the original power plant into a heated Olympic-sized pool, giving residents the only respite from the summer heat for miles around.[1]

View of Uravan looking northwest, 1978. The uranium-processing mill was literally the center of life in Uravan. This view shows the A and B plants, *center*, with the original 1914 two-story boardinghouse nearby. Across the street from the boardinghouse is the recreation center and post office. Courtesy, Ed Norton and the Estalee Silver Collection.

During the stretch-out program, the new government contract ended the boom but assured employees of continued economic security. As the housing expansion ended and the population stabilized at around 850 residents, the town still had many advantages for such a small, isolated community. In addition to a new swimming pool, Uravan boasted its own doctor, a town ball team, service organizations, clubs, and typical small-town life. When the country turned to uranium for power during the 1970s and yellowcake prices rebounded, Uravan responded with record production. But Uravan also had a deep, dark secret shared by few small towns: radiation.[2]

With a history of producing radioactive materials going back to the 1910s, a radioactive processing mill located in the center of town, 10 million tons of radioactive tailings ponds on a hill above the town, another 2.5 million tons in ponds next to the town, and unknown amounts of old radioactive tailings used as fill dirt scattered around the community, by 1980 Uravan had radon levels 10 times higher than federal standards. Although the mill was regarded as "safe," the fact that industrial limits for radiation were 200 times higher than those for the general public brought little comfort given the mill's location.[3]

To alleviate the environmental problems, Union Carbide spent $12 million trying to stabilize the tailings ponds. Then yellowcake prices tumbled. The company closed the mill for the first time in forty years and laid off half of its workforce. The mill was reopened for a short time, and Union Carbide spent the next four years trying to meet environmental guidelines. Finally, in 1984 the company closed the mill and agreed to spend another $25 million to reclaim the site. By year's end, most of the town's residents had left.

Despite Uravan's many health concerns and the dwindling uranium market, many residents did not want to leave the company town that had become their home. Locals claimed the tailings piles were not harmful, that the so-called radioactive soil produced beautiful roses and gardens, and that no one in the town had ever been diagnosed with cancer. One Uravan resident later joked that locals used to kid each other about glowing in the dark, but he wished that perception would disappear. Describing his feelings about leaving he concluded, "It makes my kids feel like they don't have a hometown."[4]

Uravan's story and the attitudes expressed by its departing residents are typical of the yellowcake towns during the commercial boom and bust of the 1970s and 1980s. Unlike the government procurement program in the 1950s, the market price of yellowcake was the driving force in the uranium industry in the 1970s. As Americans looked to nuclear power during the energy crisis, uranium prices skyrocketed and yellowcake towns prospered. But as environmental concerns became more widespread amid expanding federal regulation and were spotlighted nationally by the Three Mile Island incident in 1979, yellowcake prices fell and uranium towns declined. As Uravan residents left their homes in the early 1980s, they were part of a mass out-migration of uranium miners and millers around the West.

Although the new market was far more complicated than the government's program had been, the residents of uranium towns did not worry about the supply and demand factors. Instead, they were primarily concerned with the price of yellowcake versus the cost of producing yellowcake. If the former exceeded the latter, uranium was profitable and the towns prospered. If the opposite were true, they did not. One of the best ways to understand the connection between cost of production and selling price is through an understanding of uranium ore reserves. Because of its greater output, higher-quality ore could be processed more cheaply than lower-grade ores, which were more expensive because they provided less yellowcake. But by 1970 practically all of the cheapest reserves had been mined, and it would take a major price escalation to make the most expensive reserves profitable.[5]

For the first few years following the end of the government procurement program, the price of uranium remained low, and the yellowcake towns suffered through a prolonged depression. After commercial sales were legalized in the 1960s, expanding exploration produced a short-lived boom. But following continued delays in nuclear power plant construction, that false hope only intensified the effect of the declining market. The end of federal purchases in late 1970 terminated a major source of income for most remaining uranium mills, and the communities' futures appeared bleak. Grants was probably the most severely depressed at the time. Having lost almost 20 percent of its population since 1960 largely because of a 25 percent drop in uranium employment, the Grants area was still suffering from the withdrawal associated with its uranium dependency. A 1971 planning report described the area as in a state of decline, with poor housing and an obsolescent commercial strip.[6]

Although Moab's diversification into potash mining and tourism had decreased uranium's importance, the former uranium capital also experienced a mild slump in the early 1970s. Population, school enrollment, and mining income had fallen since 1970. The only bright spot for uranium was the Rio Algom uranium mine-mill complex being developed 25 miles southeast of town.[7]

As the government-sponsored uranium market concluded and the new commercial market began, a few uranium companies began securing contracts with private power companies. In Jeffrey City, Western Nuclear had merged with the copper mining giant Phelps-Dodge and was making its first commercial sales. Similarly, Uravan's Union Carbide had survived the stretch-out period and was moving into the new uranium market with its own private power company contracts.[8]

The boom in nuclear energy did not come as quickly as many had expected. The eight-year start-up time for nuclear power plants kept yellowcake demand initially low, and the lag kept prices down. But in early 1974 a variety of factors drove up the price of yellowcake, and a new uranium boom was on. Over the next three years uranium climbed from its traditional eight dollars per pound to more than forty dollars per pound.[9] As prices rose, lower-grade reserves near the yellowcake communities became increasingly profitable.

Despite the sense that the new boom was more corporate than individual, the rising price of yellowcake re-created many of the boomtown conditions of the 1950s. Rapid population increases once again caused housing and school shortages. Businesses expanded, more infrastructure was needed, and the communities actively affirmed their yellowcake economies, landscapes, identities, and dependency. Jeffrey City and Grants offer the best examples.

In the 1970s Jeffrey City's population exploded by 500 percent as the community shifted from a makeshift company town to a permanent city. From a 1970 population of 750, Jeffrey City grew to almost 2,500 by 1977 and to more than 4,000 three years later.[10] In Grants and Milan, population expanded almost 30 percent, as the number of residents grew from 11,090 in 1970 to 13,259 in 1978 to 15,186 by 1980.[11]

Most of this expansion resulted directly from an expanding uranium workforce. In Jeffrey City, Western Nuclear had employed around 200 workers since the 1960s stretch out; that number more than doubled from 1975 to 1976 and grew another 20 percent over the following five years.[12] Similarly, in Grants, uranium employment had been declining steadily since 1970 but began to rebound in 1974 and reached a new high of about 4,500 workers in 1976. It continued to set new records every year until 1979, when employment topped 7,500 workers.[13]

Commercial interests also grew at tremendous rates during the 1970s boom. Jeffrey City, once a company town, added a number of private business interests including a bank, bowling alley, library, a Coast-to-Coast hardware store, three churches, a clothing store, and two grocery stores. Developers even planned an enclosed mall.[14] In Grants, the area uranium workers' $46 million in annual wages brought similar expansion. New shopping centers and restaurants were built. During the most intense expansion between 1978 and 1980, annual total gross business receipts in the area grew from $1.36 million to $2.35 million.[15]

As in the 1950s, housing also expanded as population increased. In Jeffrey City, Western Nuclear constructed new housing and trailer lots, and another uranium producer, Lucky Mc Uranium Corporation, opened its own company-owned subdivision a few miles southeast of town in 1977. This area, called Green Mountain Village, had 100 mobile home lots connected to its own water and sewer system.[16] Topographical maps of Jeffrey

Jeffrey City during more prosperous times, c. 1979. This view of Jeffrey City taken during the height of the commercial boom shows a community of about 4,000. Within four years most of the buildings had been moved, and the population was less than 300. From the Jeffrey City *News*. Author's collection.

City in 1961 and 1984 clearly show an increase in the town's dimensions.[17] The Grants-Milan area experienced a similar housing boom. From 1970 to 1980 the number of housing units in Grants increased 72 percent, and Milan grew 106 percent. As in the 1950s, mobile homes accounted for the greatest increase, with more than 540 new units in each community; such homes accounted for 66 percent of all homes in Milan in 1980.[18] To accommodate this growth, new subdivisions were created, and the area within Grants' city limits more than doubled.[19]

Many of the newcomers were young people pulled to Grants by the prospect of making good money in the mines. Although they knew the potential health threat posed by radiation and radon in the underground mines at Ambrosia Lake, most were willing to risk it for the opportunity.[20] In a contemporary article, two couples who had just moved to Grants described their similarities. Both couples came to Grants to make money, and both found the housing situation difficult. They felt somewhat alone in the boomtown and did not know whether to stay. Although one family hoped to make enough money in uranium to allow them to settle elsewhere, the other couple had built a permanent house on the outskirts of town. Both couples felt Grants provided the opportunity they had expected.[21]

The tremendous growth also brought boomtown problems to the yellowcake towns. As in the 1950s, school space was an instant problem. Again, the worst situation occurred in Jeffrey City, where from 1970 to 1977 school enrollment grew more than 300 percent—from 150 students to more than 500. To accommodate such expansion, the state of Wyoming granted Jeffrey City its own school district in 1977. From a single grade school housed in Western Nuclear's Quonset building in 1957, by 1979 Jeffrey City had a new grade school, junior high, and high school.[22] Grants faced similar problems. After declining over the period 1970–1973, enrollment figures began rising in 1974. By 1976 the number of students had passed the previous high of 5,400 set during the 1950s boom. In 1978, enrollment peaked at just under 6,000 students.[23] The school district was able to accommodate most of these students thanks to the tremendous building program during the previous boom and the use of portable classrooms.[24]

The social malaise of alcoholism, drug use, child abuse, depression, attempted suicide, divorce, and other problems also appeared in the uranium boomtowns in the 1970s.[25] With its hard-working and hard-playing miners, Grants experienced jumps in alcoholism, drug arrests, and crime.[26] But in Jeffrey City, Western Nuclear's paternalism may have buffered the town from such problems.[27] Apparently, the threat of losing one's job and home because of illegal or rowdy behavior helped to maintain vigilance in the town.[28]

The yellowcake towns of the 1970s adopted uranium into their community identities but in a less blatant manner than was seen with the Uranium Cafes and Atomic Motels in the 1950s. In Grants, although the local branch of New Mexico State University offered a program in underground uranium mining training,[29] the best example of uranium's hold on the community's identity was the establishment of Cibola County in 1981. Organized to make Grants' increasing population more manageable, the new county was created by dividing the western part of Valencia County. With Grants as its seat, Cibola and neighboring McKinley County encompassed most of the uranium regions of New Mexico. Named for the famed Seven Cities of Cibola searched for by Coronado, the new county seemed to finally fulfill that elusive treasure. It was the first in New Mexico since 1949 when Los Alamos County, also tied to nuclear energy, was created.[30]

In Jeffrey City the uranium link was best exhibited by the transformation from company town to independent city. In 1977 the Jeffrey City *News* published its first edition and immediately became a big uranium booster.

Although uranium was not specifically mentioned in the first issue, its growth fueled Editor Lee Lockhart's excitement when he announced: "Today is a great day. We will long remember it as a time when the people of Greater Jeffrey City Area got their very own newspaper. It's another step along the way for this community to blossom into a full-fledged city."[31]

As the *News* projected, the basic character of Jeffrey City began to change over the next four years. Instead of fitting the company town definition of merely providing living quarters for isolated workers, the town began to build toward a future. In 1959 Jeffrey City had been little more than a small collection of trailers huddled together against the cold Wyoming wind. Less than two decades later Jeffrey City was a real town with its own emergency medical clinic, a library, law enforcement, a school board, civic groups, fraternal organizations, seven churches, youth groups, recreation clubs, private businesses, banks, three restaurants, a motel, and three gas stations. Residents were planting flowers and trees and watering their lawns. Western Nuclear paved the streets and donated land for a new gymnasium. At long last Jeffrey City was expanding beyond its original purpose.[32]

The uranium towns' identities were also bolstered by continuing projections for more growth and prosperity. The forecasts ratified growth, reassured residents that they were pursuing the right path, and promised future prosperity. In a story on the front page of the Albuquerque *Tribune* in May 1976, a University of New Mexico economist predicted that uranium would become a multibillion-dollar industry in New Mexico within ten years and that Grants would have a population of 100,000.[33] A more modest projection the following year suggested a population of 48,000 for the Grants-Milan area.[34] The most thorough study of the region predicted that it was conceivable for area uranium production to double its 1978 level by 1990 and to triple that level by 2000.[35]

A detailed report by the Wyoming State Department of Economic Planning and Development in 1978 predicted that yellowcake prices could rise to more than $100 a pound by the late 1980s.[36] The document also forecast a tripling of U.S. uranium requirements, thereby trebling Wyoming's production as well. As long as the price of yellowcake remained high and utility companies continued to build nuclear power plants, production of lower-grade ores, like those around Grants and Jeffrey City, would continue to be profitable.[37]

In addition to convincing residents of their future success, these studies also strengthened reliance on uranium. Instead of the economic diversity preached during the stretch-out period, the commercial boom rekindled uranium dependency. Although company towns like Jeffrey City were the most dependent because of their one-industry economies, Grants was similarly hooked. With the logo "Uranium Capital" still affixed to the banner of the local paper, Grants remained the king of the yellowcake towns. As the boom progressed, new mills, including solution mining projects, were planned for the area. By 1976 Grants was producing nearly all of New Mexico's 48 percent share of the nation's uranium.[38]

Although Moab also prospered in the 1970s, it lacked the uranium dependency of the 1950s. As the price of yellowcake rose in 1975, the Atlas and Rio Algom mills expanded their capacities and increased their efficiency.[39] Although uranium employment also grew, from 75 workers in 1973 to 500 just six years later, the absence of uranium symbols suggested that Moab had outgrown its uranium tie. Charlie Steen, the one-time uranium king, had left town and was in a battle with the Internal Revenue Service.[40] For a while, his mansion on the hill overlooking Moab was converted to a uranium mining museum. But this homage to the town's past proved unsuccessful, and the house was turned into a restaurant.[41] Uranium nomenclature also disappeared in Moab. The *Times-Independent* had replaced the "Uranium Capital of the World" motto in its banner with "Heart of the Canyonlands" back in the 1960s, as mentioned previously, and removed the nuclear symbol altogether in 1973.[42] In short, despite the second uranium boom, Moab's diversified economy limited the town's identity as a yellowcake community.

The growing environmental problem of mill tailings posed the only real threat to uranium towns during the 1970s boom. As mining companies increasingly turned to lower-grade ores, the volume of waste grew accordingly. Uravan faced the biggest problem. When its mill license expired in 1975, the state of Colorado did not renew it immediately but issued a temporary operations permit until further environmental studies could be done.[43] After six decades of milling radium, vanadium, and uranium, Union Carbide was running out of adequate level ground to dispose of its mill tailings. After the Club Ranch tailings ponds proved decreasingly effective in 1976, the company constructed 5 acres of new ponds at a cost of $170,000. Located on Club Mesa behind the mill and above the town, the new tailings piles seemed to provide new dumping space but increasingly became another source of problems. As production continued over the next three years and the tailings accumulated, concerns developed over the high levels of radiation and radon emanating from the piles.[44]

Moab faced similar but much smaller problems. In May 1976 the Nuclear Regulatory Commission (NRC) released the final environmental impact statement for the new Rio Algom mill. In this publication the mining company agreed to provide funds to facilitate the reclamation, stabilization, and maintenance of all properties for 50 years after decommissioning.[45] Because of its location near the Colorado River and its closeness to Moab, the Atlas mill was also a target for environmental concern. In 1976 the NRC briefly closed the mill because its mill tailings were leaking into the Colorado River.[46]

Despite these new environmental concerns, by 1979 it appeared that the uranium market had made a very successful transition from the government program to the commercial market. Yellowcake prices had grown from seven dollars to forty-three dollars per pound, lower- and lower-grade ores were becoming profitable, and the uranium towns were prospering. Jeffrey City was changing from company town to real city, and Grants reestablished itself as the uranium capital. Moab and Uravan, although not booming, were operating at peak production. The future seemed so bright, in fact, that Congress began to worry that domestic uranium production would never sustain future demand. In response, in 1974 it had relaxed the embargo on uranium imports to ensure that U.S. power plants would have enough fuel.[47]

Then the uranium market crashed as a result of oversupply. Although nuclear fuel projections had been downgraded in previous years, industry officials had believed using lower-grade ores would keep mining production strong. But as Americans reconsidered the role of nuclear energy after Three Mile Island, utility companies put on hold orders for new power plants. As yellowcake demand evaporated, the industry moved from apparent shortages to abundance, and the price plummeted. In 1977 uranium sold for almost fifty dollars per pound; by 1982 it was half that. For mining companies the falling price occurred just as increasing environmental concerns and diminishing ore grades were driving up operational costs. This deadly combination left domestic producers at risk of losing their market altogether to low-cost imports and utilities dumping their stockpiles into the market. As the collapse spread, the yellowcake communities learned quickly how uranium dependent they had once again become.[48]

Uranium companies responded to the reduced prices by cutting back on labor. In Jeffrey City, Western Nuclear laid off 118 employees in August 1980 and another 244 the following June. The president of Western Nuclear announced that the layoffs were necessitated by reduced demand and depressed prices caused by delays in the construction of domestic nuclear power plants. In 1980 the workforce had peaked at 554; by the end of 1982 it was down to 47.[49] The 8,000 Grants uranium workers, spread through 45 mines and 5 processing mills, faced similar problems. Citing the depressed uranium market, United Nuclear closed some of its mines in 1979. The following year companies discontinued work in 9 more mines. In 1981, 7 more were closed. By 1982, many of the area's mines—including Anaconda's Jackpile mine, in operation since the early 1950s—were closed.[50] These closures meant that roughly half of the area's uranium workers had been released.[51]

The effects of the uranium layoffs immediately impacted the yellowcake communities and reverberated through their uranium-dependent economies. For the one-industry town Jeffrey City, the bust was devastating. With no other major employer for miles, people who had lost their jobs packed up and left town. Post office records indicate that 243 heads of households vacated between the August 1980 layoffs and the end of the year. Another 266 filed change of address forms over the next six months.[52]

In June 1981 the Jeffrey City school board, expecting a loss of at least 250 students in the fall, terminated the contracts of 11 certified teachers. To speed paperwork, the local Job Service District scheduled a mass unemployment sign-up for all laid-off employees, but only 56 people came. By the end of the summer the *News* had folded, and some local businesses reported losses in commerce of up to 60 percent.[53] By the end of 1981 another 333 people had left town. Many stayed in Wyoming, although almost half of the departing 842 left the state.[54] By the summer of 1982 one writer suggested that Jeffrey City's streets were "as quiet as the streets in the movie *On the Beach,* after the human race has just fallen asleep for good."[55]

The story was just as bad in Grants. Mine closures and layoffs produced cutbacks that multiplied throughout the community. Mining support companies like drilling and equipment sales were the first hit, but soon all aspects of the economy were in a decline. In 1983 unemployment in the community reached 30 percent. School enrollment declined 30 percent, leading to the dismissal of 57 staff members. Housing, which had always experienced severe shortages, quickly became abundant as people began leaving town; homes purchased for $70,000 could not be sold at one-third that amount. All of this strained local government and forced Grants to cut budgets and begin desperate searches for new employment possibilities. The combined losses of jobs and home equity put tremendous pressure on many in the community, and school counselors created special programs to help elementary students cope with the change.[56]

In 1985 the last major uranium employer dealt a death blow to the uranium capital when it closed operations. On 16 January Kerr-McGee, then operating as Quivira Mining Company, closed its mines and mill at Ambrosia Lake. The following day another company that sent its ore to

Quivira closed its mine. These closings forced the layoffs of another 540 people and created more problems for the community. With professional people leaving and more than 200 houses for sale, the Grants *Daily Beacon* symbolically removed the uranium symbol and motto "Uranium Capital" from its banner.[57]

In addition to the depressed market, Uravan faced expanding environmental concerns. Despite the Three Mile Island incident in March 1979, Union Carbide officials had reported that yellowcake production would reach all-time highs that fall. The following spring, however, growing environmental worries called into question the fate of the community. The problems began with the tailings piles. In late December 1979 the Colorado Department of Health ordered Union Carbide to stop putting tailings in Pond 2 on Club Mesa above the town.[58] Almost three weeks later the company was ordered not to use nearby Pond 3 for similar reasons. With no place to deposit its mill refuse, the company closed its processing plant for four days until a temporary solution could be worked out.[59]

The growing fear of radiation and radon gas also beset Uravan. Because of the location and longevity of the mill, radiation levels were sometimes ten times the Environmental Protection Agency's (EPA) standard of 25 millirems per year. Another problem was radon, a by-product of uranium decomposition, which often collected in closed-off places such as mines and emitted from tailings piles. Because it contributed to lung cancer, the EPA had set maximum safety levels. When readings in Uravan reached ten times that amount, Union Carbide officials became worried.[60]

These growing environmental problems came just as yellowcake prices were tumbling. Company officials spent $12 million to stabilize the tailings ponds and believed a $2 million project would effectively control radiation levels. But if the radon measures could not be controlled economically, the town would have to be shut down.[61] In the spring of 1981 Union Carbide closed the Uravan mill for the first time since 1949 but promised to reopen it that fall. Citing the depressed uranium market as the cause, the company laid off half of its 180 mill workers. To minimize problems, the Colorado Department of Labor and Employment established unemployment sign-ups in the community. Finally, Union Carbide reminded workers that it had earlier signed an agreement with a Blanding, Utah, mill in case regulatory licensing prevented the company from meeting its contract commitments.[62]

Over the next two years the declining price of yellowcake continued to cause problems in Uravan. After reopening the mill and rehiring 75 percent of its furloughed workers in the fall of 1981, Union Carbide suspended production again the following summer. Another 60 employees lost their jobs when some independent mines closed.[63] The closures had a trickle-down effect on the area. One community leader reported that "it just sort of snowballed. First the miners were laid off, then the mill workers, then the truckers, then the waitresses." All told, 700 uranium jobs and 200 others—nearly 50 percent of employment in the area—were lost.[64] When the Uravan mill reopened in the spring of 1983, the attitude had changed to pessimism. With the continued decline in yellowcake prices and Union Carbide's ongoing environmental problems, many of the returning 80 mill workers realized that their jobs might be short-lived.[65]

Although it had diversified its economic base with tourism, Moab was not immune to the effects of the second uranium bust. In the fall of 1979 Atlas Corporation, owner of the Moab mill, reported that it intended to keep its 470 workers employed despite the Three Mile Island incident.[66] Two years later, however, the decline began when the Rio Algom mine-mill complex southeast of town laid off half of its 260 workers after its major customer, Duke Power, suspended purchases.[67] In January 1982 Atlas reversed its position and succumbed to the deteriorating market by releasing 175 miners and millers.[68]

By the end of 1982, the terminations began to affect the community. Unemployment rates doubled, and sales dropped almost 7 percent. Real estate prices tumbled. In response to the slowdown, the city budget was cut 22 percent.[69] In March 1984 Atlas closed the remainder of its mines and the Moab mill. Unemployment rates increased to 15 percent despite a decrease in Moab's population by 441 people since 1980. School enrollment fell by about 25 percent after rebounding to almost 2,000 students during the boom year of 1977.[70]

Moab's community leaders increasingly looked to tourism as the uranium industry dwindled. Commercials advertising the area were aired on Salt Lake City television stations, visitation increased at the area's national parks, mountain bicycling took hold, and the chamber of commerce even began a promotion touting the city dump as America's "most scenic."[71] In October 1988 Rio Algom closed its operations, and Moab's uranium industry was dead.[72] In a critical editorial, *Times-Independent* editor Sam Taylor called the closing the "end of an age that had lasted longer than anyone had imagined it would back in 1957." He said it was time for Moab's residents to "move on to other things."[73]

The yellowcake towns had a difficult time withdrawing from uranium and moving on to "other things." In every community, townspeople tried to publicize their economic plight. In June 1981 departing residents of Jeffrey

Signs at Atlas mill, Moab, Utah. The Atlas mill operated in Moab from 1955 to 1984. Since its closure, the 13 million ton tailings pile on the banks of the Colorado River, seen here against the background hills, has been a point of contention among environmentalists. Although the federal government has agreed to move the pile, there is currently no budget to do so. Photo by Michael Amundson, 2001.

City assembled on the company-owned town green for a community-wide garage sale.[74] At about the same time, Moab community leaders sponsored a "Uranium Rally" to gather government and private-sector support for the industry.[75] But instead of gathering support for their predicament, these actions clearly showed their lingering uranium dependencies.

By the mid-1980s about the only visible reminders of the once booming uranium industry were the huge piles of radioactive tailings outside the closed mills. Only 4 to 6 pounds of yellowcake were produced from each ton of ore, so these piles quickly became mountains. For the yellowcake communities, the reclamation of these wastes beginning in the mid-1980s opened the third phase of the commercial period.

As the uranium industry collapsed, the federal government reemerged as a major player in the yellowcake communities. But this time Uncle Sam was the primary environmental regulator. And instead of a boom, reclamation provided only a handful of jobs. Under the Uranium Mill Tailings Radiation Control Act of 1978, only mills that had sold uranium exclusively to the AEC prior to 1971, so-called Title I plants, were eligible for federal cleanup. Of the mills in this study, only one, the Phillips mill at Ambrosia Lake, qualified under Title I.[76]

The federal government offered no help to companies that had continued to produce yellowcake into the commercial period—including three in the Grants area and the major ones in Moab, Uravan, and Jeffrey City. These Title II companies would have to pay their own remediation costs. When those costs skyrocketed, the Title II companies argued that portions of their tailings had been made while under contract to the AEC and therefore should be partially paid for by the government. Subsequently, the General Accounting Office advised Congress that the government had a "strong moral responsibility" to assist in the cleanup of the remaining active "commingled" tailings and mill sites. After more than a decade of debate, the National Energy Policy Act of 1992 established an annual congressional appropriation to assist companies in reclaiming commingled sites.[77]

Uravan had the biggest tailings problem. After five years of trying to solve environmental problems, in 1984 Umetco Minerals, a Union Carbide subsidiary, agreed in principle to begin a multimillion-dollar remediation of the 12.5 million tons of tailings on the site. As the company complained of increasing environmental regulations, representatives of the Colorado Department of Health were embarrassed that the department still had not finalized the company's 1975 license renewal. To ensure that the site would be remediated even if Umetco left, Union Carbide had to post a $25 million bond. The process included removing any solid waste from the evaporation ponds and moving it to the tailings piles above the town. The piles would then be entombed with a 3-foot layer of clay, dirt, and crushed rock. Finally, the company would have to dig wells to monitor the radioactivity of groundwater.[78]

Although the agreement did not preclude mill operations, the continued yellowcake depression had kept the plant only partially operational since 1981. In 1984 the company officially closed the mill, and most residents had left by that December. Many who had lived in the town without documented health effects were upset that they had to leave. Over the next two years most buildings were either sold and removed or dismantled. The few people who stayed were forbidden to plant gardens in the radioactive soil.[79]

Two years later Union Carbide began a decade-long battle to decide who would provide the remediation funds. After reaching a Superfund agreement with the state of Colorado in 1986 under which the company would pay for the then $42 million project, Union Carbide began a fifteen-year cleanup. As part of this program, Uravan would officially close in 1988, and Umetco would then level the town and return it to its pre-mining and milling condition. Unwilling to shoulder the enormous cost by itself, Union Carbide sued the federal government for assistance, arguing that 55 percent of its commingled tailings had been produced for the AEC.[80]

The remediation at Grants, although not centered in the town, was similarly imposing because of the area's five operating mills. At the area's oldest mill, the Anaconda plant at Bluewater, 24 million tons of waste occupied over 340 acres. At the United Nuclear–Homestake Partners complex north of Grants, the Homestake–New Mexico Partners tailings pile contained 1.24 million tons of solids in a 40-acre area. Adjacent to this site, the Homestake-Sapin mill had produced a 20 million ton, 170-acre pile.[81]

The environmental devastation continued north of Grants at Ambrosia Lake. At the Phillips mill, the only one to close before the commercial market period, 2.6 million tons of tailings were spread out over 105 acres at an average thickness of 12 feet. Two and a-half miles west of Phillips sat the Kerr-McGee mill and the largest tailings pile in the United States. Covering 400 acres at a height of about 90 feet, the 30 million ton mound was described as a manmade mesa.[82]

Only the Phillips mill qualified for federal remediation as a Title I Uranium Mill Tailings Remedial Action Project (UMTRA),[83] so the other four plants and their tailings were left for their last owners to reclaim. Remediation projects began on these site in the early 1980s, but rising costs and continued commingled claims caused the work to continue into the 1990s.[84]

Moab's Atlas mill provided an analogous but lesser problem. Although the mill had been the only one in town, the presence of its 100 foot-high, 10 million ton tailings pile along the banks of the Colorado River above town caused much alarm. After Atlas offered $5 million to cap the pile and leave it in place, many argued it should be moved before a major flood destroyed it. Another group contended that trying to move such a mound would release dangerous materials into the air. Over the next decade the decision remained unresolved. In 1994 the NRC called for a separate environmental impact statement for the commingled tailings.[85] Finally, in February 2000 the federal government agreed to spend more than $150 million to move the pile.[86]

Jeffrey City's isolation, the very reason the town had originally been created, made its tailings problem the least serious of the yellowcake towns.

Located north of town, the commingled wastes stood 28 feet high, weighed almost 8 million tons, and covered 167 acres. To prevent the material from blowing away in the nearly constant Wyoming wind, Western Nuclear maintains a small crew to water down the wastes.[87]

Although debates continued over who should pay for the reclamation of the tailings, this phase of the commercial period brought little sustenance to the yellowcake towns. In Uravan, only a skeleton crew worked on the cleanup effort, and no one was allowed to live in town. In Jeffrey City workers chose not to live in the town rather than being barred from it. In Grants, although the presence of four remediation projects has provided a few jobs, no reclamation boom has occurred. Finally, nearly twenty years after closing, the Atlas mill in Moab remains at the center of debate over whether to cap the pile in place or move it 18 miles north of town.[88]

The yellowcake towns have taken similar paths in their efforts to rebound from the uranium bust. Three of the four communities tried to become nuclear waste sites as a means of providing new jobs.[89] When these efforts failed, the towns looked to diversify their economies through increasing government jobs and tourism. Their success has been varied. In Moab, tourism has become the "new uranium" and has once again put the town on the national map. With internationally renowned bicycling and scenery, Moab has succeeded to the point that some residents worry that newcomers and tourists will destroy that which brought them to the town.[90] Grants has also recovered—although not as quickly as Moab—thanks to the construction of three state prisons, a uranium mining museum, and increased tourism.[91]

Jeffrey City and Uravan have been less fortunate. In Jeffrey City most houses were sold and carted off after Western Nuclear sold the town in 1988. Plans to build a prison or retirement center on the site have largely failed. With weeds growing through its streets, Jeffrey City has become typical of mining boom-and-bust towns throughout the West.[92] Uravan is in even worse shape. As reclamation proceeds, every building in town except the original boardinghouse and recreational hall has been removed. Within a few years the entire valley will be restored to its pre-mining condition.[93]

By 1988, uranium mining in the United States was practically dead, and the dependent yellowcake towns felt like victims of a recurring nightmare. In the 1950s they had created an industry from scratch to help national defense, only to see it quickly exceed demand and decline. In the 1960s the yellowcake communities survived a major depression and boomed again, providing uranium fuel for nuclear power in the 1970s. But this new source also fell prey to a combination of oversupply and environmental

Grants Mining Museum and Chamber of Commerce. The Grants Mining Museum offers one of the few examples of uranium cultural heritage tourism. Visitors start at ground level and then descend by elevator into a replicated uranium mine. The self-guided tour shows the complete mining process. Photo by Michael Amundson, 2001.

concerns in the 1980s. Hurt, bitter, and unsettled, the inhabitants of the yellowcake communities were unsure why their source of livelihood had fallen apart so abruptly, and few found solace in knowing they shared much—most notably, the impact of increasing environmental regulation and the rise of the global market—with other U.S. mining and energy towns. When the Cold War ended in 1989, their situations went from bad to worse.[94]

Notes

1. Michael A. Amundson, "Uncle Sam and the Yellowcake Towns: The Effects of Federal Policy on Four Uranium Mining Communities, 1943–1988," unpublished Ph.D. diss., University of Nebraska, 1996, 72–87.
2. Ibid., 199–201, 203–204.
3. Deborah Frazier, "Uranium Wasteland Awaits Rebirth: Company Deserts Town, but Radioactive Refuse Remains," *Rocky Mountain News*, 19 February 1984, 20.

4. Deborah Frazier, "Era Ends With Closing, Cleanup of Uravan Uranium Mill," *Rocky Mountain News,* 26 July 1993, 8A.
5. U.S. Energy Research and Development Administration, *Statistical Data of the Uranium Industry* (Grand Junction, Colo.: Government Printing Office [GPO], 1976), 16.
6. Middle Rio Grande Council of Governments of New Mexico, *Summary Report: A Guide for Future Growth and Development of City of Grants and Village of Milan in Valencia County, New Mexico* (Albuquerque: 1971).
7. Richard A. Firmage, *A History of Grand County,* Utah Centennial County History Series (Salt Lake City: Utah State Historical Society, 1996), 361.
8. "Western Nuclear Gets $14 Million of Orders for Uranium Concentrate," *Wall Street Journal,* 22 December 1966; "A Resume: Colorado Plateau Operations Mining and Metals Division, Union Carbide Corporation" (Grand Junction, Colo.: 1970), on file at Umetco Minerals, Grand Junction, Colorado.
9. June H. Taylor and Michael D. Yokell, *Yellowcake: The International Uranium Cartel* (New York: Pergamon, 1979), 102.
10. Because Jeffrey City continued to be a fast-growing, quasi-company town, population figures are difficult to obtain. *In Wyoming* magazine suggested that the town's population was 4,500 in 1980, and the figures used here are from various issues of the Jeffrey City *News.* See "U_3O_8: Energy From Wyoming's Powerful Sand," *In Wyoming* (February-March 1980): 49.
11. Department of Finance and Administration, State Planning Division, *Cibola County Growth Management and Housing Plan* (Santa Fe: 1982), 38.
12. Wyoming State Mine Inspector, *Annual Report of the Wyoming State Mine Inspector* (Cheyenne: 1970–1977); "Enrollment Records of the Jeffrey City School, 1967–1992," on file at the Jeffrey City School. Postal records are from the Jeffrey City Post Office, *Change of Address Form Book, 1969–1985,* on file at the Jeffrey City Post Office (hereafter JCPO).
13. Office of the State Inspector of Mines, *Annual Report by the State Inspector of Mines to the Governor of the State of New Mexico* (Albuquerque: 1970–1977) (hereafter State Inspector, *New Mexico*); Department of Finance and Administration, *Cibola County Growth Management*; Energy and Minerals Department, Bureau of Mines Inspection, *Annual Report by the Energy and Minerals Department, Bureau of Mines Inspection, to the Governor of the State of New Mexico* (Albuquerque: 1982–1985).
14. A complete set of the Jeffrey City *News* is housed at the Jeffrey City School.
15. Department of Finance and Administration, *Cibola County Growth Management.*
16. "Green Mtn. Village Development Begins," Jeffrey City *News,* 9 June 1977. The story stated that Western Nuclear contributed $1.3 million to Jeffrey City expansion in the summer of 1977 alone.
17. *Crook's Peak Quadrangle, Fremont County Wyoming,* map (Denver: U.S. Geological Survey, 7.5 Minute Series, 1961), and photo-revised (1984).

18. Department of Finance and Administration, *Cibola County Growth Management.*

19. "City Limits to More Than Double Under Annex Plan," Grants *Daily Beacon,* 19 October 1977.

20. Robert Locke, "Grants Uranium Boom Comes to Life Again," Albuquerque *Tribune,* 5 December 1976; Olen Leonard and Lay James Gibson, "Towns of Strangers: Social Structure and the Miner Subculture in the Uranium Belt of Northwestern New Mexico," report of the Bureau of Indian Affairs San Juan Basin Region Uranium Study. Albuquerque: 1978.

21. Toby Smith, "Grants—Boomtown!" *New Mexico Magazine* (September 1979): 54–61.

22. "Jeffrey City Enrollment"; Sam Peterson Jr., interview by author, 13 May 1992.

23. Office of the Associate Superintendent for Curriculum and Accountability, "History of Enrollment for the Past 38 Years at the 180th School Day," in *Cibola County Schools 1991–92 Accountability Report,* on file at Cibola County Schools Main Office, Grants, New Mexico (hereafter *Grants Enrollment*).

24. Sue Winsor, "Centennial, 1882–1982: Grants Station, New Mexico Territory to Grants, New Mexico," Grants *Daily Beacon,* 30 April 1982.

25. Robert W. Righter, *The Making of a Town: Wright, Wyoming* (Boulder: Roberts Rinehart, 1985), 3–5.

26. Locke, "Boom Comes to Life."

27. Gary W. Malamud, *Boomtown Communities,* Environmental Design Series, ed. Richard P. Dober (New York: Van Nostrand Reinhold, 1984); V. Edward Bates, "The Impact of Energy Boom-Town Growth on Rural Areas," *Social Casework* 59, no. 2 (February 1978): 73–82; John S. Gilmore, "Boom Towns May Hinder Energy Resource Development," *Science* 191, no. 4227 (February 1976): 535–540; R. L. Little, "Some Social Consequences of Boom Towns," *North Dakota Law Review* 53, no. 3 (1977): 401–425.

28. Richard Fairservis, interview with author, 22 September 1993.

29. Department of Finance and Administration, *Cibola County Growth Management,* 57–59.

30. "King Enacts Cibola County Bill," Albuquerque *Journal,* 18 March 1981; Alley Sanchez, "Newborn Cibola County off to Enthusiastic Start," Albuquerque *Journal,* 19 March 1981.

31. Lee Lockhart, "Big News: Wyoming's Newest Newspaper," Jeffrey City *News,* 26 May 1977.

32. A city directory was printed on the back page of the 27 October 1977 edition of the Jeffrey City *News.*

33. "Uranium: Multibillion-Dollar Industry Predicted for NM; 100,000 Population for Grants," Albuquerque *Tribune,* 25 May 1976.

34. Middle Rio Grand Council of Governments of New Mexico, *Population Projections and Allocations for Grants and Milan* (Albuquerque: 1977).

35. U.S. Department of the Interior, San Juan Basin Regional Uranium Study, *Uranium Development in the San Juan Basin Region: A Report on Environmental Issues, Final Edition* (Albuquerque: Bureau of Indian Affairs, 1980), I-7 (hereafter UDSJBR).

36. Quality Development Associates, *Wyoming's Uranium Industry—Status, Impacts, and Trends* (Cheyenne: Wyoming State Department of Economic Planning and Development, Mineral Division, 1978). Even the conservative estimate suggested a leveling in the $55–$60/lb range.

37. Wyoming Department of Labor and Statistics, *Wyoming: The Uranium Industry, a Manpower Survey 1979* (Cheyenne: Wyoming Department of Labor and Statistics, 1979).

38. UDSJBR, I-11.

39. "Rio Algom Mines: Firm to Expand Utah Mill," Salt Lake City *Tribune,* 16 April 1974; "Uranium-Atlas Continue to Play a Key Role in the Economy of Southeastern Utah," Moab *Times-Independent,* 21 August 1975.

40. Raye C. Ringholz, *Uranium Frenzy: Boom and Bust on the Colorado Plateau* (New York: W. W. Norton, 1989), 267–269.

41. Both ventures were operated by Steen's son Andy. See "American Museum of Mining History Scheduled for Opening Soon in Moab," Moab *Times-Independent,* 14 August 1975; Firmage, *Grand County,* 358.

42. The motto "Uranium Capital of the World" was dropped on 28 February 1963 and the uranium symbol on 28 February 1975. During the height of the commercial boom in the late 1970s, the paper did run a special column on the uranium industry.

43. Bob Silbernagel, "Recent Spills Reveal Waste Problem," Grand Junction *Sentinel,* 9 November 1980.

44. "Employment, Spending Increase During 1975 at Union Carbide Tri-State Area of Operations," Moab *Times-Independent,* 12 February 1976.

45. "After Years, the Final Environmental Statement Issued for Rio Algom," Moab *Times-Independent,* 6 May 1976.

46. "NRC Issues Draft Environmental Statement on Atlas Uranium Mill," Moab *Times-Independent,* 15 December 1977.

47. U.S. Congress, Joint Committee on Atomic Energy, *Proposed Modification of Restrictions on Enrichment of Foreign Uranium for Domestic Use: Hearings Before the Joint Committee on Atomic Energy,* 93rd Cong., 2d sess. (Washington, D.C.: GPO, 17–18 September 1974), 235–236.

48. Anthony David Owen, *The Economics of Uranium* (New York: Praeger, 1985), 54–55.

49. Paul Menser, editor of the Jeffrey City *News,* wrote these articles tracing the layoffs: "Western Nuclear Warns of Layoff," 28 May 1981; "244 Workers Laid off by Western Nuclear Today," Jeffrey City *News Extra,* 4 June 1981. A year later Menser wrote "Jeffrey City: The Slow Death of a Boom Town" for the

Casper *Star-Tribune*, 28 March 1982, 64th Annual Wyoming Chronicle Community and Recreation Edition, 8.

50. Department of Finance and Administration, *Cibola County Growth Management*, 32.

51. State Inspector, *New Mexico*.

52. JCPO; Michael A. Amundson, "Home on the Range No More: The Boom and Bust of a Wyoming Uranium Town, 1957–1988," *Western Historical Quarterly* 26 (winter 1995): 483–505.

53. The 18 June 1981 edition of the Jeffrey City *News* contained a variety of articles related to the bust, including "Laid off Teachers to Receive Money From School District," "Unemployment Sign up Wednesday," and "Jeffrey City 'Booms' With Activity Over Weekend." On the loss of commerce, see Richard D. Lamm and Michael McCarthy, *The Angry West: A Vulnerable Land and Its Future* (Boston: Houghton Mifflin, 1982), 101.

54. JCPO; Amundson, "No Longer."

55. Geoffrey O'Gara, "Jeffrey City's Ghosts," *Western Energy Magazine* (July 1982): 25–29.

56. Sue Major Holmes, "Kerr-McGee Mine Closure Deals 'Death Blow' to Grants," Albuquerque *Journal*, 10 February 1985; Abe M. Peña, "Coming Back From the Brink," in "Cibola County Profile," *New Mexico Business Journal* (June 1992); *The Illustrated Daily: Profile of Grants, New Mexico,* prod. Karl Kernberger, 7 March 1985, videocassette; *The Illustrated Daily: Mining in New Mexico,* prod. Karl Kernberger, 25 April 1985, videocassette.

57. Holmes, "Death Blow."

58. The Nuclear Regulatory Commission, beginning in 1968, allowed several western states, including Colorado and New Mexico, to regulate and license mills in their states. They were known as "Agreement" states.

59. Ellen Wheeler, "Radioactive Tailings Focus of Debate: Future of Mill and Town at Stake," *Rocky Mountain News,* 23 March 1980.

60. Sheri Poe Bernard, "Expected EPA Rules Could Rub out Uravan," Grand Junction *Sentinel,* 9 November 1980.

61. Ibid.; Sheri Poe Bernard, "Uranium Travels Grim-Looking Path Into 'Yellowcake,'" Grand Junction *Sentinel,* 9 November 1980.

62. "Uravan Uranium Mills Face Spring Shut Down," Telluride (Colorado) *Times,* 4 December 1980.

63. Bob Silbernagel, "West End Problems Linked to Depressed Uranium Market in '80s," Grand Junction *Sentinel,* n.d. [1982].

64. Ibid.

65. Bob Silbernagel, "Uranium Mill Reopening Lifts Spirits," Grand Junction *Sentinel,* 18 May 1983.

66. Robert H. Woody, "Atlas Still Looks Strong," Salt Lake City *Tribune,* 10 November 1979.

67. Robert H. Woody, "Moab Looks Ahead to Bright Future," Salt Lake City *Tribune,* 16 October 1981.
68. Robert H. Woody, "Atlas Forced to Cut Uranium Works," Salt Lake City *Tribune,* 7 January 1982.
69. Bette Stanton, *Moab and Grand County Community Profile* (Moab: Grand County Economic and Community Development, 1992), 3–4.
70. *Moab Enrollment;* Firmage, *Grand County,* 381–383; William L. Chenoweth, "A History of Uranium Production in Utah," *Energy and Mineral Resources of Utah.* Utah Geological Association Publication 18 (1990): 123.
71. Conrad Walters, "City Puts Worst Foot Forward: Moab Says Rubbish to Any Town Thinking It Has Prettier Dump," Salt Lake City *Tribune,* 12 October 1986.
72. Firmage, *Grand County,* 384–392.
73. Quoted in ibid., 392.
74. Paul Menser, "Where's My Winnebago," Jeffrey City *News,* 18 June 1981.
75. Firmage, *Grand County,* 381–383.
76. Uranium Mill Tailings Radiation Control Act of 1978, *Statutes at Large* 92 1978), 3021; American Mining Congress, "Commingled Uranium Mill Tailings—A Historical Perspective," report (Washington, D.C.: American Mining Congress, 4 March 1985).
77. American Mining Congress, "Commingled Uranium Mill Tailings"; Energy Policy Act of 1992 (P.L. 102-486), *U.S. Statutes at Large,* 106 Stat. 2776.
78. Deborah Frazier, "Uranium Wasteland Awaits Rebirth: Company Deserts Town, but Radioactive Refuse Remains," *Rocky Mountain News,* 19 February 1984.
79. Ibid.; Kit Miniclier, "Glow of Atomic Age Dims in Uravan," Denver *Post,* 19 January 1986.
80. Lou Chapman, "Cleaning up Uravan to Cost Union Carbide $42 Million," Denver *Post,* 1 November 1986.
81. These figure are from Holger Albrethsen and Frank E. McGinley, *Summary History of Domestic Uranium Procurement Under U.S. Atomic Energy Commission Contracts: Final Report* (Grand Junction, Colo.: U.S. Department of Energy, 1982), A-54, A-58, A-63.
82. Ibid., A-47, A-51; Sherry Robinson, "Push Turns to Shove," Albuquerque *Journal,* 8 April 1990.
83. UMTRA is the federal agency that performs the remediation on Title I sites.
84. Jim Carrier, "Atomic Legacy Cleanup: Heavy Metal," Denver *Post,* 1 August 1995.
85. Albrethsen and McGinley, *Summary History,* A-89; Firmage, *Grand County,* 390–414.
86. Leon Drouin Keith, "Pact Signed to Remove Uranium From Path of Colorado River," Arizona *Daily Sun,* 12 February 2000.

87. Albrethsen and McGinley, *Summary History,* A-121; Amundson, "No Longer."

88. "Moab Uranium Tailings Near River Called a 'Time Bomb,'" Salt Lake *Tribune,* 31 July 1999.

89. For Uravan, see Katie Kerwin, "Tailings Dump Site Worries Group," *Rocky Mountain News,* 8 January 1994. The story on Jeffrey City is in "Nuclear Waste Proposal Killed," Denver *Post,* 22 August 1992, B2. Moab's controversy is covered in Firmage, *Grand County,* 377–378, 381; and Raye C. Ringholz, *Little Town Blues: Voices From the Changing West* (Salt Lake City: Peregrine Smith, 1992), 44–46.

90. Firmage, *Grand County,* 413–417; Ringholz, *Little Town Blues,* 47–49.

91. Peña, "Coming Back."

92. Amundson, "No Longer."

93. William L. Chenoweth, interview by author, 25 May 1996.

94. Duane A. Smith, *Mining America: The Industry and the Environment* (Niwot: University Press of Colorado, 1993), 163–170; Michael Malone, "The Collapse of Western Metal Mining: An Historical Epitaph," *Pacific Historical Review* 55, no. 3 (August 1986): 455–464.

Chapter 10

Conclusion

In her important book *The Legacy of Conquest,* Patricia Limerick noted that in the American West the past and present often appeared so different that it was impossible to see the many elements holding the two together. Although the notion of cowboys using computers seemed at odds with our traditional vision of the West, Limerick suggested in what she called the "persistence of continuity," that many elements of the past "were still dominant, even if they came in different clothes and in different vehicles."[1]

In much the same way, the uranium industry and the yellowcake towns appear out of place in the romantic West. The jump from modern mining of carnotite ore as a ceramic pigment to the postmodern removal of pitchblende for atomic bombs appears to be the ultimate machine in the garden of the American West.[2] But as Limerick suggested, the present can offer connections to the past, and the uranium industry offers important links to the history of both yellowcake towns and the American West.

Conclusion

Since the bust of the commercial market in the early 1980s, the uranium industry has remained inviable as it suffered through a continued depression. Uranium prices, exploration, production, and employment have dropped significantly. The federal government has offered no quotas, embargo on imports, or stretch-out contracts. This bleak picture appears to be an anomaly in uranium's colorful past. But the bust of the 1980s and 1990s shares some important attributes with the uranium market of the 1960s and western metal mining in general.[3]

Two trends that have persisted since the stretch-out period are closings and consolidation. After the plethora of closings in the 1980s described in Chapter 9, the last underground mines went on standby in early 1991, the final open pit mine closed in mid–1992, and the last conventional uranium mill terminated operations in December 1992. Consolidation also occurred frequently as companies looked to cut their losses by selling out. Since the bust, firms like General Atomics, Rio Algom Mining Corporation, and U.S. Energy Corporation have expanded their holdings at discount prices.[4]

Another connection to stretch-out economics has been increased efficiency. With yellowcake prices as low as seven dollars per pound in the early 1990s, U.S. companies were forced to adopt cheaper methods to compete in the global market. With little overhead, in situ techniques like solution, mine water, and by-product mining have succeeded on a small scale. In the first case, solutions pumped into the ground leach uranium from known deposits, and the uranium-rich mixture is pumped back to the surface and refined as yellowcake. In mine water production, naturally occurring water circulating through inactive mines is pumped to the surface where the uranium is separated. Yellowcake is also produced as a by-product from phosphate mining. Although these methods produce far less material than traditional mining techniques, they require a fairly small amount of equipment and few workers, thus making them cost-effective enough to compete in the dismal market.[5]

An important break from the past has been the increasing dependency on foreign uranium. Since the end of the embargo in 1983, the use of imported uranium has greatly expanded. From a low of 26 percent of domestic purchases in 1983, imports accounted for as much as 80 percent of the market in 1990. Although projections suggest that the completion of current contracts with importers will reduce U.S. dependency, continued low prices could exclude most U.S. companies from the competition.[6]

A major source of imports and another significant variation in historical patterns surfaced in late 1992 when the U.S. government negotiated with Russia and five other former Soviet republics to purchase uranium for

U.S. nuclear plants.[7] Although many U.S. officials saw the move as an effort to stabilize the Russian economy and the Yeltsin government, uranium producers in the United States argued that the former communist country was dumping uranium at prices below U.S. production costs. Further, Canadian officials challenged the pact under the North American Free Trade Agreement (NAFTA). Canada, which supplied 24 percent of the U.S. demand, unsuccessfully contended that the Russian-American agreement would squeeze all other foreign producers out of the U.S. market.[8]

As this latest chapter in the uranium saga is played out, the remaining yellowcake towns watch uranium prices in hopes of a comeback. Although the absence of operable mills in Uravan and Moab makes their prospects of returning to yellowcake dependency dim, Jeffrey City and Grants—each with one of few remaining functioning mills—have the capability to produce uranium again. Indeed, sporadic upturns in the price of yellowcake, combined with government approval of an environmental impact statement for a new mine, have rekindled hope in Jeffrey City for a potential uranium future.[9] The prospects are still uncertain, but the recurring faith that outside forces will resurrect the community suggests a continuity that links the yellowcake towns with major themes in the history of the American West.

The first of these ties is colonialism. Throughout the history of uranium production, outside forces controlled the fate of the yellowcake towns. The most obvious agent was the federal government. A brief recounting of history shows that during the first half of this relationship, the federal role was positive.

Beginning in 1943, the government sponsored the first yellowcake communities through the Manhattan Project. The creation of a private industry in 1946 under the Atomic Energy Commission's (AEC) incentives and subsidized market program impacted more areas. When boomtowns were created, the government provided special funding for schools and infrastructure to help offset the problems created by growth. When the tremendous growth of the industry exceeded government supplies in the late 1950s, the AEC created the allocation and stretch-out programs to keep the industry and its dependent communities alive until private power companies could take over. To ensure survival, Washington also initiated an embargo on foreign uranium purchases and passed legislation to guarantee a "viable domestic industry."

The end of the government buying program in 1970 also ended the image of the government as benevolent protector of the uranium industry. Increasingly, the yellowcake communities suffered as federally sponsored and enforced environmental laws made uranium mining and milling more and more expensive. After the commercial boom began in 1974, the inception of the split tails program and the reduction of the enrichment embargo seemed to threaten domestic producers. As supplies increased, the lack of government intervention set the industry up for a potential bust.

After the Three Mile Island incident in March 1979, increased government regulation of nuclear reactors combined with oversupply to create a second bust. With no federal watchdog, the towns collapsed. When uranium companies sued, demanding import restrictions to aid the market, the federal government decided the industry was no longer viable, thereby ensuring the towns' demise. Then, when uranium was no longer mined in any of the yellowcake communities, the federal government dictated how the tailings piles would be remediated. To offset the losses, the government offered the towns prospects of long-term jobs in nuclear storage. Finally, in a move designed to aid international relations, the federal government okayed the purchase of cheap Russian uranium for U.S. reactors. In short, the federal government encouraged the creation, expansion, overproduction, and demise of the U.S. uranium industry and the towns that supported it.

Another important colonial agent was the boom and bust of the free market. Like nearly every other commodity-based community, the yellowcake towns were creatures of market prices that were beyond their control. As long as uranium prices were high, the low-grade U.S. ore could compete. But when oversupply drove prices down, the yellowcake towns learned—as had other U.S. industries such as steel, oil, and automobile manufacturing—that other countries could offer less expensive products.

The history of the yellowcake towns also provides a meaningful correlation with the history of mining and the environment in the American West. Although uranium was far different than anything mined previously, the 1950s rush offered several connections to mining's past. Stories of Charlie Steen's uranium adventure invoke strong connections to the past. Similarly, the increasing environmental regulation and reclamation of places like Uravan share themes with other modern mining practices.

The final connection between the yellowcake towns and the West is the idea of community. Situated in isolated locations, Moab, Grants, Uravan, and Jeffrey City provided more than just refuge from desolation. With the ambition to transform themselves from company town to real city or from real city to "uranium capital," the uranium towns sought to improve community ties and unify their migratory miners. During the booms, the yellowcake townspeople constructed schools and churches, joined voluntary associations,

Radiation sign at Uravan Recreation Hall, 2001. Radiation caution signs such as this one are present throughout Uravan. Behind this stands the former Recreation Hall, one of only two buildings—the other is the original boardinghouse—that remain. Photo by Michael Amundson.

and sponsored community festivals like Moab's Uranium Days or Grants' Miss Atomic Age contest. During the busts, those remaining struggled to keep their towns alive and offered assistance to their departing neighbors. Jeffrey City's community-wide garage sale, Moab's "uranium rally," and Uravan's annual town reunion hint that the yellowcake towns offered their miners and millers a place not only to work but also to live.

Within this sense of community, the yellowcake towns offer a twist on the relationship between colonialism and boosterism in the twentieth-century American West. From the first discoveries, members of local growth coalitions publicized their towns' link to uranium through the media and town celebrations. At the same time they were reporting the news, editors also promoted their communities' and yellowcake's potential for continued growth. Civic leaders who staged Miss Atomic Age beauty contests and Uranium Days festivals linked their towns to federal coattails. Although this seemed obvious during the booms, during the busts the power of boosterism was often lost, and colonialism shouldered all the blame for economic downturns. In short, the persistence of continuity suggests that as unique as the history of uranium mining and yellowcake towns appears, strong undercurrents link them to major themes in the history of the American West.

Notes

1. Patricia Nelson Limerick, *The Legacy of Conquest: The Unbroken Past of the American West* (New York: W. W. Norton, 1988), 135–136.

2. David Lavender's firsthand account of life on Club Ranch and the development of Uravan is the best example of this transformation. See David Lavender, *One Man's West*, 3d ed. (Lincoln: University of Nebraska Press, 1977). The machine in the garden metaphor is from Leo Marx, *The Machine in the Garden: Technology and the Pastoral Ideal in America* (New York: Oxford University Press, 1964).

3. U.S. Department of Energy, Energy Information Administration, Office of Coal, Nuclear, Electric, and Alternate Fuels, *Domestic Uranium Mining and Milling Industry: 1991 Viability Assessment* (Washington, D.C.: Government Printing Office, 1992).

4. William L. Chenoweth, "The State of the United States Uranium Industry in 1992," *American Association of Petroleum Geologists Bulletin* 76 (September 1992): 1451–1542.

5. Ibid.

6. Department of Energy, *1991 Viability Assessment*.

7. "U.S. to Buy 500 Tons of Russia's Leftover Arms Uranium," *Los Angeles Times*, 25 February 1993, A12; Peter Passell, "A Deal With Russia on Uranium Draws

Protest From U.S. Industry," *New York Times,* 8 June 1994, A1; John J. Fialka, "Modern Prospector: Big Uranium Dealer Grows Rich in Market Where Few Succeed," *Wall Street Journal,* 10 June 1994, A1.

8. Rosanna Tamburri, "Uranium Pact Between U.S. and Russia Is Challenged by Canada Under NAFTA," *Wall Street Journal,* 11 April 1994, B5,

9. For stories on Jeffrey City's prospects, see "Jackpot Mine Won't Begin Mining Yet, Official Says," Casper *Star-Tribune,* 6 May 1996; Chris Tollefson, "With Rising Prices Uranium Development Expanding in State," Casper *Star-Tribune,* 15 January 1996.

Bibliography

Primary Sources

Manuscripts

Estalee Silver Collection. Estalee Silver, Grand Junction, Colorado.

Grants file. State Research Center and Archives. Santa Fe, New Mexico.

Jeffrey City file. Manuscripts Section. Wyoming State Archives and Museum. Cheyenne, Wyoming.

Moab file. Museum of Western Colorado. Grand Junction, Colorado.

Moab file. Utah Historical Society. Salt Lake City, Utah.

Pitkin, Lucien. Papers. State Research Center and Archives. Santa Fe, New Mexico.

Steen, Charlie. Scrapbook. Western History Department. Denver Public Library. Denver, Colorado.

Uranium file. Manuscripts Section. Wyoming State Archives and Museum. Cheyenne, Wyoming.

Uranium file. Mother Whiteside Memorial Library. Grants, New Mexico.

Bibliography

Uranium file. Museum of Western Colorado. Grand Junction, Colorado.

Uranium file. State Research Center and Archives. Santa Fe, New Mexico.

Uranium file. Utah State Historical Society. Salt Lake City, Utah.

Uravan file. Jack Frost. Umetco Minerals Corporation. Grand Junction, Colorado.

Uravan file. Museum of Western Colorado. Grand Junction, Colorado.

Uravan file. Western History Department. Denver Public Library. Denver, Colorado.

Interviews

1. INTERVIEW BY AUTHOR

Adams, John R., and Muril D. Vincelette. Tape recording. Denver, Colorado. 20 May 1992.

Chenoweth, William L. Grand Junction, Colorado. 25 May 1996.

Collins, Roland. Split Rock, Wyoming. 15 May 1992.

Fairservis, Richard. Tape recording. Riverton, Wyoming. 22 September 1993.

Frost. Jack F. Grand Junction, Colorado. 28 October 1993.

Frost, Jack F. Telephone interview. 1993.

Jones, Bernie. Tape recording. Grand Junction, Colorado. 28 October 1993.

Peterson, Sam, Jr. Tape recording. Jeffrey City, Wyoming. 13 May 1992.

Powell, Carol and Bill. Jeffrey City, Wyoming. 15 May 1992.

Proctor, Kelly. Jeffrey City, Wyoming. 15 May 1992.

Silver, Estalee. Tape recording. Grand Junction, Colorado. October 1993.

Silver, Estalee. Telephone interview. 12 June 1996.

2. UNIVERSITY OF UTAH ORAL HISTORY PROJECT INTERVIEWS (UUOHP): The transcripts of these interviews, conducted under the direction of Dr. Gary Shumway, are housed in Special Collections at the Marriott Library, University of Utah, Salt Lake City, Utah.

Barton, Harold. Interview by Steve Guttman and John Donnelly. No. 45. Moab, Utah. 30 July 1970.

Beach, Kenneth. Interview by Steve Guttman. No. 38. Moab, Utah. 12 August 1970.

Benedict, Marion E. Interview by Clare Engle. No. 101. Uravan, Colorado. 6 August 1970.

Boyd, Norman. Interview by Steve Guttman and John Donnely. No. 28. Moab, Utah. 4 August 1970.

Bunce, Winford. Interview by Steve Guttman and John Donnely. No. 29. Moab, Utah. 29 July 1970.

Carter, E. R. Interview by Steve Guttman. No. 33. Moab, Utah. 22 July 1970.

Corbin, J. Wallace. Interview by Steve Guttman. No. 30. Moab, Utah. 23 July 1970.

Ellinwood, Dr. and Mrs. Leroy Edward. Interview by Clare Engle. No. 178. Grand Junction, Colorado. 23 July 1970.

Haldane, William Everett and Marge. Interview by Clare Engle. No. 179. Grand Junction, Colorado. 4 August 1970.

Harrison, Duncan. Interview by Richard Gibbs. No. 93. N.P. June 1970.

Hill, John and Lorraine. Interview by Clare Engle. No. 187. Grand Junction, Colorado. 21 July 1970.

Kissinger, Jack. Interview by Clare Engle. No. 172. Uravan, Colorado. 6 August 1970.

Larrison, Mr. and Mrs. Lloyd. Interview by Clare Engle. No. 177. Uravan, Colorado. 5 August 1970.

Lewis, Elbert E. Interview by Richard Gibbs. No. 83. Grand Junction, Colorado. 30 July 1970.

Marsing, Dan and Leon. Interview by Suzanne Simon. No. 121. Moab, Utah. 10 August 1970.

Miller, Ralph, Jr. Interview by Steve Guttman and John Donnelly. No. 34. Moab, Utah. 6 August 1970.

Moore, J. P. Interview by Clare Engle. No. 184. Grand Junction, Colorado. 4 August 1970.

Moore, Mary L., M.D. Interview by Clare Engle. No. 194. Grand Junction, Colorado. 26 July 1970.

Munro, John R.J. Interview by Clare Engle. No. 180. Grand Junction, Colorado. 29 July 1970.

Pope, Mars. Interview by Steve Guttman. No. 32. Moab, Utah. 22 July 1970.

Quackenbush, Ruth M. Interview by Clare Engle. No. 196. Uravan, Colorado. 3 August 1972.

Silver, Estalee. Interview by Clare Engle. No. 171. Uravan, Colorado. 6 August 1970.

Simpson, Allan. Interview by Clare Engle, Greg Bolin, and Richard Gibbs. No. 97. Grand Junction, Colorado. 28 July 1970.

Somerville, Esther. Interview by Steve Guttman. No. 46. Moab, Utah. 11 August 1970.

Steele, Germaine. Interview by Clare Engle. No. 185. Grand Junction, Colorado. 1 August 1970.

Sundwall, Robert. Interview by Steve Guttman. No. 37. Moab, Utah. 20 July 1970.

Taylor, Samuel. Interview by Steve Guttman. No. 56. Moab, Utah. 23 July 1970.

Thull, Ralph. Interview by Clare Engle. No. 203. Uravan, Colorado. 5 August 1970.

Tomsic, Marjorie. Interview by Steve Guttman. No. 42. Moab, Utah. 5 August 1970.

Tranter, T. Dee. Interview by Steve Guttman. No. 35. Moab, Utah. 11 August 1970.

Washburn, Lark. Interview by Clare Engle. No. 198. Grand Junction, Colorado. 22 July 1970.

Newspapers

Albuquerque *Journal,* 1968–1969, 1981, 1985, 1990.

Albuquerque *Tribune,* 1969, 1976.

Arizona *Daily Sun,* 2000.

Casper *Star-Tribune,* 1982, 1993–1996.

Chicago *Sun Times,* 1954.

Denver *Post,* 1953, 1956, 1961, 1969, 1980–1995.

Deseret News, 1954–1958, 1964–1697, 1970–1984, 1988.

Grand Junction *Sentinel,* 1939, 1943, 1946, 1953, 1956, 1980–1995.

Grants *Daily Beacon,* 1950–1989.

Gunnison (Colorado) *News-Champion,* 1941.

Jeffrey City *News,* 1977–1981.

Kansas City *Star,* 1958.

Long Beach (California) *Independent Press Telegram,* 1958.

Los Angeles *Times,* 1993.

Moab *Times-Independent,* 1945–1989.

Montrose (Colorado) *Daily Press,* 1937, 1939, 1942, 1943.

New York *Herald-Tribune,* 1954.

New York *Times,* 1988, 1993–1994.

Ogden (Utah) *Standard-Examiner,* 1954, 1962, 1987.

Riverton (Wyoming) *Ranger,* 1980.

Rocky Mountain News (Denver), 1980, 1984, 1993, 1994.

Salt Lake City *Tribune,* 1953–1959, 1964–1968, 1972–1988, 1999.

San Juan *Record,* 1953, 1967.

St. Louis *Post-Dispatch,* 1953.

Telluride (Colorado) *Times,* 1980.

Thermopolis (Wyoming) *Independent Record,* 1966.

UCN Photo News, 1955–1958.

USV Photo News, 1953–1955.

Wall Street Journal, 1959–1969, 1993–1994.

Wyoming *State Tribune and Wyoming Eagle* (Cheyenne), 1966.

Government Documents

Albrethsen, Holger, and Frank E. McGinley. *Summary History of Domestic Uranium Procurement Under U.S. Atomic Energy Commission Contracts: Final Report.* Grand Junction, Colo.: U.S. Department of Energy, 1982.

Atomic Energy Act of 1946. *U.S. Statutes at Large* 60 (1946): 755–775.

Atomic Energy Act of 1954. *U.S. Statutes at Large* 68 (1954): 919–961.

"Atomic Energy Commission, Uranium Enrichment Services, Criteria." Notice. *Federal Register* 31, no. 248 (23 December 1966): 16479.

Colorado Department of Health, Radiation Control Division. *Preliminary Executive Licensing Review Summary for the Uravan Uranium Mill*. Grand Junction, Colo.: 1984.

Crook's Peak Quadrangle, Fremont County Wyoming. Map. Denver: U.S. Geological Survey, 7.5 Minute Series, 1961; photo-revised 1984.

Department of Finance and Administration, State Planning Division. *Cibola County Growth Management and Housing Plan*. Santa Fe: 1982.

Energy Policy Act of 1992. *U.S. Statutes at Large* 106 (1992): 102–486.

Huffman v. Western Nuclear, Inc. 108 S.Ct. 2087 (1988).

Jeffrey City Post Office. *Change of Address Form Book, 1969–1985*. On file at the Jeffrey City Post Office, Wyoming.

Jeffrey City School. "Enrollment Records of the Jeffrey City School, 1967–1992." On file at the Jeffrey City School, Wyoming.

Kithill, Karl L., and John A. Davis. *Mining and Concentration of Carnotite Ores*. Department of Interior, Bureau of Mines. Bulletin 103, Mineral Technology 11. Washington, D.C.: Government Printing Office (GPO), 1917.

Leonard, Olen, and Lay James Gibson. "Towns of Strangers: Social Structure and the Miner Subculture in the Uranium Belt of Northwestern New Mexico." Report, Bureau of Indian Affairs. San Juan Basin Region Uranium Study. Albuquerque: 1978.

Middle Rio Grande Council of Governments of New Mexico. *Summary Report: A Guide for Future Growth and Development of City of Grants and Village of Milan in Valencia County, New Mexico*. Albuquerque: 1971.

———. *Population Projections and Allocations for Grants and Milan*. Albuquerque: 1977.

National Environmental Policy Act of 1969. *U.S. Statutes at Large* 83 (1970): 852–856.

New Mexico Energy and Minerals Department. *An Overview of the New Mexico Uranium Industry*. Santa Fe: New Mexico Energy and Minerals Department, 1979.

Nininger, R. D., and P. L. Guarin. "S-37 and T-37 Resources of the United States." *Manhattan Project History*. Microfilm, reel 11.

Office of the State Inspector of Mines. *Annual Report by the State Inspector of Mines to the Governor of the State of New Mexico, 1952–1988*. Albuquerque: Office of the State Inspector of Mines, 1952–1988.

Office of the Associate Superintendent for Curriculum and Accountability. "History of Enrollment for the Past 38 Years at the 180th School Day." *Cibola County Schools 1991–92 Accountability Report*. On file at Cibola County Schools Main Office, Grants, New Mexico.

O'Rear, Nielson B. *Summary and Chronology of the Domestic Uranium Program (August 1966)*. Report prepared for U.S. Atomic Energy Commission, Grand Junction Office. Grand Junction, Colo.: 1966.

Parson, Charles L., R. B. Moore, S. C. Lind, and O. C. Schaefer. *Extraction and Recovery of Radium, Uranium and Vanadium From Carnotite*. U.S. Department of the Interior, Bureau of Mines. Bulletin 104, Mineral Technology 12. Washington, D.C.: GPO, 1915.

Petty, Paul V., and Devoy A. Ryan. *Grants Is Growing: School Facilities Survey Report*. Albuquerque: University of New Mexico, Department of Educational and Administrative Services, February 1960.

Private Ownership of Special Nuclear Materials Act. *U.S. Statutes at Large* 78 (1964): 602–607.

Stanton, Bette. *Moab and Grand County Community Profile*. Moab: Grand County Economic and Community Development, 1992.

Steen, Charles A., George P. Dix Jr., Scott W. Hazen Jr., and Russell R. McLellan. "Uranium-Mining Operations of the Utex Exploration Co. in the Big Indian District, San Juan County, Utah." *Information Circular 7669*. U.S. Department of the Interior, U.S. Bureau of Mines. Washington, D.C.: GPO, 1953.

Uranium Mill Tailings Radiation Control Act of 1978. *U.S. Statutes at Large* 92 (1978): 3021.

U.S. Atomic Energy Commission. "Temporary Additional Allowances, Colorado Plateau Area Carnotite-Type and Roscoelite-Type Ores." *Addition to Circular 4*. 15 June 1948.

———. "Domestic Uranium Program Circular 5, Revised." *Federal Register*. Document 53-8282. 15 October 1953.

———, Grand Junction Operations Office. "U.S. Atomic Energy Commission Announces Program to Stimulate Production of Domestic Uranium." Press release no. 96. 10 April 1948.

———. "AEC to Permit Private Sales of Uranium to Foreign and Domestic Buyers." Press release no. 213. 8 May 1958.

———. Press release no. 220. 24 November 1958.

———. "Inquiries About Uranium." Press release. 1 July 1966.

U.S. Atomic Energy Commission and U.S. Geological Survey. *Prospecting for Uranium*. Washington, D.C.: GPO, 1949, rev. 1951.

U.S. Bureau of the Census. *U.S. Census of Population: 1950*. Vol. II, *Characteristics of the Population*. Part 31, New Mexico. Washington, D.C.: GPO, 1952.

———. *U.S. Census of Population: 1950*. Vol. II, *Characteristics of the Population*. Part 44, Utah. Washington, D.C.: GPO, 1952.

———. *U.S. Census of Population: 1960*. Vol. I, *Characteristics of the Population*. Part 33, New Mexico. Washington, D.C.: GPO, 1963.

———. *U.S. Census of Population: 1960*. Vol. I, *Characteristics of the Population*. Part 46, Utah. Washington, D.C.: GPO, 1963.

U.S. Congress. *Proposed Modification of Restrictions on Enrichment of Foreign Uranium for Domestic Use: Hearings Before the Joint Committee on Atomic Energy.* 93rd Cong., 2d sess. Washington, D.C.: GPO, 17–18 September 1974.

U.S. Congress. *Review of the Status of the Domestic Uranium Mining and Milling Industry: Hearing Before the Subcommittee on Energy Research and Development.* 97th Cong., 2d sess. Washington, D.C.: GPO, 12 September 1984.

U.S. Congress, Committee on Environment and Public Works. *Domestic Uranium Mining and Milling: Hearing Before the Subcommittee on Nuclear Regulation.* 97th Cong., 1st sess. Washington, D.C.: GPO, 29 August 1983.

U.S. Congress, Joint Committee on Atomic Energy. *Atomic Energy Commission Authorizing Legislation Fiscal Year 1965: Hearings Before the Joint Committee on Atomic Energy.* 88th Cong., 2d sess. Washington, D.C.: GPO, 3 February 1964.

U.S. Congress, Joint Committee on Atomic Energy, Subcommittee on Raw Materials. *AEC Uranium Procurement Program: Hearings Before the Subcommittee on Raw Materials of the Joint Committee on Atomic Energy.* 87th Cong., 2d sess. Washington, D.C.: GPO, 18–19 June 1962.

U.S. Congress, Senate, Committee on Energy and Natural Resources. *Status of the Domestic Uranium Mining and Milling Industry: The Effects of Imports.* 97th Cong., 1st sess. Washington, D.C.: GPO, 25 September 1981.

U.S. Department of Energy. *Domestic Uranium Mining and Milling Industry: 1983 Viability Assessment.* Washington, D.C.: GPO, 1984.

———. *United States Uranium Mining and Milling Industry: A Comprehensive Review.* Washington, D.C.: GPO, 1984.

———. *Domestic Uranium Mining and Milling Industry: 1985 Viability Assessment.* Washington, D.C.: GPO, 1986.

———, Energy Information Administration, Office of Coal, Nuclear, Electric, and Alternate Fuels. *Domestic Uranium Mining and Milling Industry: 1991 Viability Assessment.* Washington, D.C.: GPO, 1992.

U.S. Department of the Interior. San Juan Basin Regional Uranium Study. *Uranium Development in the San Juan Basin Region: A Report on Environmental Issues, Final Report.* Albuquerque: Bureau of Indian Affairs, 1980.

U.S. Energy Research and Development Administration. *Statistical Data of the Uranium Industry.* Grand Junction, Colo.: GPO, 1976.

Western Nuclear, Inc., v. Huffman. 825 F2d 1430, 1433 (10th Cir. 1987).

Wyoming Department of Labor and Statistics. *Wyoming: The Uranium Industry, a Manpower Survey 1979.* Cheyenne: Wyoming Department of Labor and Statistics, 1979.

Wyoming State Mine Inspector. *Annual Report of the Wyoming State Mine Inspector.* Cheyenne: Wyoming State Mine Inspector, 1970–1983.

Secondary Sources

Books

Ackland, Len. *Making a Real Killing: Rocky Flats and the Nuclear West.* Albuquerque: University of New Mexico Press, 1999.

Allen, James B. *The Company Town in the American West.* Norman: University of Oklahoma Press, 1966.

Armitage, Merle. *Stella Dysart of Ambrosia Lake.* New York: Duell, Sloan, and Pearce, 1959.

Barth, Gunther. *Instant Cities: Urbanization and the Rise of San Francisco and Denver.* Albuquerque: University of New Mexico Press, 1988.

Bartimus, Tad, and Scott McCartney. *Trinity's Children: Living Along America's Nuclear Highway.* Albuquerque: University of New Mexico Press, 1991.

Bothwell, Robert. *Eldorado: Canada's National Uranium Company.* Toronto: University of Toronto Press, 1984.

Cottrell, Leonard S., Jr., and Sylvia Eberhart. *American Opinion on World Affairs in the Atomic Age.* Princeton: Princeton University Press, 1948.

Dannenbaum, George. *Boom to Bust: Remembrances of the Grants, New Mexico, Uranium Boom.* Albuquerque: Creative Designs, 1994.

Dawidoff, Nicholas. *The Catcher Was a Spy: The Mysterious Life of Moe Berg.* New York: Vintage, 1994.

Eichstaedt, Peter H. *If You Poison Us: Uranium and Native Americans.* Santa Fe: Red Crane, 1994.

Fermi, Rachel, and Esther Samra. *Picturing the Bomb: Photographs From the Secret World of the Manhattan Project.* New York: Harry N. Abrams, 1995.

Fernlund, Kevin J., ed. *The Cold War American West: 1945–1989.* Albuquerque: University of New Mexico Press, 1998.

Firmage, Richard A. *A History of Grand County.* Utah Centennial County History Series. Salt Lake City: Utah State Historical Society, 1996.

Ford, Daniel. *Meltdown: The Secret Papers of the Atomic Energy Commission.* New York: Simon and Schuster, 1986.

Fradkin, Philip L. *Fallout: An American Nuclear Tragedy.* Tucson: University of Arizona Press, 1989.

Francaviglia, Richard V. *Hard Places: Reading the Landscape of America's Historic Mining Districts.* Iowa City: University of Iowa Press, 1991.

Gardner, A. Dudley, and Vera R. Flores. *Forgotten Frontier: A History of Wyoming Coal Mining.* Boulder: Westview, 1989.

Gerber, Michele Stenhjem. *On the Home Front: The Cold War Legacy of the Hanford Nuclear Site.* Lincoln: University of Nebraska Press, 1992.

Gomez, Arthur R. *Quest for the Golden Circle: The Four Corners and the Metropolitan West, 1945–1970.* Albuquerque: University of New Mexico Press, 1994.

Gray, Earle. *The Great Uranium Cartel.* Toronto: McClelland and Stewart, 1982.

Greever, William S. *The Bonanza West: The Story of the Western Mining Rushes.* Norman: University of Oklahoma Press, 1963.

Griffith, J. W. *The Uranium Industry—Its History, Technology, and Prospects.* Ottawa: Department of Energy, Mines, and Resources, 1967.

Groves, Leslie R. *Now It Can Be Told: The Story of the Manhattan Project.* New York: Harper, 1962.

Gulliford, Andrew. *Boomtown Blues: Colorado Oil Shale, 1885–1985.* Niwot: University of Colorado Press, 1989.

Hales, Peter Bacon. *Atomic Spaces: Living on the Manhattan Project.* Urbana: University of Illinois Press, 1997.

Hein, Teri. *Atomic Farm Girl: The Betrayal of Chief Qualchan, the Appaloosa, and Me.* Golden, Colo.: Fulcrum, 2000.

Hevly, Bruce, and John M. Findlay, eds. *The Atomic West.* Seattle: University of Washington Press, 1998.

Hewlett, Richard G., and Oscar E. Anderson Jr. *A History of the United States Atomic Energy Commission.* Volume I: *The New World, 1939–1946.* University Park: Pennsylvania State University Press, 1962.

———. *A History of the United States Atomic Energy Commission.* Volume II: *Atomic Shield, 1947/1952.* University Park: Pennsylvania State University Press, 1969.

Hine, Robert V. *Community on the American Frontier: Separate but Not Alone.* Norman: University of Oklahoma Press, 1980.

Jackson, W. Turrentine. *Treasure Hill: Portrait of a Silver Mining Camp.* Tucson: University of Arizona Press, 1963.

Johnson, Susan Lee. *Roaring Camp: The Social World of the California Gold Rush.* New York: W. W. Norton, 2000.

Kuletz, Valerie. *The Tainted Desert: Environmental and Social Ruin in the American West.* New York: Routledge, 1998.

Lamm, Richard D., and Michael McCarthy. *The Angry West: A Vulnerable Land and Its Future.* Boston: Houghton Mifflin, 1982.

Lavender, David. *One Man's West.* 3d ed. Lincoln: University of Nebraska Press, 1977.

Limerick, Patricia Nelson. *The Legacy of Conquest: The Unbroken Past of the American West.* New York: W. W. Norton, 1988.

Loeb, Paul. *Nuclear Culture: Living and Working in the World's Largest Atomic Complex.* Philadelphia: New Society, 1986.

Look, Al. *U-Boom: Uranium on the Colorado Plateau.* Grand Junction, Colo.: Bell, 1956.

Lotchin, Roger. *Fortress California, 1910–1961: From Warfare to Welfare.* New York: Oxford University Press, 1992.

Malamud, Gary W. *Boomtown Communities*. Environmental Design Series, ed. Richard P. Dober. New York: Van Nostrand Reinhold, 1984.

Mann, Ralph. *After the Gold Rush: Society in Grass Valley and Nevada City, California, 1849–1870*. Palo Alto: Stanford University Press, 1982.

Marx, Leo. *The Machine in the Garden: Technology and the Pastoral Ideal in America*. New York: Oxford University Press, 1964.

McIntyre, Ben. *Uranium City: The Last Boom Town*. Mill Bay, B.C.: Driftwood, 1993.

McIntyre, Hugh C. *Uranium, Nuclear Power, and Canada-U.S. Energy Relations*. Montreal and Washington, D.C.: C. D. Howe Research Institute (Canada) and National Planning Association (U.S.A.), 1978.

Meyers, Robert A., ed. *Encyclopedia of Physical Science and Technology*. 2d ed. San Diego: Academic, 1992. S.v. "Uranium," by William L. Chenoweth.

Millar, Rodney D., Lane T. Neilson, and Richard E. Turley. *A Study of the Utah Uranium Milling Industry, Volume II: Utah Energy Resources — Uranium*. Salt Lake City: Mechanical and Industrial Engineering Department and Utah Engineering Experiment Station, May 1980.

Moss, Norman. *The Politics of Uranium*. New York: Universe, 1982.

Murphy, Mary. *Mining Cultures: Men, Women, and Leisure in Butte, 1914–41*. Urbana: University of Illinois Press, 1997.

Nash, Gerald D. *The American West in the Twentieth Century: A Short History of an Urban Oasis*. Albuquerque: University of New Mexico Press, 1973.

Navajo Uranium Miner Oral History and Photography Project. *Memories Come to Us in the Rain and the Wind: Oral Histories and Photographs of Navajo Uranium Miners and Their Families*. Jamaica Plain, Mass.: Red Sun, 1997.

New Mexico Energy Institute. *Uranium Industry in New Mexico*. Albuquerque: Energy Resources Board, 1976.

Newell, Maxine. *Charlie Steen's Mi Vida*. Moab, Utah: By the author, 1976.

Nichols, Maj. Gen. K. D. *The Road to Trinity*. New York: William Morrow, 1987.

Ortiz, Simon. *Woven Stone*. Tucson: University of Arizona Press, 1992.

Owen, Anthony David. *The Economics of Uranium*. New York: Praeger, 1985.

Paul, Rodman W. *Mining Frontier of the Far West, 1848–1880*. New York: Holt, Rinehart, and Winston, 1963.

Peterson, Keith C. *Company Town: Potlatch, Idaho, and the Potlatch Lumber Company*. Pullman: Washington State University Press, 1987.

Plastino, Ben J. *Coming of Age: Idaho Falls and the Idaho National Engineering Laboratory, 1949–1990*. Chelsea, Mich.: BookCrafters, 1998.

Quality Development Associates. *Wyoming's Uranium Industry — Status, Impacts, and Trends*. Cheyenne: Wyoming State Department of Economic Planning and Development, Mineral Division, 1978.

Quinn, James E. *Western Nuclear, Inc., Uranium Mill.* Denver: Denver Equipment, [1960].

Radetzki, Marian. *Uranium: A Strategic Source of Energy.* New York: St. Martin's, 1981.

Reader's Guide to Periodical Literature. New York: H. W. Wilson, 1953–1955.

Reps, John W. "Bonanza Towns: Urban Planning on the Western Mining Frontier." In *Pattern and Process: Research in Historical Geography,* ed. Ralph E. Ehrenberg. Washington, D.C.: Howard University Press, 1975.

Rhodes, Richard. *The Making of the Atomic Bomb.* New York: Touchstone, 1986.

Righter, Robert W. *The Making of a Town: Wright, Wyoming.* Boulder: Roberts Rinehart, 1985.

Ringholz, Raye C. *Uranium Frenzy: Boom and Bust on the Colorado Plateau.* New York: W. W. Norton, 1989.

———. *Little Town Blues: Voices From the Changing West.* Salt Lake City: Peregrine Smith, 1992.

Robbins, William G. *Hard Times in Paradise: Coos Bay, Oregon, 1850–1986.* Seattle: University of Washington Press, 1988.

———. *Colony and Empire: The Capitalist Transformation of the American West.* Lawrence: University of Kansas Press, 1994.

Rohrbough, Malcolm J. *Aspen: The History of a Silver Mining Town 1879–1893.* New York: Oxford University Press, 1986.

Romm, Joseph J. *The Once and Future Superpower: How to Restore America's Economic, Energy, and Environmental Security.* New York: W. Morrow, 1992.

———. *Defining National Security: The Nonmilitary Aspects.* New York: Council on Foreign Relations Press, 1993.

Rothman, Hal K. *On Rims and Ridges: The Los Alamos Area Since 1880.* Lincoln: University of Nebraska Press, 1992.

———. *Devil's Bargains: Tourism in the Twentieth-Century American West.* Lawrence: University of Kansas Press, 1998.

Schwantes, Carlos A. *Vision and Enterprise: Exploring the History of Phelps-Dodge Corporation.* Tucson: University of Arizona Press, 2000.

Schwartz, Stephen I. *Atomic Audit: The Costs and Consequences of Nuclear Weapons Since 1940.* Washington, D.C.: Brookings Institution Press, 1998.

Silver, Estalee. *Images of the Uravan, Colorado, Area 1880–1990.* Grand Junction, Colo.: By the author, 1992.

Smith, Duane A. *Rocky Mountain Boom Town: A History of Durango, Colorado.* Niwot: University Press of Colorado, 1992.

———. *Mining America: The Industry and the Environment.* Niwot: University Press of Colorado, 1993.

Bibliography

Stumpf, David K. *Titan II: A History of a Cold War Missile Program.* Fayetteville: University of Arkansas Press, 2000.

Szasz, Ferenc. *The Day the Sun Rose Twice: The Story of the Trinity Site Nuclear Explosion July 16, 1945.* Albuquerque: University of New Mexico Press, 1984.

Tanner, Faun McConkie. *The Far Country: A Regional History of Moab and La Sal, Utah.* 2d ed. Salt Lake City: Olympus, 1976.

Taylor, June H., and Michael D. Yokell. *Yellowcake: The International Uranium Cartel.* New York: Pergamon, 1979.

Titus, A. Constadina. *Bombs in the Backyard: Atomic Testing and American Politics.* Reno: University of Nevada Press, 1986.

Udall, Stewart L. *The Myths of August: A Personal Exploration of Our Tragic Cold War Affair With the Atom.* New York: Pantheon, 1994.

University of New Mexico Department of Educational and Administrative Services. *Grants Is Growing! School Facilities Survey Report.* Albuquerque: University of New Mexico, 1960.

Weart, Spencer R. *Nuclear Fear: A History of Images.* Cambridge, Mass.: Harvard University Press, 1988.

Welsome, Eileen. *The Plutonium Files: America's Secret Medical Experiments in the Cold War.* New York: Dial, 1999.

White, Richard. *It's Your Misfortune and None of My Own: A History of the American West.* Norman: University of Oklahoma Press, 1991.

Writer's Program of the Work Projects Administration of the State of New Mexico. *New Mexico: A Guide to the Colorful State.* New York: Hastings House, 1940.

Writer's Program of the Work Projects Administration of the State of Utah. *Utah: A Guide to the State.* New York: Hastings House, 1941.

Young, Otis E., Jr. *Western Mining.* Norman: University of Oklahoma Press, 1970.

Articles

Ambler, Marjane. "Uranium Industry's Expansion Prospects Bleak: Fallout From Three Mile Island Doesn't Help." *High Country News* 11, no. 16 (10 August 1979): 1.

American Mining Congress. "Commingled Uranium Mill Tailings—A Historical Perspective." Report. Washington, D.C.: American Mining Congress, 4 March 1985.

Amundson, Michael A. "Home on the Range No More: The Boom and Bust of a Wyoming Uranium Mining Town, 1957–1988." *Western Historical Quarterly* 26 (Winter 1995): 492.

———. "Mining the Grand Canyon to Save It: The Orphan Uranium Mine and National Security." *Western Historical Quarterly* 32 (Autumn 2001): 320–345.

Atlas Minerals. "Environmental Report for Moab, Utah, Facility." Moab, 1973.

"Atomic Energy: Uranium Jackpot." *Time* (30 September 1957): 89–90.

Bates, V. Edward. "The Impact of Energy Boom-Town Growth on Rural Areas." *Social Casework* 59, no. 2 (February 1978): 73–82.

Bavarskis, Justas. "The West Mines, Mills, and Worships Radioactive Fuel: URANIUM." *High Country News* 10, no. 5 (10 March 1978): 1.

"Boom That Gives U.S. Top Spot in Uranium." *U.S. News and World Report* (16 August 1957): 120–121.

"Broke and Hungry Prospector Hits Uranium Jackpot." *Business Week* (1 August 1953): 28–30.

Chenoweth, William L. "The Uranium-Vanadium Deposits of the Uravan Mineral Belt and Adjacent Areas, Colorado and Utah." *New Mexico Geological Society Guidebook,* 32nd Field Conference, Western Slope Colorado, 1981, 165–170.

———. "Raw Materials Activities of the Manhattan Project on the Colorado Plateau." *Four Corners Geological Society Guidebook,* 10th Field Conference, Cataract Canyon, 1987, 151–154.

———. "Ambrosia Lake, New Mexico—A Giant Uranium District." *New Mexico Geological Society Guidebook,* 40th Field Conference, Southeastern Colorado Plateau, 1989, 297–302.

———. "A History of Uranium Production in Utah." *Energy and Mineral Resources of Utah: Utah Geological Association Publication* 18. Salt Lake City, 1990, 123.

———. "The State of the United States Uranium Industry in 1992." *American Association of Petroleum Geologists Bulletin* 76 (September 1992): 1451–1542.

"The Cisco Kid." *Time* (3 August 1953): 60–61.

Curran, Thomas F.V. "Carnotite in Paradox Valley, Colo." *Engineering and Mining Journal* 92 (30 December 1911): 1287–88.

———. "Carnotite-I." *Engineering and Mining Journal* 96 (20 December 1913): 1165–67.

"Exploration Widens the Uranium Ore Belt." *Business Week* (3 March 1951): 102–104.

"Freeze on Uranium." *Time* (11 November 1957): 114–115.

Gilmore, John S. "Boom Towns May Hinder Energy Resource Development." *Science* 191, no. 4227 (February 1976): 535–540.

"High-Powered Rush for Uranium Claims." *Life* (17 September 1956): 57–62.

"The History of a Successful Uranium Venture." *Wyoming* 1 (June-July 1957): 28–31.

Hough, Henry W. "Starvation in the Midst of Plenty." *Uranium* (February 1958): 4–5.

"How to Find Uranium." *Time* (21 April 1947): 86.

"How to Hunt for Uranium." *Popular Science* (February 1946): 121–123.

Huffard, J. B. "Corporation Acquires Additional Vanadium Property in Colorado." *Carbidea* (February 1929): 5.

Little, R. L. "Some Social Consequences of Boom Towns." *North Dakota Law Review* 53, no. 3 (1977): 401–425.

"Lost Creek Expanding." *Uranium* (April 1957): 30.

"Lost Creek Mill at Home on the Range." *Uranium* (February 1957): 30.

Lundquist, A. Q., and J. L. Lake. "History and Trends of the Uranium Plant Flowsheet." *Mining Congress Journal* (November 1955): 42.

Malone, Michael. "The Collapse of Western Metal Mining: An Historical Epitaph." *Pacific Historical Review* 55, no. 3 (August 1986): 455–464.

"Man in Search of Million: Negro Prospector Seeks Fortune in Uranium Boom." *Ebony* (February 1955): 16–22.

McEvoy, J. P. "Uranium's New Horatio Alger." *American Mercury* (November 1953): 15–18.

Meyers, Burt. "Uranium Jackpot." *Engineering and Mining Journal* 154, no. 4 (September 1953): 72–75.

———. "Big Boom at Big Indian." *Engineering and Mining Journal* 155, no. 4 (April 1954): 96–99.

Newell, Maxine. "The Scrapbook." *Canyon Legacy: Journal of the Dan O'Laurie Museum, Moab, Utah* 14 (summer 1992): 16–17.

Nicholson, Kenneth C. "Early Carnotite Mining in Colorado." *Engineering and Mining Journal* 159, no. 6 (June 1958): 100–101.

O'Gara, Geoffrey. "Jeffrey City's Ghosts." *Western Energy Magazine* (July 1982): 25–29.

"Out Where the Click Is Louder." *Time* (18 July 1949): 53.

Payne, Bill. "Lights Dim for Domestic Uranium Producers." *Natural Resources Journal* 29, no. 4 (fall 1989): 1079–91.

"Pay-offs for Many in Giant Uranium Jackpot." *Life* 41 (10 December 1956): 133–134.

Peña, Abe M. "Coming Back From the Brink," in "Cibola County Profile." *New Mexico Business Journal* (June 1992).

Robbins, William G. "The 'Plundered Province' Thesis and the Recent Historiography of the American West." *Pacific Historical Review* 55, no. 4 (November 1986): 577–597.

Smith, Toby. "Grants—Boomtown!" *New Mexico Magazine* (September 1979): 54–61.

"Special Report: Striking It Rich in the A-Age." *Newsweek* (19 April 1954): 100–105.

Steen, Charles A. "A Timely Statement From Charles A. Steen." *Uranium* (February 1958): 14.

Sullenberger, Robert. "100 Years of Uranium Activity in the Four Corners Region." *Journal of the Western Slope* 7, no. 4 (fall 1992): 1–18.

"Survey of Wyoming Uranium." *Uranium* (August 1957): 16.

Tennyson, Dora. "The Trailer That Led to Millions." *Trailer Life* (April 1954).

"Top of the News." *Uranium* (March 1957): 7.

"Top of the News." *Uranium* (July-August 1958): 6.

"Top of the News." *Uranium* (November-December 1958): 6.

"U_3O_8: Energy From Wyoming's Powerful Sand." *In Wyoming* (February-March 1980): 49.

"The Uranium Boom." *Time* (13 October 1952): 95–96.

"Uranium Jackpot." *Time* (30 September 1957): 89–90.

"Uranium Makes a Wilder West." *Life* (19 July 1954): 12–15.

"Western Nuclear Corp." *Uranium* (August 1957): 12.

"Western Nuclear Corp. Is the New Name for Lost Creek Oil and Uranium." *Uranium* (May 1957): 26.

"With Nowhere to Go, Uranium Sits It Out." *Business Week* (30 November 1957): 116–117.

Winters, Wayne. "Uranium Boom at Grants." *New Mexico Magazine* (March 1951): 13–15, 52.

Videocassettes

The Illustrated Daily: Mining in New Mexico. Prod. Karl Kernberger. 25 April 1985.

The Illustrated Daily: Profile of Grants, New Mexico. Prod. Karl Kernberger. 7 March 1985.

Town on a Powder Keg: A Video Tape Production on the Industrial Emergence of Moab, Utah. Prod. Daniel Albert Keeler. University of Utah, 1966.

Unpublished Theses and Dissertations

Amundson, Michael A. "Uncle Sam and the Yellowcake Towns: The Effects of Federal Policy on Four Uranium Mining Communities, 1943–1988." Ph.D. diss., University of Nebraska, 1996.

Devers, Victor L. "A History and Economic Analysis of the Uranium Industry in New Mexico." M.A. thesis, University of New Mexico, 1962.

Eastman, John F. "Blue Collar Community: A Descriptive Analysis of the Family Life Style of Uranium Workers in an Atypical Social Environment." M.A. thesis, University of Wyoming, 1972.

Bibliography

Hardcastle, John A. "Halfway Between Nobody Knows Where and Somebody's Starting Point: A History of the West End of Montrose County, Colorado." M.A. thesis. Utah State University, 1998.

Keeler, Daniel Albert. *Town on a Powder Keg: A Video Tape Production on the Industrial Emergence of Moab, Utah.* M.A. thesis, University of Utah, 1966.

Kiner, Phil Eugene. "A Case Study of Rural Employment in Wyoming's Uranium Sector." M.A. thesis, University of Wyoming, 1973.

Shumway, Gary Lee. "A History of the Uranium Industry on the Colorado Plateau." Ph.D. diss., University of Southern California, 1970.

Unpublished Papers

Burwell, Blair. "Construction, Operation, and Maintenance Report of Uranium Sludge Plants Operated by the United States Vanadium Corporation in the Colorado Area." In files of William Chenoweth, Grand Junction, Colorado.

Hahne, F. J. "Early Uranium Mining in the United States." Paper presented at the annual symposium of the Uranium Institute. 6–8 September 1989. London. In files of Jack Frost, Umetco, Grand Junction, Colorado.

Harvey, Curn C. "Grants, New Mexico: The Uranium Capital." Paper prepared for the U.S. Navy Department. History file no. 26, State Research Center and Archives, Santa Fe, New Mexico.

Van Sell, Tandie. "The Early History of Uravan and Uravan Area." Tms. In possession of Estalee Silver, Grand Junction, Colorado.

Web Pages

National Atomic Museum: http://www.atomicmuseum.com.

Uravan Home Page: http://www.uravan.com.

Virtual Nuclear Tourist: http://www.nucleartourist.com.

World Nuclear Association: http://www.world-nuclear.org.

Index

Page numbers in italics indicate illustrations.